PRACTICE PLACEMENT IN SOCIAL WORK

Innovative approaches for effective teaching and learning

Edited by Avril Bellinger and Deirdre Ford

First published in Great Britain in 2016 by

Policy Press
University of Bristol
1-9 Old Park Hill
Bristol
BS2 8BB
UK
t: +44 (0)117 954 5940
pp-info@bristol.ac.uk
www.policypress.co.uk

North America office:
Policy Press
c/o The University of Chicago Press
1427 East 60th Street
Chicago, IL 60637, USA
t: +1 773 702 7700
f: +1 773-702-9756
sales@press.uchicago.edu
www.press.uchicago.edu

British Library Cataloguing in Publication Data
A catalogue record for this book is available from the British Library

Library of Congress Cataloging-in-Publication Data
A catalog record for this book has been requested

ISBN 978-1-4473-1861-3 paperback
ISBN 978-1-4473-1860-6 hardcover
ISBN 978-1-4473-1864-4 ePub
ISBN 978-1-4473-1865-1 Mobi

Cover design by Hayes Design
Front cover image: istock
Printed and bound in Great Britain by CMP, Poole
Policy Press uses environmentally responsible print partners

This book is dedicated to our friend and colleague Diane Garrard, who stood up to injustice in all its forms without flinching. Her humour, reliability, plain-speaking and humanity have held us steady.

Contents

Foreword

The social work placement has always been an Other Place; this is its power. When students enter a placement, they have the chance of an altered state, an experience of creativity that comes from, hopefully, a destabilising and disorienting space. That is the radical vision, so powerfully articulated in this book – to contrast with the tired cliché that the student goes on placement 'to put into practice the knowledge they have acquired in college', 'theory into practice'. It is a hope for transformational learning contrasted with the passing on of existing mindsets.

More transformational still is the notion of an Other Place *created* by the students themselves (and, in some cases, by service users too). Rather than placements passively awaiting their apprentices or, at best, valuing the coming students as a resource, these Other Places are services generated by students to provide services that would not exist without them. Here, then, is A Place that fully integrates learning and practice through the agency of social work. Of course, these Other Places do not happen without tremendous persistence, wisdom and bravery to ensure that they are sustainable and that they are safe places, both for the student's learning and, most of all, for those who use their services.

Over the years, the happenstance that characterised the social work placement – a Nowhere Land that could be magical or dire but was always unchartered – quickly started to experience the glare of scrutiny. With this attention came audit, regulation and control; this Other Place did not escape the obsessive mapping that bisected and dissected professional life throughout the public sector. The 'guidance' became oppressive, the bullet-pointed lists of injunctions and imperatives longer than the placement documentation itself. Nowhere was this more strongly evidenced than in the decision about a student's ability or suitability for social work – the assessment. This decision, always complex, became deadeningly complicated.

Complication is a ball of wool that has become knotted, unravellable, unusable; complexity, on the other hand, is devising patterns and using the wool to turn these patterns into beautiful, wearable garments. Social work education will always be complex but it has become unhelpfully and tediously knotted. Take the long strands of criteria for student competence on placement – if we were to replace them simply with questions, would we lose anything?

- How does the student's work promote social justice?
- To what extent are the student's actions fair and compassionate?
- How does the student demonstrate integrity?
- How does the student understand and use discretion?

'Where is safeguarding and risk?', the traditionalist asks. We might reply: 'Are these concerns not embedded in the four questions, each of which requires us to interrogate social work practice and learning more thoroughly than a list of standards or indicators?' 'Us' is the student, service user, practice educator, tutor.

It is good to remind ourselves that students respond in different ways to these Other Places. When researching non-traditional placements, as they were then known, I came across four students placed together to develop a community resource in partnership with a group of service users. Three of the four thrived in this environment, but the fourth felt it to be a deeply Alien Place. He was an 'A' student when it came to writing essays, but his level of bewilderment was too great for him to experience that hoped-for 'creative disorientation'. To what extent, then, do we wrap the placement around the student and how much do we expect the student to make their own adaptations? Is this Other Place a safe place for the student – for instance, if this 'A' student is a lone, black, gay man in an exclusively female, white, straight Place? So, there is a trade-off between the student's responsibility to be proactive and the Other Place's capacity to home him/her – and, of course, there is the university's obligation to support and develop these homes.

How do we make the classroom an Other Place, and should we? The college setting is often referred to as 'The Course', as if it is the default location for social work education; yet, practitioners consistently report placements as what they remember most (that goes for me too). *Practice-led* class curricula are not easily established in the university environment and are open to a kind of academic snobbery, even though theorising from and about professional practice is arguably a more complex activity than theorising an unapplied discipline. A practice-led curriculum is a noble attempt to integrate students' learning between Both Places.

Social work placements have not wholly escaped their Cinderella status but 'the practicum' has gained recognition in some quarters as a way of teaching and learning in its own right, aspiring to become the *signature pedagogy* of social work (Wayne et al, 2010) – a place of renewal for social work, perhaps even a rekindling of the original spirit that infused the early Settlements, with a sense of mutuality and reciprocity between students and teachers, and students and service users. The social work placement is not an outpost of the university, a testing ground for the bubbling theories concocted in the academy; this Other Place is a laboratory in its own right.

It is evident that there are many challenges. First, how to create space for this Other Place within what are known as statutory placements? We should not abandon these spaces as lost to transformational learning, but engage with them. There is no reason, for instance, why students should not develop an innovative group-work service within a statutory agency as a way of meeting needs that service users might themselves find transformational. Another challenge is to make these innovative Other Places sustainable and not dependent on the inspirational leadership of an individual. Last but not least is how to keep this sense of an Other Place alive when the student has become an experienced practitioner and he or she has habituated to it, when looking *in to* has become looking *out from*. Many find a new and welcome destabilisation and disorientation by studying to become practice educators, so their Place can become an Other Place through the eyes of their students.

This is a book with local roots and global spread. The editors and contributors are to be congratulated on the compilation of a book that illuminates our understanding of social work practice education – past, present and potential. Hard-hitting in its critical analysis, the book nevertheless gives us cause for hope and numerous practical ways to keep true to a vision of practice education that is, in itself, true to social work.

Mark Doel
Emeritus Professor, Sheffield Hallam University

Reference

Wayne, J., Raskin, M. and Bogo, M. (2010) 'Field education as the signature pedagogy of social work education', *Journal of Social Work Education*, 46(3): 327–39.

Notes on contributors

Carole Adamson is a Senior Lecturer at the University of Auckland, New Zealand, where her teaching and research interests focus on best practice, mental health, occupational resilience and stress, disasters and social work curriculum development.

Sallie Allison's background is in adult social care. For the last 10 years she has been a Practice Educator/Lecturer with students at Plymouth University.

Cherie Appleton is the Director of Practicum in the social work programmes in the University of Auckland, New Zealand. She is passionate about research and teaching in field education, transfer of learning and building ethically robust practice frameworks. Cherie and Carole see themselves as *wahine toa*, strong women.

Avril Bellinger is a registered social worker who led the Centre for Practice Learning at Plymouth University until she retired in 2013. Founder and chair of the charity Students and Refugees Together (START), she actively maintains her commitment to social work education as social action. Her National Teaching Fellowship, granted in 2008, endorsed her commitment to social justice through practice, teaching and research. Her publications reflect this commitment.

Geraldine Blomfield is a Practice Educator/Lecturer and a registered social worker. Geraldine's background is in adult mental health and generic social work. Geraldine has a Masters in Understanding and Securing Human Rights.

Pete Brown is a retired Royal Navy chef now in his final year of social work education.

Dawn Clarke, now a freelance consultant, managed statutory and third sector services for 30 years.

Michael Cook is from Bradford, West Yorkshire and recently graduated from the Plymouth University BA (Hons) Social Work programme.

Deirdre Ford is a registered social worker and Lecturer in Social Work who gained the Practice Teaching Award in 1996. For ten years she combined an academic career, including placement co-ordination, at Exeter University with practice in the field of learning disabilities and mental health prior to taking up a full-time post at Plymouth University in 2002. She has worked extensively with service user and carer groups in education and practice.

Kate Hazel has been a registered social worker for 25 years. She is a qualified Practice Educator, a member of BASW and a Fellow of The Royal Society of Arts (FRSA). Kate's social work career includes working at senior levels in the areas of child protection, mental health, probation and practice education with adults, children and families in all sectors of the community. Kate currently works as an independent social worker and an Independent Practice Educator.

Christopher Higgins is a mature social work student currently in the final year of his studies.

Hannah Jago is a Plymouth University graduate, who is currently practising social work in adult social care.

Margaret Jelley (MSW) is a Lecturer/Practice Educator at Plymouth University with over 20 years' social work experience in various settings.

Annastasia Maksymluk is a Lecturer in Social Work at Plymouth University. A registered social worker, Annastasia has worked in adult mental health services. She is passionate about the arts and this is reflected in her research interests which include arts-based methods within the classroom, and the relevance of autoethnography for the social work curriculum.

Julie Mann has been a Lecturer in Social Work at Plymouth University since 2002. She completed the GSCC Practice Teaching Award in 2004 and has co-led training for Practice Educators since 2007. She was a social worker in London and then Devon for 16 years, and was Programme Lead for the Diploma in Social Work at East Devon College for four years. She is a registered social worker.

Dean Matthews, care leaver, is a third year BA (Hons) Social Work student at Plymouth University.

Beth Moran is a Social Work Lecturer at Plymouth University. Her research interests include student peer learning, interprofessional working and health and social care provision.

David Neal is a Lecturer and Practice Educator based in the Centre for Practice Learning, Plymouth University. A registered social worker, he worked as a senior Social Worker with the Royal Navy before starting his academic career.

Angie Regan is a registered social worker with 20 years' experience in child protection. Currently working as a Practice Educator at Plymouth University, Angie has considerable experience in teaching, supporting and assessing social work students.

Victoria Sharley is a Doctoral Researcher at Cardiff University. Prior to commencing her research in identifying child neglect in schools, Victoria practised as a specialist Domestic Violence and Abuse Social Worker in statutory Child Protection services for three years.

Hayley Smith is a postgraduate of both social work and education. Twenty years of practice experience led her into social work education and here she remains, working for Plymouth, Bristol and The Open University.

Sharon Soper is a Practice Educator/Lecturer and a registered social worker and family therapist still in practice. Sharon has published work about service user involvement in social work education and practice with asylum seeker and refugee families. Her interests include equality, social justice, human rights, and also social media.

Dr Doris Testa is a Senior Lecturer at Victoria University, Melbourne, Australia. Passionate about education and welfare she registered as a social worker in 1992. Her publications include articles and joint chapters on supervision, teaching and learning strategies, and working with people from diverse backgrounds.

Dr Joanne Westwood is a Senior Lecturer in Social Work at the University of Stirling where she is Programme Director for qualifying social work programmes. A qualified social worker who practised with children and families in England, Joanne has edited a book about using social media in social work. She has worked with practitioners, students and academics to support their developing social media strategies for teaching and practice.

Andy Whiteford is a Practice Educator, Lecturer and HEA Teaching Fellow. Following an early teaching career within the 'small school' movement, Andy qualified in social work in 1992. He worked in the probation, youth justice and drug treatment sectors. An interest in practice teaching led onto higher education teaching in 2001. Currently studying for a Master's degree in Education, Andy is particularly interested in advancing transformative, experiential teaching and learning.

Daniel Wilding is an undergraduate student social worker and producer, writer-director of short films. This is his first academic publication.

Introduction

Avril Bellinger and Deirdre Ford

Texts such as this edited collection invariably comment on the prevailing climate as a time of substantial change and conflict for social work, both in the UK and globally. It would be fair to say, however, that the scale of change and conflict in the second decade of the 21st century is unprecedented. Nationally, the global economic downturn, creating austerity, political instability, insurmountable pressures on services and frequent regulatory shifts by way of solution, is having catastrophic effects on systems of state welfare and the well-being of the poorest groups and communities. For those professions charged with giving support to disenfranchised people in each society, the struggles to combat capitalist forces have diverted attention from the persistent erosion of professionalism and autonomy. Questions about whether social work is defined by the state or a function of the state in the UK, or whether it can maintain its independent professional identity, appear to take precedence over its ability to intervene effectively in the face of expanding social need exacerbated by economic, climate and social factors. Social work's commitment to social justice and interventions based on relationships can be hard to maintain through the prevailing techno-managerial processes and an increasingly disconnected 'universal' service.

As state solutions fail and communities are left to manage their own difficulties, this edited collection aims to inspire new thinking to meet these challenges with professional education that is fit for purpose. It is a learning resource that seeks to liberate social work educators from conventional approaches to placement-finding and student learning. The book captures diverse voices presented in different formats. Framed within a critical analysis of social work as social action, it provides an internationally relevant collection of practical examples to show what is possible when practice education is held fully in dynamic tension with academic learning, and when student learning is shaped by practice imperatives and concerns. We are privileged as editors to have worked alongside many of the authors and have been motivated by admiration for their work to bring this collection together. Our intention is to celebrate good practice and to share innovation and the potential to develop creative spaces even within restrictive environments. Readers are presented with practical guidance grounded explicitly in theoretical frameworks. Chapters are informed by scholarship and pedagogy specific to adult learning in practice settings.

While this is a book about practice learning, inevitably reference is made to learning in the university setting as well. Traditionally, in social work education delivered by universities and colleges, the fieldwork element has been ascribed lower status than classroom-based teaching. It is our assertion, however, that the two sites are neither separate nor in competition with each other, but, rather, are in dynamic interaction. Students should not be left with the burden of making the connections between them, as is frequently the case. Incorporating the voices of students and practitioners, the book is intended to counter these trends, challenging the received wisdom that professional practice is best learned through an apprenticeship model.

Educators face significant challenges in seeking to develop opportunities for learning and professional development that instil the values of the profession in students and equip them for the complexities of practice in an uncertain world. In Chapter Thirteen, we reflect on the nature of these challenges and examine the status of practice education in professional programmes, offering an alternative perspective that removes the traditional academic–practice divide.

The chapters promote knowledge generation, not just knowledge application. Practice has been seen as a place where students apply knowledge to practice rather than these being in dynamic interaction. This book is the latest attempt to countermand such an approach. The book also aims to show what can be achieved, for example, through working with students as co-creators of knowledge for practice. In Chapter Two, Hayley Smith and Vicky Sharley use an auto-ethnographic approach to explore the impact of an international placement on both student and tutor. In Chapter Six, Annastasia Maksymluk offers an accessible, arts-based technique developed in a statutory setting to help students learn how to reflect and to explore power relationships without defensiveness.

Two chapters deal with the difficulties for minority group students in all aspects of their education. Chapter Four and Chapter Five highlight parallel concerns in the experiences cited by black and minority ethnic students and by men in social work. In Chapter Four, Sharon Soper and Geraldine Blomfield offer a challenging insight to white readers about the progression of black students, and guidance for those who want to avoid replicating conventional barriers to professional and higher education. Both chapters may prove to be uncomfortable reading for white female educators, in particular. They are original, however, in refreshing the literature about the experiences of both of these groups on social work programmes. They offer provocation but also strategies to create more open learning environments.

Contributors confront placement shortages, in the state sector especially, by providing a range of creative strategies that are a direct response to human need, unfettered by managerialist imperatives. Three chapters focus specifically on developing alternative placements. The first, Chapter One, reflects on student-led services in Australia and the UK to consider the factors that contribute to their sustainability. Chapter Seven is deeply embedded in scholarship about the connection between social work and the natural world. Andy Whiteford draws on extensive personal commitment and charts his journey in engaging placement students in outdoor settings to emphasise the connection between people and planet. Chapter Nine is a polyphonic account of developing capacity for final placements in the 'third sector' or non-governmental organisations (NGOs). It is worth noting that the practice described here is constrained by current UK standards that, in an attempt to be protective of professionalism, are simply restrictive. This chapter is included as an example of good-quality practice wherever guidelines do not preclude it.

Illustrating the diversity of affiliation, Kate Hazel provides an outsider perspective on working as a practice educator in Chapter Three. As an independent social worker, she shows the value of the critically reflective position that practice educators need to adopt alongside the students with whom they work.

Information technology gateways are increasingly presented as the way to access information and financial support. Virtual reality is an important dimension of 21st-century life. In Chapter Eight, Joanne Westwood provides an introduction to the new possibilities posed by the application of social media to practice education, its benefits and potential risks. She poses reflective questions throughout the chapter to help practice educators engage with this new area. Similarly, other contributors summarise their learning for the reader to make their ideas as accessible as possible.

Chapter Ten, by Dave Neal and Angie Regan, bears testimony to the importance of utilising practice educators with a pedagogic qualification to undertake the practice observation of students. In Chapter Eleven, Julie Mann offers both a conceptual framework and guidance about the content of such training. Not all students can succeed. Cherie Appleton and Carole Adamson use a Māori construct in Chapter Twelve to support educators and students in making judgements about student progression based on integrity.

At a time of acute student placement shortages for all professions, this book proposes original solutions to maintain high-quality opportunities for students. It is essential reading for all those responsible for fieldwork education worldwide, both in social work and in professions where practice learning is a requirement. With an emphasis on creativity and innovation, it is also relevant for educators charged with developing work-based learning opportunities in health and social care disciplines.

The book offers readers an opportunity to see social work in action through education and will, we hope, provide ideas and encouragement. It is full of examples of what can be achieved, even under difficult and repressive conditions.

ONE

Student-led services

Avril Bellinger and Doris Testa

Introduction

Applicants for social work courses will often explain their motivation as 'wanting to make a difference' in people's lives. Even in relatively resource-rich nations like the UK and Australia, there are deepening social inequalities and a tightening of access points to service entitlements. As state resources are reduced, preventive practice can be perceived as a luxury and problems are dealt with only when they reach crisis point. Practice education is an opportunity to harness students' idealism, respond directly to need, redress social injustice, create positive alternatives and promote significant learning. Student-led services, staffed principally by students undertaking fieldwork placements, offer beneficial results both for society and for the quality of professional education. However, developing and maintaining this provision can be complex and challenging.

This chapter provides critical reflection on the common features of one student-led service in Australia and another in the UK. Both services operated for a number of years and each is the subject of publications (Butler, 2005, 2007; Testa, 2011). The phenomenon of student-led services is placed in the historical and international context of the health and social care literature. Each service is then described in sufficient detail for the reader to understand the origins of the initiative, the learning opportunities provided to students and its development over time. In conclusion, factors that are generative and protective of such innovations are identified in order to encourage others to take such initiatives.

Literature review

There is a well-established tradition of students on professional courses providing services to groups and communities as a mutually beneficial part of their training. Much of the literature originates in the US, where Moskowitz et al (2006) found that over 30 US medical schools had student-led clinics as part of the educational experience available to students. The health insurance system in the US has meant that, historically, people in poverty and those who were homeless were unable to access preventive health services. These communities are therefore the most likely to be served by student initiatives. They offer new entrants to the profession an introduction to the relationship between health and social justice (Marmot, 2005) while providing otherwise unavailable services to a group with complex needs. Research has shown that such exposure can result in higher levels of student professional satisfaction (Fournier et al, 1993) and may encourage graduates to work in similar settings when qualified (Tavernier et al, 2003). Student-led provision is not restricted to the US, or to medicine. Aiken and Wizner (2004) review the history of law clinics in the US. They reflect on the outcome of the competing claims of social injustice and academic imperatives over three decades and affirm the importance of activism in education. Occupational therapists have developed a concept of 'role-emerging' placements for final-year students (Wood, 2005; Thew et al, 2008). In such placements, students are given the task of creating an occupational therapy service in an agency where none has previously existed. The results are rich in terms of learning. International research identifies key themes in relation to role-emerging placements, indicating that these are emotionally highly charged learning experiences that make a demand on students to plan and think more carefully, and to learn to collaborate with other disciplines, which encourages the development of their professional identity (Dancza et al, 2013).

In social work, students are being taught to recognise and respond to social inequality. The settlement movement was fundamental in its social activist orientation, providing accommodation for students within disenfranchised communities to facilitate mutual learning and benefit (Gilchrist and Jeffs, 2001). Although the original, Toynbee Hall (see: www.toynbeehall.org.uk), still serves its local community, regrettably very few of these centres remain. In 2012, the famous Hull House settlement in Chicago, initiated by Jane Addams, went into administration after 120 years of community provision. Smaller-scale initiatives around the world have most commonly been led by activist academics. Examples include the law centre for Roma people set up by Diana Videva in Bourgas (Videva, 1998), students from Hong Kong working with communities in mainland China prior to unification (Wong and Pearson, 2007), students working with people displaced by the forest fires in Greece to prevent the loss of land rights (Pentaraki,

2011), and students from the College of Social Work in Mumbai working in police stations to improve police interactions with people living in the Dharavi slum (Muzumdar and Atthar, 2002). There are many other examples of students working alongside disenfranchised individuals and groups and achieving extraordinary results. The question therefore arises: why are student-led services for social work the exception rather than the norm?

Specific projects

Example one: Students and Refugees Together

Students and Refugees Together (START) began as a service provided by social work students for people seeking asylum in the UK in 2001. Changes of law and policy in 1999 meant that people seeking asylum in the UK were segregated from mainstream society. In an attempt to control all aspects of immigration and to deter people from choosing the UK as a 'soft option', the government set up the National Asylum Support Service. This department's brief was to control all aspects of people's lives and movements until a decision was made about whether they had leave to remain. While some people were held in detention centres, the majority were 'dispersed' to cities around the country. Accommodation was provided through contracts with private companies and people were given a minimal allowance for subsistence. People had neither choice nor influence over where they were sent and were unable to work or relocate while waiting for a decision. Frequent changes of law over this period resulted in situations that were complex and very specific to each individual or family. Indeed, inefficiencies in the bureaucracy meant that people could wait several years for a decision.

A strategic decision to avoid clustering meant that people from all nationalities were dispersed to one city in the south-west of England, Plymouth. A family could find that there was no one else in the city able to speak their language. In 2001, the national census showed that the city had an unusually low (0.6%) black and minority ethnic population and was ill-prepared for the arrival of people with diverse cultures and languages. Boswell's (2003: 324) research in the UK and Germany found that 'social tension is usually highest in areas with relatively small numbers of people seeking asylum and with little experience of integrating other groups'. Individuals and families dispersed to the city were both exposed and isolated. One of the authors had previously explored ways of enabling students to move from the 'colour-blind' approach prevalent in the region (Jay, 1992; Dhalech, 1999) to one that was culturally sensitive and anti-racist (Butler et al, 2003). The dispersal of people seeking asylum presented an opportunity for activism through education with the potential of mutual benefit.

Families waiting for a decision had no recourse to mainstream advice or welfare services and were only provided with support to enable their school-age children to attend full-time education. The visionary manager in the education department used the small stream of funding from central government to employ a specialist teacher, who ensured that children had school uniforms and transport and worked with city schools to provide a welcoming environment. Families trusted this teacher and brought all kinds of other questions and problems to her – letters from the immigration service, health problems and racist abuse – often out of working hours. Her manager grew increasingly concerned about the pressure on her as the number of families increased. One of the authors, then a university placement coordinator, and the teacher's manager lived in the same village and a chance conversation between them generated the possibility of students 'filling the gap'. They brought together a small group of concerned professionals to explore ways in which a service could be developed using student resources to offer families support that was otherwise unavailable.

The primary considerations were the safety of service users and the educational needs of students. Work allocation and weekly supervision were to be provided by the teacher together with the local authority referral coordinator, who was also known to the families. Frustrated by the necessity to turn the families away, the coordinator had undertaken independent research and had amassed substantial information about the resources that asylum seekers could access. The university provided a qualified practice educator, who agreed to oversee the service development and to provide professional supervision. Her work included regular supervision, observations of the students' work with service users and assessment, which incorporated feedback from service users and other professionals. Three students were invited to undertake this placement and learning agreements were drawn up. Shortly before the placement was due to begin, it became clear that the education service was unable to accommodate the students and a decision had to be made to withdraw or to make other arrangements.

Motivated by the extreme neglect of the needs of families at that time, the group decided to go ahead. The practice educator met with the students in her own home on the first day and the students accepted that they *were* the service (Butler, 2005). Although formally part of the education service and social services departments, with combined supervision from staff of both agencies, the students were doing work that was outside the remit and beyond the eligibility criteria of both. They had to develop information management formats and procedures for a virtual organisation, which enabled them to explore the ethics and practicalities of bureaucratic systems. Each student worked with between two and five families for their placement and each was able to demonstrate the full range of social work competence through providing a needs-led, strengths-based holistic service. In the first two years, placement patterns on the undergraduate and postgraduate courses enabled a service to be provided from September to June. In that time, 14 students provided services to 21 families, comprising 35 adults and 68 children. The families came from 10 different countries of origin and spoke 11 different first languages. An analysis of the student experience of these first two years and details of the work undertaken can be found elsewhere (Butler, 2007). What follows here is an account of the organisation's development as a student-led service.

In 2003, a final placement student on the undergraduate programme challenged the steering group's acceptance that the service would have to close in the summer because of the absence of student placements. She worked alongside the group to fund-raise for a temporary part-time continuation worker so that families would not be left without a service. The remarkable achievements of students working without agency resources provided evidence to support major fund-raising activity. In 2003, the organisation won a major Lottery grant and also a government contract and was able to employ six full-time members of staff. Although welcome, this rapid expansion shifted the focus from students and refugees towards internal organisational issues. The steering group became trustees and the organisation was registered as a business and charity. Policies and procedures had to be produced, contracts complied with, employment issues resolved, and financial governance assured. Student activity in this period was significantly reduced as START strove to achieve recognition as a reputable non-governmental organisation. When the Lottery grant ended in 2006, START had to reduce to three members of staff in order to survive. The contract to deliver a refugee housing support service provided the core funding but additional funding sources ensured that people could still be offered a holistic service at whatever point of the immigration journey they had reached. This funding crisis acted as a catalyst to enable START to return to its original values of being a non-hierarchical learning organisation. No single manager was appointed; instead, the three staff (two student supervisors and the administrator) now jointly manage the organisation. Students are the majority workforce and a flow of around 20 each year undertake their placements there. Although the majority are social work students from all over Europe, there are regular occupational therapy placements, as well as students from business studies, geography, clinical psychology and other subject areas.

The organisation provides a range of services, particularly to people with leave to remain, and works closely alongside the organisations that offer advice to those waiting for a decision. Community activities such as a women's group, fortnightly cultural kitchen, gardening and walking projects provide a range of access points for people wanting help. Student capacity means that the individual casework service can be highly responsive and driven by service user need rather than by eligibility criteria. This flexibility allows people to have support with realising their ambitions and aspirations, as well as with finding housing, work and health care. By 2013, in 10 years as a registered charity, START has provided 2,536 refugees with an individual casework service and 189 students with professional placements.

Reflecting on the beginnings of the organisation and on its development, the point at which START was most vulnerable was when it attracted major funding. Interestingly, this period of rapid growth coincided with a reduction in the number of students and a move towards a more conventional arrangement in which staff outnumbered students. It is common for students to be seen as a burden on busy staff rather than as a resource and the author has argued elsewhere that this same error is made in respect of refugees even though both groups are potentially high contributors in transition (Butler, 2005). The young organisation's focus on internal and structural factors deflected attention from the core values on which it was based. The painful process of downsizing was informed by these values, which continue to provide a consistent basis for decision-making.

Example two: Social Work Students in Schools

The Social Work Students in Schools (SWSiS) initiative began in 1994 and was located in a Catholic primary school situated in the western suburbs of Melbourne in the Australian state of Victoria. Although school-based social work had been the norm in local public schools, in Catholic Church schools, social workers were not included in pupil welfare or pupil well-being approaches. The SWSiS programme was an initiative developed and adopted by the principal of the Catholic primary school in response to a gap in the pupil welfare resources located in the school site.

Characterised by social and economic disadvantage, the school has a richly diverse population, with some 28 cultural backgrounds. The school's ethos and values stress inclusivity regardless of difference. Even so, its socio-economic status meant that it had limited social, cultural and human resources that it could deploy to well-being programmes. Thus, SWSiS was born of a realisation that if programmes were to be added to address social, emotional, educational, spiritual and/or cultural well-being and to free teachers to attend to their main task of teaching, then other resource possibilities needed to be explored.

The principal, a qualified social worker, decided to approach social work field placement coordinators first at Victoria University, Melbourne, and then, as the programme developed organically, other schools of social work in order to discuss the placement of social work students within the school setting. Initially, Victoria University agreed to place two social work students within the school to complete their 70-day field education placement. Over time, the other five Victorian universities expressed interest in placing their students in the school setting. Between 1994 and 2005, 79 social work students, drawn from the six Victorian universities offering the Bachelor of Social Work, completed their field placement at the school.

Underpinned by a socio-ecological perspective and the health-promoting school discourse, the SWSiS initiative targeted the whole school environment. Taking a whole-school approach to programme delivery, the main emphasis was to intervene early on before factors affecting pupil achievement, such as family poverty, experience of forced migration or non-English-speaking carers, became too complex or too established. In so doing, the SWSiS initiative took account of the child's total environment and the factors that impinge on their well-being and learning.

The introduction of social work students to the well-being programmes was an attempt to ensure that, once introduced, programmes were sustained over time. Over a period of 12 years, social work students led or co-led, with their social work peers, 19 well-being programmes. Each targeted one or a number of interventions located along a continuum:

- *Primary prevention:* lunch programme; breakfast club; and school camp.
- *Early intervention:* classroom programme; grants and submission writing (eg advocacy for camp fees); parent engagement research (eg parents as partners in the swimming and camp programmes; parents' experience of enrolment processes and policy); programme-

based research (eg breakfast club research; scoping of the need for after-hours care; bullying audits); and community development programmes (eg artist in residence).

- *Intervention:* transition programme; welfare referrals; and after-hours school care.
- *Restoring resilience:* SEASONS programme (for grief and loss).

From a social work education perspective, SWSiS was purposefully structured to emphasise the three characteristics of professional practice – theory, practice and research – and it guided the social work students through the process of integrating theory and practice (AASW, 2006, 2012). Social work students were allocated responsibility for a particular well-being programme and participated in weekly/bi-weekly individual and group supervision. The social work students also participated in all other staff, school and community activities.

As stated earlier, SWSiS lasted 12 years and while the analysis of the model can be found elsewhere (Testa, 2010), there were some significant factors that impacted on the cessation of the programme one year after the principal left the school. Specifically, this can be attributed to the initiative's lack of insertion in the formal and professional structures of the school operations. While the programme developed organically, what did *not* develop was a strategic plan for it to be embedded in the vision, understandings, formal work assignments and decision-making processes of the whole-school approach to pupil well-being (Nutbeam, 1992, 1998; Kouzes and Posner, 2006). These will be discussed in the following section.

Following the principal's departure from the school in 2005, the Catholic Education Office invited her to work as a project officer and establish social work student units in Melbourne Catholic primary schools. During 2006, the project involved work with 10 Catholic primary schools implementing the SWSiS programme, redesigning and restructuring SWSiS as a template for other Catholic schools in Melbourne. However, the student-led service did not continue.

On reflection, the SWSiS model's implementation was dependent on the school's socio-ecological discourse and cross-disciplinary collaboration being embedded in the formal and professional structures of the school operations. Embedding this model, or any model, was predicated on the stakeholder's understanding and acceptance of the SWSiS model. Analysis of SWSiS data pointed to the difficulties that often occur when different disciplines come together to take action (Lee, 2004; Nutbeam, 2004) without having first negotiated the organisational culture that is needed to sustain such a collaboration.

As Kouzes and Posner (2006) argue, a collaborative culture is one characterised by stages that shift organisations from being loose associations to full collaborative partners. This requires the key stakeholders to work with all involved through processes that make the case for change, assist all to have a shared vision and develop effective and responsive practices to implement this shared vision. It also ensures that key leaders and stakeholders model and encourage effective collaborative practice. In the case of the SWSiS initiative, it appeared that in its organic development and duration, the foundations and opportunities necessary for collaboration were missing or were left to chance. This affected the longevity and effectiveness of the initiative. The stages missing in the introduction and development of the SWSiS initiative and the steps that would have addressed the omissions are as follows:

- *The development of shared cross-disciplinary attitudes.* This could have been achieved through purposefully structured forums within which staff, social workers, parents and the wider community shared, mapped and understood their contribution to pupil well-being, and within which they shared knowledge and learnt together how to support and guide each other's contribution to well-being programmes.
- *The understanding and development of effective and responsive cross-disciplinary knowledge.* All stakeholders would be involved in the design, evaluation and implementation of well-being programmes. This shared knowledge would increase the broad ownership and understanding of the SWSiS programme. It would also provide all stakeholders with a forum in which to advocate, explain and promote their cooperative contributions to pupil well-being.
- *The development of cross-disciplinary skills.* A purposeful, sequential and reasoned phasing-in of the components of the SWSiS model would include ongoing training for the stakeholders. This training would help stakeholders move beyond the traditional disciplinary silo approach to a cross-disciplinary, well-articulated, well-understood socio-ecological approach to pupil well-being that could be periodically evaluated.

Had the steps just outlined been considered and acted puon, perhaps the processes and practices would have changed the school's culture to more accurately reflect both an understanding of the health-promoting discourse and an understanding of how cross-disciplinary collaboration can establish and sustain a health-promoting school. The absence of this planning and the eventual cessation of the initiative highlight the attention that must be paid when attempting to promote and embed such models of student-led social work programmes within school-based health promotion strategies. Without such planning, the social work students' input may remain in the margins of mainstream schooling rather than becoming embedded.

Although social work students continue to work in schools, providing them with opportunities for well-being programmes that may not otherwise be available, the ongoing work to shift organisational cultures remains a challenge. Failure to embrace a strategically planned holistic approach to pupil well-being evident in the original school meant that it lost the SWSiS initiative when the head moved on, even though a form of the programme was embraced by other Catholic schools. This exemplifies the pivotal role that leadership plays in implementing and sustaining change.

The challenge continues of enabling schools to see social work students as a force for change and as effective contributors to health promotion. Instead, they are viewed as workers who will focus solely on direct casework with pupils and their families without addressing the underlying systemic causes of health disparities.

Reflections

Although these two examples of student-led services responded differently to diverse groups of people, it is worth noting that both originated within the education system. The school environment is one in which family difficulties can be apparent but there are rarely resources within the education services to respond to their needs holistically. Services must address both well-being *and* achievement if pupils are to have a successful passage through schooling and eventual participation in the social and economic fabric of society. Schools have a role in developing children's social, human and cultural capital, all of which are implicated in well-being and achievement, and all of which are driven by global, national and local policy mandates. However, schools are also balancing the dual concerns of productivity and welfare. Likewise, mainstream welfare services have to balance the rights of individuals to equitable services in times of austerity and must direct provision to targeted problems according to specific criteria.

The structural impediments to balancing operational output demands and well-being are related to the level of resources available. These resources are bounded by the socio-economic and cultural circumstances of the organisation and its stakeholders. The more social, cultural and human capital located in the community stakeholders, the greater the resources available. In both projects, the community resources were very limited and students provided the investment to undertake essential preventive work that was not otherwise possible.

Both examples confirm the contribution that students are able to make to wider society in the process of developing their professional identity. With careful leadership and consistent support, students can provide services to some of the more excluded members of society across a spectrum of intervention levels. Although statutory interventions such as child or adult protection are beyond their remit and capability, students may be able to alert responsible agencies earlier than would otherwise be the case. They are able to form trusting relationships with children, families and individuals and to intervene positively to prevent more serious difficulties arising. In a global economy where resources are increasingly under pressure, mainstream social work services tend to be directed to situations that meet strict eligibility criteria and that have deteriorated to a point at which intervention cannot be avoided. In both examples outlined earlier, students have been able to prevent such situations arising and to work alongside people to increase their resilience and social capital.

Making student-led services a reality

The terms 'service learning' (Chupp and Joseph, 2010) or 'fieldwork' capture the dual function of such arrangements, whereas words like 'placement' or 'practicum' may appear to privilege a student learning agenda. For example, while the placement of white American social work students in an African-American church is seen as generally beneficial for both parties (Moore and Collins, 2002), it is acknowledged that the experience is not always successful. Chupp and Joseph (2010) critique the placement of students within excluded communities as potentially reinforcing students' negative stereotypes and exploiting already oppressed people. In their view, care should be taken to ensure that the arrangements are directed to impact on the students, the community and the educational institution in equal measure. It may be that the benefit to the institution of law and medical students having access to complex work ensures the continuation of student-led services. However, even in disciplines where this arrangement is the norm, there is significant critique about their purpose and values (Aiken and Wizner, 2004). For professions like social work, however, the more contested view of professional practice and the potential risk to students and to service users seem to render these structures fragile and dependent on individual commitment.

Drawing on the substantial experience of student-led services that have endured over time, the authors have identified a number of protective factors that fit broadly within three categories. Building on the conclusions of Chupp and Joseph (2010), it is clear that for such initiatives to succeed, they must attend to the needs of service users and the educational needs of students in equal measure. They must also be mindful of their impact on the existing formal structures within and alongside which they work.

In terms of service users, priority must be given to ensuring that their needs are held as primary and never exploited for the benefit of student learning. Students bring energy and fresh ideas to their work, which can be of enormous benefit to people who are otherwise neglected by state provision. These groups of people are already at risk and must not be made more vulnerable by the services provided. This places an additional onus on those providing the support. They must be competent enough to fulfil the students' needs for developmental supervision and be knowledgeable about the particular field in which the students are working. In the case of SWSiS, the head was also a social worker and so had this competence. However, this exposed a vulnerability in the programme when she left. In START, the staff are employed as student supervisors and they themselves work within the fast-changing world of refugee policy.

With regard to student learning, we must remain alert to the danger of exploiting the most vulnerable people in society for educational purposes. Equally, we must guard against the risk of abusing student labour in an attempt to redress social injustice (Aiken and Wizner, 2004; Chupp and Joseph, 2010). With high-quality developmental supervision and teaching, it is possible to maintain the balance between the right of the public to good-quality services and the right of students to professional education.

In relation to organisations, care should be taken to recognise that although students add value to existing provision, they are not cost-neutral. Investment in office accommodation, running costs for activities and basic administrative costs must also be factored in. Structures that promote learning are those that are non-hierarchical and it can be challenging to persuade large organisations to be open to unconventional practices and to share ownership. This was a key factor in the closure of the SWSiS student-led programme and it is why START became an independent charity. START's independence promoted close working relationships with both higher educational providers and the relevant traditional organisations, rather than being dependent on either of them for continuation. The consistent change of personnel as students finish their placement and new students begin can be seen as disruptive and problematic for relationships with service users and other agencies. If managed well, however, this flow of students maintains a learning organisation culture (Gould and Baldwin, 2004) and freshness of approach.

Organisations that use student labour to deliver services are likely to be developed by individuals as a response to particular and localised conditions. If the provision is to persist over time, the organisational structure needs to take account of these factors and not be dependent on the continuing availability of the originators. Personal commitment and investment are essential in the early stages. However, mainstream organisations will always tend to be ambivalent towards such organisations because of the fragility of student services and the fact that, by their very existence, they highlight inadequacies in existing services.

Students come into social work wanting to make a difference in people's lives and can learn substantially from being allowed to do so. As educators of professionals who are charged with promoting 'social change and development, social cohesion, and the empowerment and liberation of people' (IFSW, 2014), we have a responsibility to educate through responding to social injustice. There is no shortage of unmet need in society and we hope that this sharing of our experience will encourage others to be brave, to manage risk responsibly and to work alongside students to respond positively and proactively to policy and cultural changes.

References

AASW (Australian Association of Social Workers) (2006) *Practice standards for social workers in schools*, Melbourne: AASW.

AASW (2012) *Australian social work education accreditation standards*, Canberra: AASW.

Aiken, J. and Wizner, S. (2004) 'Teaching and doing: the role of law school clinics in enhancing access to justice', Georgetown Law Library, Georgetown, US, Open Commons: 997–1011.

Boswell, C. (2003) 'Burden-sharing in the European Union: lessons from the German and UK experience', *Journal of Refugee Studies*, 16(3): 316–35.

Butler, A. (2005) 'A strengths approach to building futures: UK students and refugees together', *Community Development Journal*, 40(2): 147–57.

Butler, A. (2007) 'Students and refugees together: towards a model of student practice learning as service provision', *Social Work Education*, 26(3): 233–46.

Butler, A., Elliott, T. and Stopard, N. (2003) 'Living up to the standards we set: a critical account of the development of anti-racist standards', *Social Work Education*, 22(3): 271–82.

Chupp, M.G. and Joseph, M.L. (2010) 'Getting the most out of service learning: maximising student, university and community impact', *Journal of Community Practice*, 18: 190–212.

Dancza, K., Warren, A., Copley, J., Rodger, S., Moran, M., McKay, E. and Taylor, A. (2013) 'Learning experiences on role-emerging placements: an exploration from the students' perspective', *Australian Occupational Therapy Journal*, 60(6): 1–9.

Dhalech, M. (1999) *Challenging racism in the rural idyll. Final report of the Rural Race Equality Project Cornwall, Devon and Somerset 1996–98*, Exeter: NACAB.

Fournier, A.M., Perez-Stable, A. and Greer, P.J., Jr (1993) 'Lessons from a clinic for the homeless: the Camillus Health Concern', *Journal of the American Medical Association*, 270: 2721–24.

Gilchrist, R. and Jeffs, T. (2001) *Settlements, social change and community action: good neighbours*, London: Jessica Kingsley.

Gould, N. and Baldwin, M. (eds) (2004) *Social work, critical reflection and the learning organisation*, Aldershot: Ashgate Publishing.

IFSW (International Federation of Social Workers) (2014) 'Global definition of social work'. Available at: http://ifsw.org/policies/definition-of-social-work/

Jay, E. (1992) *Keep them in Birmingham: challenging racism in South West England*, London: Commission for Racial Equality.

Kouzes, J.M. and Posner, B.Z. (2006) *The leadership challenge* (vol 3), Hoboken, NJ: John Wiley & Sons.

Lee, T. (2004) 'Cultural change agent: leading transformational change', in C. Barker and R. Coy (eds) *The power of culture: driving today's organization*, New South Wales: McGraw Hill, pp 37–67.

Marmot, M. (2005) 'Social determinants of health inequalities', *The Lancet*, 365(9464): 1099–104.

Moore, S.E. and Collins, W.L. (2002) 'A model for social work field practicums in African American churches', *Journal of Teaching in Social Work*, 22(3/4): 171–88.

Moskowitz, D., Glasco, J., Johnson, B. and Wang, G. (2006) 'Students in the community: an interprofessional student-run free clinic', *Journal of Interprofessional Care*, 20(3): 254–59.

Muzumdar, K. and Atthar, R. (2002) 'Social work placements in police stations: a force for change', in S. Shardlow and M. Doel (eds) *Learning to practise social work: international approaches*, London: Jessica Kingsley Publishers, pp 43–58.

Nutbeam, D. (1992) 'The health promoting school: closing the gap between theory and practice', *Health Promotion International*, 7(3): 151–3.

Nutbeam, D. (1998) 'Evaluating health promotion – progress, problems and solutions', *Health Promotion International*, 13(1): 27–44.

Nutbeam, D. (2004) *Theory in a nutshell: a practical guide to health promotion theories* (3rd edn), New South Wales: McGraw Hill.

Pentaraki, M. (2011) 'Grassroots community organising in a post-disaster context: lessons for social work education from Ilias, Greece', in M. Lavalette and V. Ioakimidis (eds) *Social work in extremis. Lessons for social work internationally*, Bristol: The Policy Press, pp 51–64.

Tavernier, L.A., Connor, P.D., Gates, D. and Wan, J.Y. (2003) 'Does exposure to medically underserved areas during training influence eventual choice of practice location?', *Medical Education*, 37: 299–304.

Testa, D. (2010) 'Silos to symphonies: social work and its contribution to student wellbeing programs within a Victorian Catholic school', PhD thesis, Victoria University, Australia.

Testa, D. (2011) 'School social work: a school-based field placement', *Aotearoa New Zealand Social Work*, 23(4): 14–25.

Thew, M., Hargreaves, A. and Cronin-Davis, J. (2008) 'An evaluation of a role-emerging model for a full cohort of occupational therapy students', *British Journal of Occupational Therapy*, 71(8): 348–53.

Videva, D. (1998) Untitled paper given at international conference, Bourgas Free University, Bulgaria.

Wong, Y. and Pearson, V. (2007) 'Mission possible: building social work professional identity through fieldwork placements in China', *Social Work Education*, 26(3): 292–310.

Wood, A. (2005) 'Student practice contexts: changing face, changing place', *British Journal of Occupational Therapy*, 68(8): 375–78.

TWO

International placements: learning from a distance

Hayley Smith and Victoria Sharley

Introduction

These reflections were compiled following a three-month international social work placement in 2010. One of the authors, Victoria, was located within a women's refuge in Napier, New Zealand, working predominantly with a group of Māori women and children. Victoria was supported via videoconferencing by her tutor, Hayley Smith. The placement was assessed on Victoria's return to the UK through an observed presentation to academics, students and practice educators.

Drawing on the principles of auto-ethnography, this chapter focuses on understanding the relationship between self, others and the concept of cultural identity (Chang, 2008). It explores the multiple layers in the authors' consciousness to connect the personal to the cultural, first through their outward interpretations of the social and cultural aspects of their experiences, and then inwardly examining the impact of the relationship to self (Ellis and Bochner, 2000). The authors present individual narratives from tutor and student perspectives that are not only confessionally emotive, but also intrinsically connected with each other's learning journey.

The structure encourages readers to interpret the authors' creative expressions for themselves, offering a narrative that transcends personal experience to engage in a cultural interpretation of relationship-based practice education (Chang, 2008). The chapter focuses upon three themes: *isolation*, *the changing nature of the relationship* and *shared learning and reciprocity*. These themes were drawn from the authors' reflective 'letters to self', written independently after completion of the placement and reorientation of the student to the university. Each theme begins with an extract from both the tutor's and student's 'letter to self'.

Theme 1: Isolation

Victoria

> I don't believe you are the least bit aware of the magnitude of what you are thinking about undertaking.... You are placing yourself for three long months in an area you are barely familiar with, living and working with strangers of a vastly different cultural upbringing, and doing so alone. That said, the being alone part will actually materialise in being the largest factor that allows you to grow as an individual more than you imagined possible. The usual product of years of experience and learning – squeezed right down into a few mere months. It is just magical.

There was a sense of extreme isolation that manifested during my international placement in New Zealand, which acted as a significant catalyst in progressing my learning. This came as a real surprise given that my placement was in an English-speaking country that was already very familiar to me from a tourist perspective. My identity as a white Western female located my position within the cultural minority – not only in the women's group, but also within the agency's workforce, which was representative of the service user demographic.

As time passed, it became evident that New Zealand English held many mysteries, with the connotation of words often leaving me without the assumed subtext from my own cultural upbringing. This resulted in 'talking past one another' in practice, naively stuck in ineffective communication where I was unable to overcome the cultural dissonance (Metge and Kinlock, 1978; Metge, 2010). Consequently, my contributions to group work were often ignored or dismissed by participants. My accent and British intonation not only caused an additional obstacle, but were also interpreted by the group as an indication of personal wealth and educational privilege. This left me feeling incredibly lonely, isolated and misunderstood by those around me.

Throughout the three months, I was challenged by assumptions about, and perceptions of, me in a post-colonial country. I experienced emotional solitude at personal, cultural and structural levels (Thompson, 2010). This created a feeling of intense division, not only from the people with whom I practised, but also from anything of familiarity or fundamental understanding. A vivid memory was a sense of separation from the deep-seated cultural comprehension, where we are secure in knowing the unwritten rules and social norms that guide us in our day-to-day life (Barlow, 2007).

This isolation was not simply that of being in a foreign physical environment, or of being a solo traveller, it was more complex emotionally and compounded by the socio-political framework. The women's refuge where I was placed was a service that responded to a hidden and taboo social issue, sited at a secret geographical location in the region, and protected via a PO Box postal address (Whebi, 2009).

Retrospectively, such loneliness and separation probably began long before I found myself in placement (Pinkola Estes, 1992). As an individual, I have always felt a distance from those around me. I have had a naive desire to change the world somehow, and 'make a difference' to the lives of people in need of support, but had never really understood my driving force behind it (Whebi, 2009). I have travelled far, striving to realise this expectation, and experienced many cultures in the process (Magnus, 2009). However, the identification and planning of the placement for six months prior to departure was a time-consuming and solitary process. I was anxious about what the agency might expect, my role within its remit and the assumptions held by us both (Walker et al, 2008; Magnus, 2009). Undertaking this extraordinary learning opportunity alone and suddenly finding myself completely submerged within another culture simply magnified my feelings of peer division in the learning community. This was particularly so when I had completed the three-month placement and returned to my familiar learning environment at the university.

My practice sensitivity is heavily entwined with my sense of creativity (Rowe, 2003). While on placement, I drew upon the processes of reflective free writing and journaling as techniques for self-evaluation when I was unable to draw upon my established support systems in the UK (Magnus, 2009). I tried to connect with my new physical environment through exploration and photography of the surrounding landscape congruent with a Māori cultural and spiritual perspective (Munford and Sanders, 2011). My aim was to construct a world-image identity when I was struggling to make sense of the socially constructed world in which I found myself (Zaph, 2005). The combination of these methods proved to be an invaluable vehicle for self-reflection. They enabled more explicit articulation of my deeper learning within this cultural context, while simultaneously offering a creative healing process for what proved to be isolating and often confusing experiences (McNiff, 2004; Magnus, 2009).

Such feelings of division, helplessness and anxiety were heavily moderated through the use of two communication strategies while in placement (Magnus, 2009): peer support and supervision with my tutor via videoconferencing. Regular video calls with another student who was undertaking an international placement in Australia offered unrivalled mutual support and deep peer comprehension of the emotional solitude that I was experiencing (Munn-Giddings and McVicar, 2006). It quickly became apparent that having a solid framework of academic support to alleviate the rising sense of fear and isolation was a sheer necessity. I recall the huge significance and comfort in planned videoconferencing supervision times with my tutor and the reassurance this provided through a visual connection with a familiar face from my own culture in my home country (Panos, 2005).

Hayley

> Remember that not all students will necessarily experience what you did when you went away to another country to work for the first time, they may feel more comfortable more quickly. Equally, I would encourage you to reconnect with that feeling of isolation and confusion about not knowing any of the 'rules' when a student shares this with you.

Isolation is a recurring theme echoed by many students who have undertaken international placements (Panos, 2005), but I wondered what that meant. I began by reflecting on my own experience of travel and revisited what feeling isolated meant to me and whether it was part of the motivation for going overseas. There may be something deliberate in placing oneself in an unfamiliar setting as a way of confronting self in the face of isolation. Solo travel exacerbates this, generating a unique set of circumstances that stimulates our thinking in a new way (Lang and Crouch, 2009). This connection seems more profound as we recognise that the social work task is largely working with people who are in some way isolated and marginalised (Gair, 2008).

I questioned from my own experience how isolated I had felt prior to my travels, whether I had felt displaced within my own context before I left (Pinkola Estee, 1992), then transported this feeling with me overseas in such a way that the unfamiliarity of the new context legitimised its presence; a recognition that the emotional space is validated by the geographical one.

Isolation can be defined as 'a lack of contact between persons, groups or whole societies' (Collins Dictionary, 2014); it can be tangible (I am alone here, literally and physically) and it can be invisible (I am surrounded by people with whom I have no connection). My own previous experience of not knowing 'the rules', and not having any real anchor point, was something that generated its own isolation. Over time, and as the familiarity of a new setting increased, the potency of that feeling diminished. As a tutor supporting this adjustment for students, it has proved helpful (though not essential) to be able to connect personally to that place of vulnerability experienced through my own solo travels.

Lang and Crouch (2009) explore the phenomenon of 'frontier' lone travel and their study produces some interesting key themes that motivate individuals to undertake these journeys. Their findings suggest that travel provides, among other things, an opportunity for reflection; it instigates challenge (personally and professionally) and promotes reaching for self-actualisation (Lang and Crouch, 2009).

Addressing isolation is challenging; balancing support without intruding, while also recognising the needs identified. Videoconferencing offered us both the opportunity to literally see one another, and this visibility enabled me to read non-verbal cues about wellness, as well as listen to the narrative. Students similarly report that being able to see someone familiar is comforting and immediate (Panos, 2005).

Theme 2: The changing nature of the relationship

Victoria

> Although you are aware the university's support will be limited, you haven't yet given sufficient thought to what impact this will have if things become difficult or problems arise: both personally and professionally. During the difficult times, the depth and length of the working relationship with your tutor will be crucial in enabling you to feel understood, when no-one around you holds a similar perspective at all.

I remember a considerable shift from the didactic, micro-learning environment I had become accustomed to within the relationship. The transformation began to emerge alongside the heightened cultural uncertainty and unfamiliarity that I was experiencing in a challenging and unknown practice context with a predominantly Māori group of women and children (Magnus, 2009). The multifaceted student–tutor relationship that developed had an incredible impact upon the way I learned throughout the remainder of my final academic year (Gardner and Lane, 2010). Its profundity remains and still offers me a means to approach and make sense of my life (Reed-Danahay, 1997). It provides a learning framework that continues to inform my ongoing maturation and personal development (Skovholt and Ronnestad, 1992; Eraut et al, 1998).

What took place was an evolution from my familiar position as a receiver of information to one of continuous reflection with my tutor. I held shared possession of the space to explore and revise the way I understood the territory, history and culture of the people I was supporting (Lyon and Brew, 2004). This encouraged my voice through reflective practice. Through the sharing of power with my tutor (Helms and Cook, 1999), I rapidly progressed from the role of 'map reader' to that of 'map maker' while being isolated within a new and uncharted global landscape (Lester, 1999, cited in Cooper, 2008). I was developing a dynamic competence to create my own map, representative of my interpretation of the situation, and responsive to the cultural needs of the group I was working with (Doel et al, 2002; Williams and Rutter, 2010). This approach not only broadened my professional capability, but deepened my motivation to learn (Barnett and Coate, 2005) while also increasing my desire to apply such knowledge to my relationship-based practice during placement (Knowles, 1990; Magnus, 2009).

Having been taught by my tutor through the second year of the degree, I had some insight into the way she approached academic learning with elements of origination and imagination. This offered me reassurance and informed my expectations about our shared preference for learning through visual and artistic methods. This sense of creative association reduced the power imbalance within the relationship early on, and provided me with a bridge of consistency that enabled both our roles and our working relationship to extend far beyond the student–tutor boundaries. It facilitated a fresh educational platform, where it became possible for a mutual, reflexive exchange to take place (Gardner and Lane, 2010). What occurred was an unexpected intimacy, which initially felt unusual, a little uncomfortable and most definitely exposing (Kadushin, 1976). The relationship changed and became reflective of the new learning environment in which I found myself (Orchowski et al, 2010). It now incorporated professional and personal facets requiring a greater alliance of trust and commitment to what, at times, proved an unpredictable learning exchange (Grey, 2002).

Reciprocity, openness and trust were the three fundamental values that strengthened the bond between us (Rogers, 1990). I remember feeling completely overwhelmed when I needed to confide both personal and professional dilemmas in the same supervision session via videoconferencing even though the relationship between us was well-developed. I had an overriding feeling of vulnerability through being on the other side of the world, reliant on one person to offer some sort of shared recognition fitting with my personal meaning system. My capacity to be open and honest, and trust my tutor, underpinned my ability to learn effectively while in a place of geographical and emotional isolation. While I was able to increase my self-awareness and self-confidence and to develop more fully as a reflexive practitioner (Barnett and Coate, 2005), I believe an absence of reciprocity, openness, trust or creative association would have left the connection faulty and mistrustful, with the organic process of development un-nurtured and unable to unfurl into its full potential.

Hayley

> What you do well is relate to and understand their emotional place. Remember that part of your role, Hayley, is to make connections with students to develop their learning and help them pull theory forward into their practice. Again, this was helpful this summer and last year, when you related this to Maslow, supporting them to meet their basic needs to enable them to move onward and upward.

This key theme relates to the changing nature of the tutor–student relationship, which remains a challenge for me. I wondered if offering personal aspects of my experience might expose vulnerability in my confidence to offer knowledge and constructive teaching as part of the student–tutor relationship. It made me question whether this might blur the edges of the established professional working relationship (Kadushin, 1976). However, my own integrity and recognition of the essential position of self in any relationship resolutely drove me forward, as Butler et al (2007: 282) state: 'the use of self in relationship building should continue to be central to a profession such as social work'.

I recognise that in this aspect of the letter to self, I am trying to redefine the edges that are familiar and safe. I talk about 'developing their learning' and 'pulling theory forward into practice' as though they are the most important things I should do. Yet, supporting students on international placements demands a move beyond that safety. Connecting with them emotionally is fundamental to providing a different kind of safety.

It is important to recognise that students undertaking international placements are trusted to manage some of the core requirements that we would normally perform. This contributes to shifting the intimacy within our regular supervision, where additional aspects of professional issues and personal experience collide. Separation of these is more complicated as discussion inevitably weaves between the two – personal wellness impacting on professional understanding of situations.

On several occasions I have been left wondering which of us feels more vulnerable: the tutor supporting aspects of student self that are beyond usual expectations, or the student recognising a need to share them in order to make sense of their experience. Perhaps because we both feel this so intensely, the unfamiliar personal–professional territory might become something that unites us.

I recognise that there is a danger here of over-identifying with their placement experience. However, Karpetis (2011: 1159) suggest that a student–tutor supervisory relationship 'significantly influences the nature of the learning environment'. This encourages me to embrace what I bring and not see it as a contaminant. One of the four key significant aspects of my role that was highly valued involved simply 'being there' (Bellinger and Elliott, 2011: 716), providing consistency and stability.

The changing nature of intimacy starts early in the spring term prior to departure, when discussions with students about international placements raise the question of mutual trust. Part of the preparation (Magnus, 2009) involves moving out of the hierarchical place where student and tutor inhabit different spaces, and agreeing to share a new platform together, which can feel risky. I need to be able to trust what that student will do with the information we share, as they do with me. It can feel like a leap of faith. The preparatory conversation sets the parameters, something Butler et al (2007: 292) suggest might be 'both risky and exciting'.

In my letter to self, I state that part of my role is to 'make connections' with students; yet, equally, I know that there is a chance I may not find one. How supportive can I be if all I do is detach myself and hold a very formal place? Implicit in this aspect of my letter is an expectation of good modelling in the relationship, something that demonstrates depth and commitment to the work. I clearly assume that I will 'hold' students in some way, supporting their confidence to explore personal and professional boundaries, much as I feel I am exploring mine. To facilitate both aspects within this relationship requires that, as the tutor, I offer a stable platform of personal accountability, while retaining the 'capacity to be present in the professional relationship' (Butler et al, 2007: 293). This investment and subsequent development can feel meteoric but is only possible when both tutor and student have the courage to enter into something that is unexplored.

Each international placement will bring its own uncertainties as the variables of countries and cultures unknown clearly contribute to the unpredictability. Mason (1993) suggests that we work most effectively from a place of 'safe uncertainty'; therefore, the tension for me as the tutor is around defining and maintaining that relative safety.

Theme 3: Shared learning and reciprocity

Victoria

> You believe that your planning and preparation for the trip will carry you through the experience, keep you safe in your expectations of what the learning will be, and where it will come from – and although you think you know what to absorb and digest in advance of your departure – simply, you don't. You will be working as a professional who is accountable for your practice within an unfamiliar and complex cultural environment. It will take you to your absolute limit – and change you intrinsically as a person.

Looking back on the experience as a whole, this final theme of shared learning carried – and continues to carry – the greatest weight in my overall professional development. This deep learning was not achieved solely because of the rich opportunity that offered unfamiliar fundamentals of 'being'; it allowed a chance to muse and contextualise alternative ways of thinking. I believe the extent and significance of the learning was directly linked to the isolation from the abundant transmission of information that I was accustomed to while on campus (Light et al, 2009).

The cultural seclusion I experienced instigated a new sense of professionalism and accountability to a degree that I had not previously encountered as a student (Barnett and Coate, 2005). I found that I could not avoid the feeling of professional responsibility growing within me, reifying ownership of my learning while on placement (Knowles, 1990; Race, 2010).

This feeling continued to resonate deeply, captured in daily practice comparisons, while I shared accommodation with the refuge manager who was my practice supervisor. The presence of such an organic interchange catapulted forward my understanding about the principles of shared learning: exchanging ideas and concepts, and exploring cultural representations and reflections in order to make sense of situations at personal and cultural levels (Magnus, 2009). This was further reflected at a structural level, where the absence of a linear management structure in the refuge highlighted equitable contribution in the decision-making process (Wenger, 1998).

Embracing a new model of community knowledge, I looked to the Māori culture surrounding me to encompass its core principles in my individual practice. A pivotal moment in my learning was the identification and use of a Māori genealogical concept that offered a bridge of cross-cultural understanding. This enabled me to have a meaningful connection with the women I was supporting (Metge and Kinlock, 1978; Metge, 2010). I was looking out from a position within the Māori culture. This proved absolutely key in expanding my understanding of the events in the lives of the women that I was working with, as well as those in my own learning relationship with my tutor (Devo and Schlesinger, 1999; Gutierrez et al, 2000).

The working relationship between me and my tutor evolved considerably throughout my three months in New Zealand. As I became more reflective about the impact of the culture in which I was submerged, the depth and intensity of reflexive conversation between us increased, and brought with it a powerful exchange. This was in stark contrast to how, as the passive student, I had previously 'banked' information for use later (Freire, 1996).

As my placement progressed, the reflections I brought to the exchange with my tutor became more refined. I found myself beginning to look 'out from', rather than 'in to', the cultural environment that I was in. I felt that our learning relationship prioritised the profundity of a shared belief system, a meaning system that superseded individualism. In doing so, a space was created for a dynamic learning environment, which was supportive and encouraging (Jones, 1995).

On my return to the UK, I drew on creative and visual representations to connect international experiences to personally significant areas in the New Zealand landscape congruent with Māori culture (Suopajarvi, 1998; Zaph, 2005). My aim was to convey the notion that who I was and how I now understood the world had become strongly rooted in my overall sense of self, creativity, place and, most profoundly, the people with whom I had stood beside (Spretnak, 1991, cited in Zaph, 2005; Sharley, 2012). When I was later reoriented at the university, it therefore felt natural to attempt to suffuse my cultural understandings with my learning. I sought permission for my mother, who had been a consistent and supportive figure throughout my international placement journey, to be present at my observed presentation. Initially, my tutor dismissed the request, which I found extremely frustrating. I was already experiencing confusion and difficulty resettling alongside my peers, and I was left questioning why the 'learning exchange' so preciously manifested between me and my tutor now appeared not to function effectively. My mother being there was a representation of my position within my ancestry; a piece of my own cultural identity – of who I am, and how I was beginning to understand my place in the world through another culture's eyes. Her presence that day represented the relational and familial cultural bridge to the Māori understanding of 'whānau' or wider family grouping (Love, 2008). Bringing a support person or family member to a meeting at work, an interview or significant event is widely accepted practice in New Zealand culture. My mother's attendance formed the connection between my individual understandings of both communities. This reified my experiences from the three months as a whole, illustrating the deep sense of understanding I had achieved, while also enabling me to share this in the context of my own culture (Ruwhiu, 2008; Munford and Sanders, 2011).

Hayley

> I think it is all too easy to undervalue what you offer by being interested and connected to the global world, enjoy the learning you receive, Hayley, as well as what you give, allow yourself to be open to learning with students who will educate you along the way with their journey; you don't always need to have all the answers, just be the listener.

This has probably been the single most valuable lesson I have learnt in my role as a practice tutor: to receive learning and not feel as though my only role was to give, to educate or to inform. It is humbling to be taught by students, and, in some ways, is a relief to have permission not to have knowledge about everything.

By recognising this reciprocal arrangement, we experience learning through 'engagement' rather than 'transmission' (Light et al, 2009), which enables us both to hold an element of power and authority in the relationship and value one another's contribution. When the student was overseas, I could enjoy and engage with the experience, reducing any distraction from hierarchical or academic expectations. It became a mutually dependent learning activity, modelling Lave and Wenger's (1991: 30) 'communities of practice', where each participant teaches another, moving from 'legitimate peripheral participation' to a central point of learning. This reciprocity and intensity of experience gained by relinquishing a position of perceived authority effected change for us both.

Repositioning of self was most evident on the student's return when she asked if she could invite a family member to her observed presentation. The presentation forms part of the assessment process, exploring how the experience shapes the student's understanding of social work and how she might use it to inform practice in the UK. My immediate response to the request was to simply disregard it, believing that it was not sincere. I was distracted by culturally normative requirements of academic rigour and had lost the intimacy of the relationship we had established, simply because the geography had changed. Kadushin (1976) suggests that tutors can often revert to a more academic stance when faced with the challenge of student emotion. On reflection, the introduction of Victoria's family to the process extended that intimacy into an environment that I was less comfortable with. Perhaps the geographical distance had supported my ability to connect in this way, but bringing that back to my familiar professional world felt uncomfortable.

In fact, the presence of family was a significant factor for her, and when she challenged me on the importance of family in relation to her social work experience in New Zealand, I recognised my oversight. I realised that my views of the programme and assessment requirements were fundamentally rooted in a white, Western perspective.

As Cook (quoted in Orchowski et al, 2010: 55) suggests: 'supervisors who are committed to training supervisees in culturally competent and ethical practice must accept and withstand feelings of vulnerability associated with their own disclosure of their racial and ethnic identity'.

As a result of this challenge, my understanding of self, as well as my implementation of our social work programme, was transformed. The request was an opportunity to embrace the cultural engagement that Victoria had experienced and to use it to develop my understanding of social work in the UK. This challenged me considerably as the tutor. It also reminded me about the courage that I needed to build on this shift in my position, to maintain this position of vulnerability for all placements.

Transformative learning (Mezirow, 2000) is not the sole domain of students. Having the courage and humility to learn together is, I would argue, a prerequisite to supporting international placements, and challenges the conventional tutor role. This ratifies and consolidates my desire to set clear expectations for the student–tutor relationship before departure and on return. By doing so, it is acknowledged that vulnerability exists for us both, but also that there is the opportunity to share in a rich source of learning (Karpetis, 2011). Without this, reciprocity of learning is limited, maintaining the default positions of tutor/student and potentially limiting the experience for us both.

Conclusion

The exposure to self that this international placement offered and the writing of this chapter have been significant for us both. Initially, we recognised that a pivotal learning moment had been our mutual experience, but neither of us anticipated what revelations would appear two years later when we reflected as colleagues. Supporting an international placement, and maximising learning, require courage and skill as both participants engage in an environment with little experience or ability to feel 'culturally competent' (Laird, 2008). What we now understand is that we can apply knowledge and skills from our own context with cultural sensitivity and that this starting place can be the springboard for mutual growth. Embarking on this journey enabled us both to move from 'map readers' to 'map makers', and was always going to require us to explore terrain that was not always predictable or comfortable, but with a belief that the investment is worthwhile.

Recognising students' ability to teach as well as learn enabled us both to take risks with our development. The organic shift from transmission to transformational learning (Light et al, 2009) was enhanced by the factors and variables unique to the placement setting. It was a journey across a landscape of obscure, often invisible, obstacles stumbled upon and navigated with academic trepidation because so much was unprecedented.

A lack of conformity releases a potential to be transformational (Mezirow, 2000) and reinforces that social work need not be defined by parameters of culture, nationality or location. It is not about a singular aspect of the experience originating from a binary position, such as a white Western female living and working in a predominantly black community, nor is it about comparing practice and approaches to specific dilemmas between countries. It is about utilising all aspects of self, building a relationship on foundations of trust. Employing technology through Web-based supervision, blogs or emails to enhance supervision content can certainly support this experience but the fundamental requirement was about embracing the intimacy that this generated. At times, it felt risky for tutor and student alike, but, ultimately, it supported our growth.

International placements are ambitious and exposing. They are expensive financially and emotionally but, equally, fulfilling if both student and tutor yield to their teaching. The mutual sense of responsibility, vulnerability (Gingras, 2012) and equality of privilege is something neither of us anticipated, or, indeed, appreciated to the full, until the completion of this chapter.

References

Barlow, C.A. (2007) 'In the third space: a case study of Canadian students in a social work practicum in India', *International Social Work*, 50(2): 243–54.

Barnett, R. and Coate, K. (2005) *Engaging the curriculum in higher education*, Maidenhead: Open University Press.

Bellinger, A. and Elliott, T. (2011) 'What are you looking at? The potential of appreciative inquiry as a research approach for social work', *British Journal of Social Work*, 41(4): 708–25.

Butler, A., Ford, D. and Tregaskis, C. (2007) 'Who do we think we are? Self and reflexivity in social work practice', *Qualitative Social Work*, 6(3): 281–99.

Chang, H. (2008) *Autoethnography as method*, Walnut Creek, Canada: Left Coast Press.

Collins Dictionary (2014) 'Isolation'. Available at: http://www.collinsdictionary.com/dictionary/english/isolation

Cooper, B. (2008) 'Continuing professional development: a critical approach', in S. Fraser and S. Matthews (eds) *The critical practitioner in social work and health care*, London: Sage, pp 222–37.

Devo, W. and Schlesinger, E.G. (1999) *Ethnic-sensitive social work practice* (5th edn), Boston, MA: Allyn and Bacon.

Doel, M., Sawdon, C. and Morrison, D. (2002) *Learning, practice, and assessment*, London: Jessica Kingsley.

Ellis, C.S. and Bochner, A.P. (2000) 'Autoethnography, personal narrative and personal reflexivity', in N.K. Denzin and Y.S. Lincoln (eds) *Handbook of qualitative research* (2nd edn), Thousand Oaks, CA: Sage, pp 733–68.

Eraut, M., Alderton, J., Cole, G. and Senker, P. (1998) *Development of knowledge and skills in employment*, Research Report No. 5, Brighton: University of Sussex Institute of Education.

Freire, P. (1996) *The pedagogy of the oppressed* (3rd edn), London: Penguin Books.

Gair, S. (2008) 'Walking a mile in another person's shoes: contemplating limitations and learning on the road to accurate empathy', *Advances in Social Work and Welfare Education*, 10(1): 19–29.

Gardner, L.D. and Lane, H. (2010) 'Exploring the personal tutor–student relationship: an auto-ethnographic approach', *Journal of Psychiatric and Mental Health Nursing*, 17: 342–7.

Gingras, J. (2012) 'Embracing vulnerability: completing the autofictive circle in health profession education', *Journal of Transformative Education*, 10(2): 67–89.

Grey, D. (2002) *A briefing on work-based learning*, Generic Centre Assessment Series No 11, London: Higher Education Academy.

Gutierrez, L., Yeakley, A. and Ortega, R. (2000) 'Educating social workers for practice with Latinos: issues for a new millennium', *Journal of Social Work Education*, 36: 541–60.

Helms, J.E. and Cook, D.A. (1999) *Using race and culture in counselling and psychotherapy: theory and process*, Needham Heights, MA: Allyn & Bacon.

Jones, B.J. (1995) *The Indian Child Welfare Act handbook: a legal guide to the custody and adoption of Native American children*, Chicago, IL: American Bar Association.

Kadushin, A. (1976) *Supervision in social work*, New York, NY: Columbia University Press.

Karpetis, G. (2011) 'A relational approach to the evaluation of the practice performance of social work students in Greece: the supervisors' perspective', *British Journal of Social Work*, 41(6): 1158–75.

Knowles, M. (1990) *The adult learner – a neglected species* (4th edn), London: Golf Publishers.

Laird, S. (2008) *Anti-oppressive social work: a guide for developing cultural competence*, Los Angeles, CA: Sage Publications.

Lang, J.H. and Crouch, G.I. (2009) 'Myth, adventure and fantasy at the frontier: metaphors and imagery behind an extraordinary travel experience', *International Journal of Tourism Research*, 11(2): 127–41.

Lave, J. and Wenger, E. (1991) *Situated learning: legitimate peripheral participation*, Cambridge, Cambridge University Press.

Lester S. (1999) 'From map-reader to map-maker: approaches to moving beyond knowledge and competence', in D. O'Reilly, L. Cunningham and S. Lester (eds) *Developing the capable practitioner: professional capability through Higher Education*, London, Kogan Page, pp 45–53.

Light, G., Cox, R. and Calkins, S. (2009) *Learning and teaching in higher education: the reflective professional* (2nd edn), London: Sage.

Love, C. (2008) 'Cultural origins, sharing, and appropriation – a Māori reflection', in G. Burford and J. Hudson (eds) *Family group conferencing: new directions in community centred child and family practice* (2nd edn), Piscataway, NJ: Transaction Publishers, pp 15–30.

Lyon, P.M.A. and Brew, A. (2004) 'Reflection on learning in the operating theatre', *Reflective Practice*, (4): 53–66.

Magnus, P. (2009) 'Preparation for social work students to do cross-cultural clinical practice', *International Social work*, 52(3): 375–85.

Mason, B. (1993) 'Towards positions of safe uncertainty in human systems', *Journal of Systemic Consultation and Management*, 4: 189–200.

McNiff, S. (2004) *Art heals: how creativity cures the soul*, Boston, MA: Shambhala Publications Inc.

Metge, J. (2010) *Tuamaka: the challenge of difference in Aotearoa New Zealand*, Auckland: Auckland University Press.

Metge, J. and Kinlock, P. (1978) *Talking past each other: problems of cross cultural communication*, Wellington: Victoria University Press.

Mezirow, J. (2000) *Learning as transformation: critical perspectives on a theory in progress*, San Francisco, CA: Jossey-Bass.

Munford, R. and Sanders, J. (2011) 'Embracing the diversity of practice: indigenous knowledge and mainstream social work practice', *Journal of Social Work Practice: Psychotherapeutic Approaches in Health, Welfare and the Community*, 25(1): 63–77.

Munn-Giddings, C. and McVicar, A. (2006) 'Self-help groups as mutual support: what do carers value?', *Health and Social Care in the Community*, 15(1): 26–34.

Orchowski, L., Evangelista, N.M. and Probst, D.R. (2010) 'Enhancing supervisee reflectivity in clinical supervision: a case study illustration', *Psychotherapy, Theory, Research, Practice and Training*, 47(1): 51–67.

Panos, P. (2005) 'A model for using video conferencing technology to support international social work field practicum students', *International Social Work*, 48(6): 834–41.

Pinkola Estes, C. (1992) *Women who run with the wolves: contacting the power of the wild woman*, Croydon: CIP Group UK.

Race, P. (2010) *Making learning happen* (2nd edn), London: Sage.

Reed-Danahay, D.E. (1997) *Auto-ethnography*, Oxford: Berg.

Rogers, C. (1990) 'The interpersonal relationship in the facilitation of learning', in H. Kirschenbaum and V. Henderson (eds) *The Carl Rogers reader*, London: Constable, pp 304–22.

Rowe, D. (2003) *Depression: the way out of your prison*, East Sussex: Routledge.

Ruwhiu, L. (2008) 'Indigenous issues in Aotearoa New Zealand', in M. Connolly and L. Harms (eds) *Social work: contexts and practice*, Australia and New Zealand: Oxford University Press, pp 107–20.

Sharley, V. (2012) 'New ways of thinking about the influence of cultural identity, place and spirituality on child development within child placement practice', *British Adoption and Fostering Quarterly Journal*, 36(Autumn/Winter) (Special issue: Multiculturalism, Identity and Family Placement): 112–17.

Skovholt, T.M. and Ronnestad, M.H. (1992) 'Themes in therapist and counselor development', *The Journal of Counseling and Development*, 70(4): 505–15.

Spretnak, C. (1991) *States of grace: the recovery of meaning in the postmodern age*, New York, NY: Harper Collins.

Suopajarvi, L. (1998) 'Regional identity in Finnish Lapland', paper presented at the Third International Congress of Artic Social Sciences, Copenhagen, Denmark.

Thompson, N. (2010) *Anti-discriminatory practice*, Basingstoke: McMillan.

Walker, J., Crawford, K. and Parker, J. (2008) *Practice education in social work: a handbook for practice teachers, assessors and educators*, Exeter: Learning Matters.

Wenger, E. (1998) *Communities of practice: learning meaning and identity*, Cambridge: Cambridge University Press.

Whebi, S. (2009) 'Deconstructing motivations: challenging international social work placements', *International Social Work*, 52(1): 48–59.

Williams, S. and Rutter, L. (eds) (2010) *The practice educator's handbook*, Exeter: Learning Matters.

Zaph, M.K. (2005) 'Profound connections between person and place: exploring location, spirituality and social work', *Critical Social Work*, 6(2). Available at: http://www1.uwindsor.ca/criticalsocialwork/

THREE

The outside looking in: an independent social worker's experience of practice educator work

Kate Hazel

Introduction

This chapter will present the particular contribution that independent social work can make to practice education. As a disabled social worker who is currently working independently, I will also explore some of the unique strengths that I believe independent social workers (ISWs) can bring to the task of creating learning experiences for students and service users. I will offer some of my own aspirations and thoughts about the possibilities that may be available to ISWs in the future given the current climate in social work education. Ways in which we can work more inclusively with all partners will be explored to ensure that we continue to contribute to providing high-quality practice learning for social work students.

My social work journey

I became an ISW partly through necessity and partly through a professional desire to continue to practise social work. At the time, I had a county-wide job in child protection, needed to have a hip replacement and was offered ill-health retirement by the local authority. I had spent much of my career trying to hang on to my direct practice, but the higher I climbed the social work ladder, the less I felt able to practise the very skills I was trained to offer. The focus of my work was increasingly unbalanced in favour of 'process'. At that time, there were no options for me to combine the two. My expertise did not always feel valued, and combined with the fact that I have never been any good at coordinating outfits and accessories, a prerequisite it seemed for women working at a senior level, it was never going to work! The environment did not feel very inclusive to me then. I still wanted to practise as a social worker but I struggled to find the right place to do this. Independent social work has been my chosen way to remain in practice. It enables me to work routinely with core social work values and place the building of relationships at the centre of all that I do. This chapter will demonstrate why independent social work is such a good fit for practice education.

I have contributed to the provision of many different forms of social work services. In the past 23 years I have spent 10 years working in the community and voluntary sector, often in multidisciplinary teams; five years as a senior manager in the statutory sector and as a practice educator for 14 years. For the past eight years I have been self-employed as an ISW across agencies and with all ages. I undertake a wide variety of tasks, from assessment in child protection through to writing funding bids to develop innovative services, for example, for parents with learning disabilities. I work in partnership with those who use services and their carers. In practice with children, I engage with the whole family where this is safe and appropriate.

The work I do is commissioned and time-limited, with a clear role, purpose and outcomes. I liaise with many different people, from government departments through to health services and statutory social care providers. I firmly believe that asking people who use services how they experience them is key to developing effective services. I work closely with the voluntary sector in ways that help to recognise and value their unique expertise in providing less formal ways of working with, and meeting the needs of, some of the most vulnerable children and adults in our society. I have also worked with others to set up and support a few charities along the way.

My approach and commitment to my own good practice and learning as a social worker and practice educator fit well with Wenger's (1998) 'communities of practice' model. From my own experience, I would argue that, in large organisations such as local authorities, these communities of practice can be difficult to sustain. This can manifest itself as an internal conflict – where the need to follow policy and protocol dominates, and the ability to inspire, create, reflect and learn can be neglected and undervalued. The danger is that we can, at times, lose both our own individuality and our sense of what our shared purpose is. Service users can become treated as, and feel like, 'thresholds' and 'packages of care' deemed to be deserving or undeserving of what we as a profession can provide, rather than people with individual needs and expectations of what social work can offer in times of crisis.

Working as an independent social worker

In 2013, there were over 2000 ISWs registered as members of the British Association of Social Workers (BASW). This represents 12% of the total membership of the professional organisation in Britain, a figure BASW anticipates will increase significantly as public sector cuts and social work reforms continue to affect the demographics of the social work profession (BASW, 2012). In my opinion, ISWs are now, more than ever, becoming a distinct and visible group of qualified social workers who are largely skilled practitioners and managers. Many have become disillusioned with the process issues and administrative tasks of the role, which have reduced the opportunities to practise high-quality direct work. Many ISWs, like me, continue to work as registered social workers and as practice educators.

In my view, social work is a generic profession and interventions need to be across the whole micro–macro range. As an ISW, I have continued to work across the sectors, with a wide range of people facing numerous issues in their lives. Regardless of whether the work has been requested by a local authority, a health trust or an education or a voluntary organisation, I engage directly with people at all levels. Whatever I do is based on their particular needs in order to effect positive change and outcomes. I have found that it is only possible to zigzag professionally in this way because, in my current role as an ISW and practice educator, I have remained open to the possibilities that are offered. I have taken a few risks and been able to critically analyse and reflect on situations. I can manage high levels of uncertainty, and can overcome and reduce barriers to good practice. In my experience, there are some fundamental core qualities that ISWs need to possess in order to undertake such a wide variety of tasks. These include expertise, diplomacy, integrity, credibility, the ability to assess and manage risk, a strong sense of professional and personal self, emotional resilience, confidence in own abilities, and knowledge of limitations. Independent work in a wide variety of environments also requires me to challenge my identity, beliefs, assumptions and stereotypes. It stimulates my own professional learning.

ISWs must be clear about how they make evidence-based judgements and stay up to date with changes in legislation and policy in local, national and global contexts. ISWs have to be self-reliant, seeking support and guidance when necessary. All this, I have found, must be supported by strong supervision, which, for me, is provided through monthly, self-funded individual supervision by a qualified psychotherapist who also provides external supervision to local authority social care teams. Taking an active role in social work education and training helps to keep me up to date with my own continuing professional development, and I remain vigilant regarding the current external influences and rhetoric that can appear to destabilise our skills, self-worth and value.

Often, the work requires me to ask difficult questions of organisations and to say the unsaid. Sometimes, I work with other social workers, but I frequently work alone or with colleagues from a variety of backgrounds, such as counselling, family therapy, psychology and youth work. The qualities of an ISW outlined earlier are transferable to a range of social work situations and, in my view, are equally relevant to practice education. I believe that ISWs have a unique perspective to offer to social work education in terms of their expertise and position.

Independent social worker practice and social work education

As an ISW, I am able to adopt a theoretical framework that has integrity and relevance for my practice (Brookfield, 1995). A variety of theories have impacted on my practice as a social worker. The intention I bring to my professional role, which, in turn, arises from my own values, culture and identity, is most closely aligned to the principles outlined in the 'social pedagogy' model. This term has been used to describe a range of work that straddles both social work and education in a way that I believe is highly relevant to my work as an ISW and as a practice educator. Cannan et al (1992: 73) define social pedagogy as 'a perspective, including action, which aims to promote human welfare through child-rearing and education practices; and to prevent or ease social problems by providing people with the means to manage their own lives, and make changes in their circumstances'. As a branch of study, Hamalainen (2003: 78) writes, 'Social pedagogy can be integrated with, for example, social work education and social workers can specialise in this approach'.

Often described as education in its broadest sense, social pedagogy focuses on the social relations that can exist between service users and professionals. The roots and prevalence of the social pedagogue movement in relation to social work are mainly found in Northern European countries such as Germany and Denmark. These countries 'report much better outcomes for their children, particularly those children who are "parented" by the state' (Meachin, 2012). Thus, my approach to practice combines:

> 1) a focus on the importance of relationships, particularly those based on equality and inclusion
> 2) an approach to practice which promotes risk-taking
> 3) a focus on the person as a whole, who is influenced by, and influences, the environment around them, be that the level of family/personal relationship, community and prevailing culture or the wider social and economic environment. (Hatton, 2013: iii)

In the UK, pockets of social pedagogy practice can generally be found in childcare, though, in my own work, I have applied these principles in an effective way when working with adults and in groups. For me, social pedagogy represents a process that can influence what already works and, crucially, gives particular recognition to what is often undervalued: in this case, *ourselves* in the social work role and profession. It values dialogue and critical reflection as a means of understanding, and making sense of situations and interactions. Social pedagogy views risk-taking as an educational objective. In my experience, this can clash with organisations that prioritise health and safety above the use of creative approaches. Similarly, the concept of learning in social pedagogy recognises and promotes the need for working together to enable change through organisational structures by valuing the workforce.

Hamalainen (2003: 76) writes: 'While political action strives towards a goal affecting the external elements of society, that is, structures, institutions and legislation, pedagogical action aspires to changing society by influencing the personal in society, that is, people, morals and culture.' Therefore, the interaction between the social worker and the service user is educational in relation to their personal development, human growth and identity.

In social pedagogy, the pedagogue is the 'practitioner', a term familiar to social workers. I see myself in this role when working both as an ISW and a practice educator, which I view as interlinked and not separate. I use the 'Three Ps' model to guide and inform my practice, which Hamalainen (2003: 76) describes as an 'educational orientation in which the world, people, society, social problems and social work are observed through social pedagogical glasses':

- The first, 'Private' (or privacy), I use to draw out information from a service user or a student rather than primarily focusing on me imparting information to another.
- Second, 'Personal' is linked intrinsically to reflection, primarily by asking myself questions, such as 'Am I moving too fast/too slow for this service user or student?' In order to apply this, a large helping of honesty with self is required.
- The third principle is 'Professional'. Critical reflection is applied here in order to remain objective. For example, when a service user or a student may appear to be disrupting a situation in their life or their learning, I would try to focus on where the service user or student is coming from in order to make sense of why this behaviour is happening now.

This model informs my practice as both an ISW and practice educator by affirming my commitment to a truly holistic approach. I believe that it is vital to work with others by progressively guiding them, rather than reactively addressing problems as they arise.

As previously discussed, the pedagogical principles of inclusion, equality and adopting a holistic approach in social work apply both to my own practice as an ISW with service users and in my practice education role with students. ISWs possess many of the skills that mirror those required to supervise and support student learning. We are flexible, autonomous and routinely contracted to undertake work that requires our independent thought.

In my experience, this unique perspective proves particularly useful when helping students retain a questioning approach within organisations and structures that may have specific procedures about how the social work role is defined and implemented within their own agency. Students can experience confusion or conflict when an agency has expectations different from theirs as to what is required of them in their social work student role. This can either increase their anxiety levels or undermine their motivation to question policy or procedure as it relates to the experience of service users.

Personal foundations for the practice educator role

> The objectives of the practice teacher cannot change. They must in future continue to be the sensitive articulation and evaluation of imagination, experience and behaviour. These terms – though they are not the ones usually used to define

> it – are the integrating expressions of practice. (England, cited in Lawson, 1998: 267)

The words of Hugh England still ring true for me in relation to the vital role that practice educators can and do contribute to practice learning.

As it is for most social work students, my first experience of someone whose role it was to support my learning in practice came on placement, when I was observed in my direct work. I can still vividly remember the sheer terror I felt at having a highly experienced practitioner sitting in a tiny interview room with me and the young man I was meeting with in order to compile a bail report at my first placement. The setting was a probation hostel for men who were either awaiting trial or had been previously convicted of committing serious sexual offences against children and/or women. Textbook practice it was not! As a learning opportunity, it was priceless. The young man, who on previous meetings had barely paused for breath in our conversations, now chose this opportunity to clam up completely. To cut a long story short, I ended up talking with him about our shared interest in late 1970s' punk bands in a desperate bid to find some common ground. I encouraged him to make links between the dates and references of the release of punk singles with significant life events in order to gain information needed to produce a social history of his family background and chart the potential triggers that led him to start offending.

What I learned from the observer's feedback that day has remained central to my practice as both a social worker and as a practice educator who now undertakes observations:

- You have to build a relationship in order to do the work. Often, circumstances dictate the need to do this very quickly and in times of crisis; therefore, a wide variety of effective communication skills is required (Kohli and Dutton, 2010).
- The importance of awareness of self: for example, listening to your intuition and what it is telling you, and reaching into the gaps in the situation and what is not being said (Fook, 2002).
- Trusting and drawing on your personal resources and creativity.
- Adopting a holistic approach to all areas of work and especially to any form of assessment.
- Learning can be drawn from many situations. It is crucial that you are open to learning from all sources, can reflect on this, can increase self-awareness and can integrate it into your practice, adapting your approach where necessary.

- Recognising the importance of feedback and guidance. Students want and need specific examples of how their practice can be developed to achieve progression.

The observer was one of the first people to truly inspire me to want to work with students after I qualified. I was highly motivated and began to supervise social work students and others within 18 months of completing my own training. I completed my Practice Teacher Award in 1999, and 16 years on, I am still doing it!

When I first began supervising students in Bristol, as a practice teacher in the 1990s, I worked closely with a community and voluntary sector student training unit. This organisation, which was partly funded by the local authority and the government regulator at the time, provided additional support and training to non-statutory agencies and placement supervisors, which were free and accessible. The unit was staffed by qualified social workers who were experienced in working in both statutory and voluntary sectors. This expertise enabled them to negotiate placement opportunities in a diverse range of settings, with a particular focus on increasing placements where students could gain skills and knowledge in working with disabled people, black and minority ethnic communities, and lesbian and gay services. Any identified potential learning gaps were addressed through additional learning opportunities. The unit provided a meeting point for seeking feedback from people using services who wanted to become more involved in supporting social work learning. Regular reviews of placement settings took place in order to ensure that good standards of practice opportunities and regular, challenging supervision were available.

Bellinger (2010) describes how, historically, non-statutory agencies were often highly regarded as placement sites, with a number of student units, such as the one I worked with, being set up to facilitate student learning, often in diverse, small, user-led agencies: '...the assumptions of students, teachers and employers [are] that the best placements are those in fieldwork teams where learning is framed by organisational procedures and bureaucratic process and where students can model their practice on that of experienced professionals' (Bellinger, 2010: 2453). Bellinger (2010: 2453, emphasis in original) observes that:

> if we collude with the view that they are the *only* place where students can learn real social work, then apprenticeship is privileged as a model of professional learning and the

definition of social work is mistakenly aligned with statutory agency fieldwork.

Widening the net – valuing practice learning opportunities from all sectors

As a profession, social work is in the midst of major change. Governing bodies continue to offer guidance on the changing expectations of social workers in the UK in ways that can often feel like the role, purpose and responsibilities of a social worker are being destabilised in favour of a more general social care title. This comes at a time of global economic crisis and some of the most radical reviews of social policy that Britain has experienced since the 1940s.

We will all experience differences in how these changes are implemented in the agencies that we are commissioned to work with, and the cultural shifts in approach that may be needed to adapt our practice. The impact of future changes in terms of how social work is delivered, and by whom, remains to be seen. I genuinely hope that this will include recognition of the valuable and unique contribution that is made to our profession by ISWs. Now, more than ever, we will need to continue to assert our own worth, take greater responsibility for our specific professional identities and contribute wherever we can to preserving the integrity of social work:

> It is recognised that 25% of social workers are *not* employed by local authorities, but by national and voluntary organisations, the private sector and as self-employed independent social workers. It is anticipated that this proportion may increase in the future. (SWRB, 2012: 2, emphasis added)

Within the same proposals, there is a recognition by the Social Work Reform Board (SWRB) that:

> Further work is needed to consider how voluntary organisations, dependent on a range of different and often shrinking funding streams can be resourced to support their social workers and develop CPD [continuing professional development] activities as part of local and national networks and how independent workers can benefit from these proposals. (SWRB, 2012: 2)

This statement does at least acknowledge our role as a growing contributor to the profession.

I have frequently worked with students who enter into their training with a firmly held belief that real social work takes place only in the statutory sector, as if this is somehow where your role, responsibilities and statutory powers appear to give you the tools to do your job (Bellinger, 2010). In my opinion, this misperception, if not explored and challenged, can disadvantage and narrow students' ability to value, question and learn from all their learning opportunities. Social work is a complex profession that can feel overwhelming. Anything that appears to simplify this and put a clear framework around it is seductive as a way to minimise the anxiety felt by the enormity of the task and potential risks that can arise in the lives of the people we aim to support. I am not suggesting that it is not crucial for students to experience and understand the statutory powers and responsibilities that social workers hold. However, due to pressure from public sector cuts, government policy could be pushing statutory employers to favour cost reduction over quality. An overemphasis on training social workers to work in local authority roles will mean that graduates qualify without the breadth of transferable skills, knowledge and experience required to undertake social work tasks in an ever-widening range of settings and situations. Walker et al (2008: 19) write that:

> systems to ensure agency accountability have led to the development of detailed procedures as a response. While these have conferred powers on practitioners, they have also restricted professional autonomy, leading to tensions between government and those paid by the state to support vulnerable people.

As the numbers of available placements in the statutory sector continue to decrease, there will be a need to develop a greater number and range of appropriate placements and partnership arrangements with non-statutory agencies, particularly those who are commissioned to undertake some of the legal responsibilities of the local authorities in their areas. I have been involved in negotiating and supporting the practice learning of students undertaking placements in both statutory and voluntary agencies. Some of the non-statutory settings I encountered had not previously offered social work placements to final-year students. In order both to meet the individual student's learning goals and for the agency to provide the complexity and level of work required, additional practice learning opportunities needed to be created. In these situations, I ensured that the opportunities were identified, discussed and agreed between the student, myself and the placement supervisor prior to the placement start date. For example, one student arranged a meeting with a specialist solicitor to increase knowledge of the key aspects of legislation arising in work with women and children seeking refuge from domestic violence situations. Further opportunities were identified to ensure that the student had a period of shadowing a range of professionals as part of their practice learning. This included: an independent domestic violence advocate, who was a qualified social worker employed by the local authority; officers from the police protection unit; a specialist immigration lawyer; and a specialist family lawyer. Several other measures were added to enable the student to carry out assessment work, taking into account the transient nature of the people who lived in the setting and overcoming some of the barriers that this created in planning specific pieces of work. These developments enabled the student to gain a different cultural experience outside their own lived experience and to undertake reflection on their own values, beliefs and attitudes in order to focus on the people they were working with.

In one academic year, of the five students I worked with during their final third-year placements, only two were supervised by a qualified social worker and only one of these was specifically employed and referred to in their job role as a social worker. One student was placed in a local authority child protection team and the other in a local education authority Pupil Referral Unit, where the student was supervised by a family support services manager. The voluntary sector placements were in a women's refuge, a drug and alcohol addiction treatment service, and a service for young people leaving care.

All of these students worked alongside other social workers in their placements and were, without doubt, providing a social work service using core social work skills, methods and knowledge on a daily basis and with great impact. On the whole, the students themselves appeared to have little difficulty in recognising how their knowledge and skills were applicable and could be easily used within these settings and with the diverse groups of people using the services. They needed to ensure that they understood what the statutory powers were and how these may be implemented alongside legislative frameworks in each given setting. ISWs are in a good position to enable this learning.

Supporting innovative practice learning

While writing this chapter, I have reflected on how independent social work is evolving and contributing to the design and delivery of social work, including statutory intervention. A government initiative that places ISWs at its core is that of Social Work Practices. They were conceived as autonomous practices, similar to GP practices, which would contract with local authorities to provide services, initially, to looked-after children.

Munro's (2011) Review of Child Protection considers the place of Social Work Practices in the future design and delivery of social work services. Prior to this, ISWs, myself included, tended to work in a more separate, often isolated, way, often without any formal attachment to a particular team. Following the review group recommendation, five Social Work Practices were set up in England between 2009 and 2010. An independent evaluation commissioned by the Department for Education found a mixed response to the efficacy and outcomes of the pilot. I was interested to see that one of the authors who contributed to the evaluation report is an ISW. From the evaluation, it is clear that each Social Work Practice had a very different organisational structure, such as a social enterprise, and the findings do not really clarify whether this impacted on the outcomes either way. Nevertheless, feelings of being better supported were reported by carers of children, and staff felt more positive about their work and spent more time in direct work with children, families and carers. However, the report acknowledges that 'changes in the political and economic context have had mixed effects for the pilots' and that 'implementation has seen considerable dilution or adaptation of the original theoretical SWP [Social Work Practice] model' (Stanley et al, 2012: 7).

In conclusion

Change can be positive; it is also necessary to adapt in order to survive. We owe it to our profession and to all of us who work in it to make the future of social work as sustainable as possible. Time will tell if we are able to achieve this without compromising the very essence of what we do and why we do it. As the numbers of statutory social work placements either remain static or diminish, and with changes in local authority policy in terms of preferred training routes – the return of internal training opportunities – I can see the potential for a pivotal shift in the perception of, and increase in the numbers of, exciting opportunities outside government agencies. At the end of the day, we are all working with either the same or similar groups of people. It is just that the services provided are delivered in different ways by people with different job titles. Whether our job title is 'social worker' or not, we are all aiming to work with people to achieve positive change.

I believe that social work skills and methods are highly transferable. It is because I have always held this view that I have been able to remain in direct social work practice for such a long time. I have adapted my approach to suit what is needed by the people I am working with at any time. After I qualified, it was the methods of work used by organisations and the interest they inspired in me regarding the issues faced by the service user groups that drew me to posts that often did not have the words 'social worker' in the title. Nonetheless, they demanded social work skills and expertise in order to deliver effective services. Before I became self-employed, I had held at least six different posts in social work. Only one of those posts had the job title of 'social worker', and only two of these posts were within the statutory sector. Regarding the definition of a social worker set out by the International Federation of Social Workers, Lavalette (2011) exposes the inconsistency in the title only being applied to those who carry a recognised qualification from a national regulatory body. He argues that, if this is so, then there are many state social workers not undertaking social work and there are a range of unqualified individuals engaging in social work activities, tasks and functions.

To everyone involved in practice learning, I therefore want to offer the following advice:

- Be mindful of failing to recognise the important part that non-statutory experiences can play as part of your overall social work practice learning in providing essential support to the lives of service users and carers.
- Be flexible and open to learning that can be gained from a wide range of settings.
- Keep updated on all current reforms.
- Chart the progress, outcomes and evaluation of practice from government recommendations such as Social Work Practices – what new opportunities can be created for learning in these structures?
- Use your voice. Take a proactive approach to engaging in the debates surrounding social work reform. Ask questions and seek feedback on how current changes to social work education and training may offer additional opportunities in your future work and how.

For me as an ISW today, the benefits of involvement in practice education are significant. Being part of student education reduces the isolation that can be part of being an ISW. It provides a space for me to reflect on my own professional identity with other social workers in social work education. It helps me to feel a valued part of current and future social work practice. Undertaking practice observations provides me with an amazing 'mystery social worker' opportunity. A bit like a mystery shopper, as part of the observation process, I get to visit agencies that I may not otherwise come across. Although it is only a snapshot, it offers the chance to meet with the people who use those services and with staff teams and to gauge their effectiveness. Sometimes, they even offer me work!

From my own experience, some of the benefits brought to practice education by ISWs are as follows:

- First and foremost, ISWs are practitioners. Students frequently tell me how much they value the input of practitioners as part of their learning. Students I have worked with have often been keen to learn more about how I practise social work in an independent role. As the ISW role develops, it is important that students experience the diversity of ways in which the 'traditional' role of the social worker is changing.
- ISWs lead the way in devising innovative services with people who directly use and benefit from them.
- ISWs already work in partnership with others, and so have an important role to play in bridging the gap between the practice and academic worlds. We can increase partnership working to improve the quality of placements and practice learning opportunities.

Above all, as ISWs, we enter the world of welfare provision from an unprotected and personally invested place, thereby offering students and programmes a unique perspective. We bring an ability to 'think outside of the box' offering a more objective, contextualised and sometimes wider view on practice.

References

BASW (British Association of Social Workers) (2012) The British Association of Social Workers: membership department. Available at: www.basw.co.uk

Bellinger, A. (2010) 'Talking about (re)generation: practice learning as a site of renewal for social work', *British Journal of Social Work*, 40: 2450–66.

Brookfield, S. (1995) *Becoming a critically reflective teacher*, San Francisco, CA: Jossey-Bass Publishers.

Cannan, C., Berry, L. and Lyons, K. (1992) *Social work and Europe*, London: Macmillan.

Fook, J. (2002) *Social work: critical theory and practice*, London: Sage.

Hamalainen, J. (2003) 'The concept of social pedagogy in the field of social work', *Journal of Social Work*, 3(1): 69–80.

Hatton, K. (2013) *Social pedagogy in the UK*, Lyme Regis: Russell House Publishing.

Kohli, R. and Dutton, J. (2010) 'Brief encounters: working in complex, short-term relationships', in G. Ruch, D. Turney and A. Ward (eds) *Relationship-based social work: getting to the heart of practice*, London: Jessica Kingsley Publishing.

Lavalette, M. (2011) 'Social work in extremis – disaster capitalism, "social shocks" and "popular social work"', in M. Lavalette and V. Ioakimidis (eds) *Social work in extremis: lessons for social work internationally*, Bristol: The Policy Press, pp 1–14.

Lawson, H. (1998) *Practice teaching: changing social work*, London: Jessica Kingsley.

Meachin, H. (2012) 'Hayley Meachin blog for World Social Work Day', posted on 19 March. Available at: http://www.huffingtonpost.co.uk/hayley-meachin/world-social-work-day-201_b_1365618.html (accessed February 2013).

Munro, E. (2011) *The final report of the Munro Review of Child Protection*, London: Department for Education.

Stanley, N., Austerberry, H., Bilson, A., Farrelly, N., Hargreaves, K., Hollingworth, K., Hussein, S., Ingold, A., Larkins, C., Manthorpe, J., Ridley, J. and Strange, V. (2012) *National evaluation of social work practices*, London: Department for Education.

SWRB (Social Work Reform Board) (2012) 'Proposals for implementing a coherent and effective national framework for the continuing professional development of social workers'. Available at: http://www.scie-socialcareonline.org.uk/proposals-for-implementing-a-coherent-and-effective-national-framework-for-the-continuing-professional-development-of-social-workers/r/a11G00000017r8SIAQ

Walker, J., Crawford, K. and Parker, J. (2008) *Practice education in social work: a handbook for practice teachers, assessors and educators*, Exeter: Learning Matters.

Wenger, E. (1998) *Communities of practice: learning, meaning and identity*, Cambridge: Cambridge University Press.

FOUR

'Do you have to be white to pass this course?' Developing support for black and minority ethnic students in a predominantly white area

Sharon Soper and Geraldine Blomfield, with Monica Mullings and Sibonginskosi Ndimande

Introduction

'Do you have to be white to pass this course?' These are the words of one black student speaking in a support group, exasperated and frustrated from the discomfort and isolation felt as a result of failing grades, impenetrable feedback, isolation and a sense that it is all *you*, not the system. This chapter outlines our response to that student's plea.

Sharon Soper and Geraldine Blomfield are lecturers/practice educators for social work programmes at Plymouth University. Social workers by profession, Sharon is still in practice and works predominantly with children and families where there has been abuse, loss and or trauma, while Geraldine's background is in adult mental health. Our role in higher education is to support and to facilitate the learning of adults who want to become professional social workers. It is specifically focused on supporting student learning through their practice experience. As argued in Chapter Thirteen, however, the practice learning experience of social work students should not be dislocated from academic learning within the institution. We therefore place student experience in the context of learning in higher education.

We are both interested in the issues of inequality and oppression that blight the lives of the people we have worked with. Sharon is a mixed-heritage woman brought up in a very deprived area of Manchester and raised by a mother who valued education and prided herself on making sure her children achieved at school in order to escape poverty. Geraldine was brought up with seven siblings in South Africa during the apartheid system. Geraldine belongs to a tribe called 'The Coloureds' (a name given by the South African regime during apartheid and still in use) and also comes from a very deprived area. Her experience of migrating to England was that if you are in a different country, you are expected to fit into the institution's rules and regulations, however oppressive they may appear, and that it is not possible to bring about change.

While it is important to challenge the idea of black and minority ethnic (BME)[1] people as 'victims', this can lead to a dangerous cycle of focusing attention away from institutional practices and social oppression, and towards the individual actions and attitudes of BME students (Freire, 1970). Furthermore, this can also contribute to the 'colour-blind' assumption that all students have a universal experience of education. This assumption can become embedded within all university processes, such as recruitment, progression, teaching and assessments (Cheetham, 1982; Ahmed et al, 1986; Sedlacek, 1987; Ahmad, 1990). In understanding the multifaceted nature of oppression, a term coined by black feminists in the 1970s is useful: 'intersectionality' (Crenshaw, 1989) describes how different biological, social and cultural differences cannot alone adequately describe the impacts of societal oppression and that a broader and more layered perspective is required. This term emerged as black working-class women felt that the experiences of white middle-class women could not adequately represent their own. It is now an important sociological concept through which to understand the interplay between gender, class, race, ability, sexual orientation and multiple dimensions of disadvantage. No one system of oppression can be understood alone – each reinforces the other. Therefore, being a black woman and suffering oppression is not only about being black, but also about interrelating gender inequalities. The interplay of gender (and other systems) is hard to quantify. The ideas behind intersectionality are useful in understanding the experience of the BME students on the course.

At first, the failure rate of BME students at our institution was the most noticeable to us. The students did not particularly seek us out as black members of staff, but Sharon was having very uncomfortable conversations with white colleagues about the failure of BME students to progress on the course: conversations like 'making allowances for English as a second language will dumb down standards', and 'X always plays the race card'. These conversations located the failure to achieve and progress within the BME students themselves. We knew, from experience and research, that where a whole group is underachieving, it is unlikely to be something individual to each of them and more likely to be caused by structural inequalities and barriers.

The research on attainment differences of BME students compared to their white counterparts is complex and multilayered, and a simple explanation does not exist. However, the Higher Education Academy found that:

> Even controlling for a wide range of factors thought likely to contribute (such as economic background, age, gender, whether a student lives at home, term-time working, parental income and education, having English as an additional language, entry qualifications and prior institution attended) coming from a minority ethnic community has a statistically significant and negative effect on degree attainment. (Broecke and Nicholls, 2007: 4)

BME students on the social work course were failing to progress to the next year and this was the catalyst for action. This trend is by no means peculiar to South-West England, but has been the subject of a major study by the National Union of Students (NUS, 2013) of black student experiences. This research found that the students' previous experience of education had a strong impact on their degree studies. Black students were often from lower social-economic groups and may not have had access to high-standard education in their formative years. The same survey reported that students suffered from widely held stereotyping and low expectations in previous (and higher) educational establishments.

Focusing on the actual student experience in the classroom, another study looked at multiply-marginalised student groups. They found that subtle marginalisation in the learning and teaching environment contributed to students feeling disempowered (Bernard et al, 2013). Something often reported during our support and mentoring meetings with students on the social work course (and reconfirmed in this study) was that the students felt marginalised and that their experiences were of little worth. In the study, they found that curriculum design, teaching and learning strategies did not deal with the students' experience in the classroom (Bernard et al, 2013).

The NUS study found that greater levels of dissatisfaction with higher educational institutions included experiences of teaching and learning and the institutional environment. Moreover, the students' experience of racism had a massive impact on their 'self-esteem, confidence, motivation, and desire to continue their education, reporting that they felt marginalised and socially excluded' (NUS, 2013: 4).

Class discussion about anti-oppressive practice and the use of language seemed to work against the students in our setting. Use of the term 'lady' over 'woman', for example, was understood differently between different cultures; spirituality and religion was viewed and talked about in slightly disrespectful ways. Anti-oppressive practice standards (Butler et al, 2003) had become dogmatic and oppressive, and we undertook research to investigate and to change this (Boyce et al, 2008).

Whenever BME students are in the minority both in practice and in the classroom, discussing such topics as identity will become much more loaded. Black students often chose to stay peripheral for multiple reasons (discussed later) or were perceived as 'angry'. This must also be coupled with research that points to a lack of diversity in teaching and curriculum design and the sense that BME students feel that their own perspective is missing or marginalised from discussion and learning (NUS, 2013).

This is not to accuse educators or supervisors of purposely oppressing their students. However, the theories on which most models and measurements are based, and by which we assess and gauge learners, often have their roots in a white, middle-class, Eurocentric and mainly male perspective, and those who sit further from that fall short. Psychology, for example, has striven to explain human development, interactions and functioning based on normative standards that have been widely shown to be culturally inadequate (Robinson, 2009). Dadzie (1993) stated that the presence of black students has challenged university curricula and the dominant traditional philosophy of teaching and learning. We can see this in practice when one of the BME students received feedback from the marker about her assessment structure: 'If you invite me to your house for dinner, I would expect a three course meal and not a bowl of soup as the main meal'. However, in some cultures, a bowl of soup is often the main and only meal for the family. The student did not understand the metaphor and had no confidence to say so to the marker. Feedback on written work and practice was often found to be loaded with cultural meaning that was not accessible to the students.

We had hoped from our research (Boyce et al, 2008) that recommendations that students 'engage in the debate' in a safe environment, rather than thinking that they needed procedural knowledge that they could get wrong or right, would negate some of the earlier failings. Nevertheless, the experience of BME students remained difficult. One process that seemed to be at play was that of students wondering what the assessor wanted, from an outside white perspective. This, coupled with their experience of feeling more isolated and invisible, had a tremendous emotional impact on students. Some said that they would be mindful of not wanting to be the expert talking on behalf of all black people. They also did not want to cause discomfort for their white peers (a feeling we understood very well). In one session, Sharon, with another colleague, was addressing students about race equality, social justice and human rights. Sharon checked in with the three black students afterwards to ask if they had been comfortable in the session. One answered that they had decided to sit apart from each other for fear of seeming like a black group; there were three of them in a classroom of 70 white students! This internalised racism particularly affects BME people when in a virtually all-white setting (Johnson-Ahorlu, 2012). Similarly, students were often the only BME person in the placement agency.

The context for a support group

As research indicates, part of the structural problem in bridging the gap for the BME student is that staff do not see their lack of success as a problem (Woodfield, 2012). Although this was partly the case in our institution, it was also a unique environment, which meant that something positive was much more likely to happen. There was support from our manager to take forward an initiative, a unique blend of academics and researchers and colleagues who viewed BME experiences as important and worthy of time and energy. Our research (Boyce et al, 2008) had been supported by many, including students, service users and carers. The request for ethical approval had been guided by a leading academic in the subject of language and discrimination (Harrison, 2006, 2009) and had been nurtured by another academic in this field (Phillips, 2010).

This positive environment fits well with Thompson's (2005) personal, cultural and societal (PCS) model of anti-discrimination, where the context at a macro level is as important as the micro and meso levels, and each influences the other. Not only did the political context fit the Race Relations (Amendment) Act 2000, and the higher education Widening Participation agenda, but the personal (our relationships to staff and students, previous history) and the cultural (programme values around anti-oppressive practices) contexts were strong. This provided a rich and supportive environment for an initiative to take place.

At the beginning, a meeting was arranged with black students for an informal discussion about what was happening for them. The level of mistrust between academics and students was most shocking for us, with only one student attending this meeting. This student had consulted with the other BME students who chose not to attend. The meeting had a profound effect on both of us. Sharon felt something akin to 'survivor's guilt' on leaving that meeting and we were galvanised to do something by the overwhelming anger and sadness at what we were hearing.

We have had to reflect on our own adaptation to living and working in a white institution and how much we challenge and how much we let go by. How much emotional investment should we put into supporting students or trying to tackle the structural inequalities within the systems in which we work? Not to do this can feel like a betrayal on a bad day, but is also necessary for survival. This is described by Hirschfield and Joseph (2012: 213) as 'identity taxation'.

It was through critical reflection that we could unpick our own feelings and assumptions, locating them within belief systems informed by experiences. Social work is a profession that can have great influence over the lives of vulnerable communities and groups, including those who are perhaps voiceless or oppressed. Practitioners must be able to give conscious consideration to their actions and beliefs, to examine ethical dilemmas, and to make judgements that are not based on their own prejudices (Larrivee, 2000). Through these reflections, we put forward the idea of creating a safe space for black students to meet to bridge the gap between student, placement agencies and academia.

We engaged with students by introducing developmental support sessions once a month during their lunch break. Interestingly, only women chose to attend. The discussions in these sessions were directed and determined by the group. These began as informal meetings away from the university with an open-door policy and an emphasis on creating a safe space.

Support groups as a safe space

A safe space was a place where an equalising of power was always striven for – an open stance to co-construct meaning with students – and a place to hear the student's journey, including the intersection of other forms of oppression linked to heritage, class and identity. Writing about reality and reflection-in-action, Schon (1987) observes that beneath the practitioner's reflection-in-action is a constructionist's view based on personal views, perceptions, appreciations and beliefs rooted in our own life experiences. This was vital to understanding ourselves in relation to the students and the students in relation to each other. It would be fair to say that we were all on a journey (Schon, 1987).

Linked to this was a shared experience regarding the impact on thought and behaviour of a wider construction. It was an important prerequisite that each of us acknowledged that institutional racism (Carmichael and Hamilton, 1968; Macpherson, 1999) was felt by all those present, every day in many ways. This was our starting point. We knew from experience that where discrimination and oppression are concerned, trying to convince people of what you are feeling is wearing and isolating. Well-meaning people try to excuse what is being said in a variety of ways to lessen their, and they hope your, discomfort. Common discourses are: 'I'm sure that is not what was meant, are you being a bit sensitive?'; and 'What about [enter some other hierarchy of oppression to be compared with], it's even worse for them?'. A 'colour-blind' approach becomes a default position that does not facilitate the expression of marginalised and isolated voices.

One area of shared experience with the students was around the process of feeling invisible. Both staff and students understood and felt this. It played out in the non-acknowledgement of people's lives within their work. For example, a student who had been through the asylum process with their own loss of power and statelessness felt dismissed in her efforts to relate this to a child in the care system. The BME students shared the experience of putting ideas forward that were not heard until they were repeated by another student or colleague. In response, Geraldine and Sharon started to overemphasise each other's ideas in meetings, and certain allies recognised this process also. We encouraged the students to try out other ideas to combat and protest against invisibility. We played with a concept of our own making called 'the visible invisibility'. Black students and staff in many ways feel *highly visible* but then experience the *invisibility* described earlier. As a mixed-race child in an all-white Catholic school, Newton (2011) called it being a 'noticeable nobody'.

We made it possible to question the expertise of others and promote the student's own voice, validating them and their perspective. In turn, we had a perspective that was valued by the course and agency partners because it was based on hearing the black student's experience that had become silenced. This could, in turn, be used as vehicle to effect change among those involved in teaching, whether on placement or in the classroom. Freire (1970) defines education as the place where the individual and society are constructed. If we are to be teachers who 'liberate' students, as he terms it, we need to be in a mutually created dialogue with our students. This is a vital context for learning to take place.

The student response

Initially, students were angry with us as representatives of the oppressing institution. We should have known how impossible that learning in this environment was going to be; after all, we had already been through it and survived the system. The anger reduced as we co-constructed the processes and learning happening between us. However, there was a huge expectation from students that you, as a black professional, should make it right for the next generation.

The power imbalance and trust had to be worked on, which in an assessment role, would have been difficult. However, in a practice-oriented facilitative role, it fitted well. There was a very deep well of emotion expressed and we needed our practitioner and group work skills to contain highly expressed emotion. This is where we were asked 'What is it they want us to write about?', as trying hard and getting it wrong was a common experience. We were discovering what our wider staff group needed to learn so that black students could trust their own perspectives and value their own experiences.

Goldberger et al (1996) identified five stages of knowledge development from their research into the way women learn. The first two of these comprised silence and believing that the only form of knowledge was external and invested in others. Their work proposes that the achievement of the fifth stage, where knowledge is tentative, dynamic and constructed through the self, is reached through processes of critical reflection (Brookfield, 2009).

Black students are often in the first two stages of the model: those of 'silence' and 'received knowing', not trusting their own knowledge and looking for the outside expert. This was often expressed in terms of wanting the 'correct' answer: 'What is it the assessor is looking for?' Confidence in personal knowledge was at a very low point and breaking through the silence was part of the support offered.

In the study undertaken by the NUS (2013), the students described a concept of inferiority complex or self-fulfilling prophecy, also known as the 'Pygmalion' effect (similar to the internalised racism mentioned earlier). Many respondents suggested that it was difficult not to internalise negative assumptions about their identity, particularly when these had been ingrained from a young age (NUS, 2013). Through critical reflection in a safe space, the students could stand outside those oppressive ways of being seen. However, structural oppression is still reconfirmed every day in every way via teaching, learning and media and societal discourses (Thompson, 2005). Through a critically reflective process, confidence can grow in intuitive and personal knowledge and then be very tentatively shared in a safe group space. One student said:

> "Attending the BME sessions was therapeutic for me because I realised in those meetings that I was not alone. I felt empowered by listening to other people's experiences and how they managed to cope. As for me, I had a very bad experience in my first year, the group of white girls that I was selected to work with refused to work with me, they said they didn't understand my accent and I was left to do a presentation on my own. Sharing these kind of experiences with my BME colleagues gave me hope and courage to persevere. These sessions provided emotional and social support. I have made friends for life, we have stayed in touch and as professionals continue to provide support for each other."

With increased trust we could unpack personal reflections on identity, practice, writing and relationships through the group process. This is where we discovered many misunderstandings in relationships: feeling set up to fail; the complexity of understanding white Eurocentric feedback; and the experience of being on placement in a predominantly white area. For example, students talked about their supervisors' shock at the strategy of telephoning a service user before visiting so that they can hear the student's accent in order to lessen the surprise of unexpectedly seeing a black person at their door. They spoke of the multiple and constant ways in which they were made to feel different and alien, through comments by service users and other professionals about their name, their appearance or any other particular characteristic. Students shared strategies, such as having an internal model of defiance to help hold mental health and spirit together. Others spoke of resolving to let people in to decrease isolation, and the importance of focusing on building a relationship. Feminist writers have long since exposed the innate inequalities that Eurocentric and patriarchal systems perpetuate and proposed alternative narratives of learning and knowing. The idea that knowledge is emergent within the learner and that the teacher facilitates its coming into consciousness is described by some authors as 'the teacher as midwife' (Belenky et al, 1986). Working with students in this way gave rise to a number of initiatives, briefly presented in the following.

Mentoring scheme

Mentoring is the support given by one individual to another through regular contact over a period of time within a personal relationship. According to Cropper (2000), for mentoring to be successful, it needs to be framed within an anti-oppressive and anti-racist model, which includes both the personal and political arenas. Initial attempts at setting up mentoring were unsuccessful as insufficient time had been given to identifying and analysing the problem (Bolman and Deal, 1991). We had not been aware that our efforts might be perceived as an individual solution to a structural problem, with the underlying causes neither recognised nor addressed. Argyris and Schon (1976) refer to this as 'single loop learning'. We were tackling the symptom while failing to seek out the cause (Cropper, 2000) and, as a result, not challenging these structural inequalities.

Although the course had a bank of mentors, we became increasingly aware that the wider social issues impacting on the lives of students were not being addressed in these sessions (Gulum and Zulfiqar, 1998). We have since consulted with the BME students involved in the group to develop a training session for mentors. A former student said:

> "On mentoring, I would say it helped me with an understanding of the challenges faced by black social workers in practice. My mentor helped me understand that I needed to be resilient as the struggle continued in practice. I feel that I benefited a lot having a social worker as a mentor. I am in practice now and am grateful each day for his advice."

Our practice further developed by working in partnership with mentors and encouraging them, wherever possible, to become critical friends to the programme. This is a good method for making resources go further. More importantly, being a critical friend provides an opportunity for mentors to feed back to the programme about the structural challenges faced by BME students both in placement settings and in the classroom. The outcome of partnership working with mentors was an effective combination of formal and informal forums for discussion with mentors and students (Neathey et al, 2005).

According to Bhatti-Sinclair (1996), black professionals have been asked to intervene at crisis points for BME students. Although care was taken to avoid this, one student said: "I seem to have just black professionals supporting me. I have a black practice educator, mentor and cultural tutor. I feel like I am disadvantaged by not having a white perspective."

An assumption had been made that black professionals would be better equipped to support black students. The statement by the student encouraged us to have open and honest dialogues with colleagues, leading us to be mindful of our unintentional practices that might not, as we would have hoped, be perceived as support.

There is a danger of assumptions around 'blackness'. It made us realise that we had a lack of white mentors for students. Brinson and Kottler (1993) and Thomas (2001) agree that developing trust in cross-cultural mentoring is crucial to developing a supportive relationship. While we may have similar experiences of discrimination, there will also be extreme differences according to particular ethnic groups and other social divisions. Our historical backgrounds and experiences (apartheid South Africa and inner-city Manchester) have a massive impact on our practice delivery. A particularly positive development was when students in our developmental sessions volunteered to become peer mentors themselves for students at all stages of the programme.

Twilight evenings

Time to develop the initiatives and a small budget enabled us to also hold what we called 'twilight evenings'. This was a space where we invited the BME social work students to meet and talk with BME social workers and other professionals who were interested in offering mentoring. These were like pre-support groups and matching events, with food so that people could fit it into the end of their working day. We found that the informality of these sessions meant that BME social workers relaxed into sharing their own challenges as former learners and as current professional social workers.

Outcomes

BME students gained the confidence to engage with other activities within the university. For example, they became involved in giving presentations, they became ambassadors for the course and they are in the process of co-writing a paper with academics about their experiences. Collaborative working has led to the students having a sense of control and ownership over BME support initiatives, which has, in turn, contributed towards their sustainability and a possibility of improving the chance of success for future students. Even so, it has been an uphill struggle to get newly enrolled social work students to engage with the group. We would talk to newly arrived first-year students about the existence of support, which, in hindsight, drew attention to the BME students in their first week here. To discuss so publicly the existence of a group that ghettoised, or branded, BME students as a generic group was not appealing to the new students. To identify this group as one in need of additional learning support made new students anxious and scared by the thought that they might need a special group. They were new to the course and were hearing that they required additional help. As a result, we changed our strategy and now advertise the support in student handbooks and online, lobbying tutors to mention the support in their sessions and individual discussions so that students do not feel different from other students in the group. There remain only a small number of BME students in each cohort but the progression of those involved has significantly improved. The original group has bridged a gap in attainment over the three years of the project and all have graduated as social workers.

Conclusion and future practice

As black staff, accepting a position as an authoritative voice has not sat easily with us. After talking about a process where the students felt put in the position of the expert, talking on behalf of others rather than for themselves, we have gone through a similar process. Setting up the groups and critically reflecting on our own practice has enabled the voices of the students and our own to become merged. We have gone through our own transformation during the life of this project through supporting black students. We have taken on an academic persona that can influence practice through research and dissemination. We have a very specific perspective locally (Dhalech, 1999) and one that can be expanded to encompass other, more rural, universities. We have spoken at conferences and involved outside speakers to help train the staff group in cultural capability as a part of our continuing professional development. In times of austerity, collaborating with students for better outcomes is even more important than it has ever been.

We do, however, have words of caution as our efforts have not changed the central, most organising, influences of institutional racism, and, therefore, without constant attention, the default position is inaction. We found we had less BME students to work with after this initiative and working on admissions, access and equality of opportunities poses ever-greater challenges to us. We are not complacent, however. Our struggles continue.

Recommendations

We recognise that supporting BME students in a predominantly white environment is a complex and multilayered task. From our experience, we offer the following strategies:

- tackling the effects of institutionalised racism at more strategic levels, notably, on recruitment, retention, attainment;
- continue engaging practice agencies and the university in the debate and keep BME issues on the agenda at a strategic level to effect change;
- engage male students with the project;
- develop training packs in collaboration with BME students for potential mentors and cultural tutors;
- develop a process for multicultural mentoring;
- lobby academics to be part of the BME initiative by becoming cultural tutors within the wider university;
- develop a 'critical friend' group that can feed back concerns that affect BME students in the programme; and
- seek external supervision for staff members who are directly involved with the BME initiative.

For anyone seeking to provide support to BME students in a predominantly white environment, we would advocate that a safe space should be provided as a priority so that student voices can be heard, however difficult the message may be to hear for well-intentioned white people.

Note

[1] The term 'BME' is used to refer to people who are African, Arab, Asian, Caribbean and mixed-heritage. In some studies, the term 'black' is used and refers to the same group.

References

Ahmad, B. (1990) *Black perspectives in social work*, London: Tavistock.

Ahmed, S., Cheetham, J. and Small, J. (eds) (1986) *Social work with black children and their families*, London: Batsford.

Argyris, C. and Schon, D.A. (1976) 'Single-loop and double-loop models in research on decision making', *Administrative Science Quarterly*, 21(3): 363–75.

Belenky, M., McVicker Clinchy, B., Goldberger, N. and Mattuck Tarule, J. (1986) *Women's ways of knowing: the development of self, voice and mind*, New York, NY: Basic Books.

Bernard, C., Fairtlough, A., Fletcher, J. and Ahmet, A. (2013) 'A qualitative study of marginalised social work students' views of social work education and learning', *British Journal of Social Work*, 44(6): 1–16.

Bhatti-Sinclair, K. (1996) *Developing black mentors and consultants schemes*, Southampton: CEDR, University of Southampton.

Bolman, L. and Deal, T. (1991) *Reframing organizations: artistry, choice, and leadership* (3rd edn), San Francisco, CA: Jossey Bass.

Boyce, P., Harrison, G., Jelley, M., Jolley, M., Maxwell, C., Soper, S., Wattam, E. and White, G. (2008) 'Review of the anti-racist standards within anti-oppressive practice: executive summary', unpublished research, CEPPL, Plymouth University.

Brinson, J. and Kottler, J. (1993) 'Cross-cultural mentoring in counselor education: a strategy for retaining minority faculty', *Counselor Education and Supervision*, 32(4): 241–53.

Broecke, S. and Nicholls, T. (2007) *Ethnicity and degree attainment*, Report RW92, London: Department for Education and Skills. Available at: http://webarchive.nationalarchives.gov.uk/20130401151715/http://www.education.gov.uk/publications/eOrderingDownload/RW92.pdf

Brookfield, S. (2009) 'The concept of critical reflection: promises and contradictions', *European Journal of Social Work*, 12(3): 293–304.

Butler, A., Elliott, T. and Stopard, N. (2003) 'Living up to the standards we set: a critical account of the development of anti-racist standards', *Social Work Education*, 22(3): 271–82.

Carmichael, S. and Hamilton, C. (1968) *Black power: the politics of liberation*, Harmondsworth: Penguin.

Cheetham, J. (1982) *Social work and ethnicity*, London: Allen and Unwin.

Crenshaw, K. (1989) 'Demarginalizing the intersection of race and sex: a black feminist critique of anti-discrimination doctrine, feminist theory and antiracist politics'. Available at: http://philpapers.org/archive/CREDTI.pdf

Cropper, A. (2000) 'Mentoring as an inclusive device for the excluded: black students' experience of a mentoring scheme', *Social Work Education*, 19(6): 597–607.

Dadzie, S. (1993) *Working with black adult learners. A practical guide*, Leicester: National Institute of Adult Continuing Education.

Dhalech, M. (1999) *Challenging racism in the rural idyll*, London: National Association of Citizens Advice Bureaux.

Freire, P. (1970) *Pedagogy of the oppressed* (30th anniversary edn), London: Bloomsbury.

Goldberger, N.R.E., Tarule, J.M.E., McVicker, C. and Belenky, M.F.E. (1996) *Knowledge, difference, and power: essays inspired by 'Women's ways of knowing'*, New York, NY: Basic Books.

Gulum, B. and Zulfiqar, M. (1998) 'Mentoring: Dr Plum's elixir and the alchemist's stone', *Mentoring and Tutoring*, 5(3): 19–26.

Harrison, G. (2006) 'Broadening the conceptual lens on language in social work: difference, diversity and English as a global language', *British Journal of Social Work*, 36(3): 401–18.

Harrison, G. (2009) 'Language politics, linguistic capital and bilingual practitioners in social work', *British Journal of Social Work*, 39(6): 1082–100.

Hirschfield, L. and Joseph, T. (2012) 'We need a woman, we need a black woman: gender and cultural taxation in the academy', *Gender and Education*, 24(2): 213–27.

Johnson-Ahorlu, R.N. (2012) 'The academic opportunity gap: how racism and stereotypes disrupt the education of African American undergraduates', *Race, Ethnicity and Education*, 15(5): 633–52.

Larrivee, B. (2000) 'Transforming teaching practice: becoming the critically reflective teacher', *Reflective Practice*, 1(3): 293–307.

Macpherson, W. (1999) *The Stephen Lawrence inquiry, report of an inquiry by Sir William Macpherson of Cluny*, Cm 4262–1, London: Home Office.

Neathey, F., Regan, J. and Newton, I. (2005) *Working in partnership in higher education: final report*, London: Universities and Colleges Employers' Association.

Newton, T. (2011) 'Embracing otherness, embracing myself', TED talks, July. Available at: http://www.ted.com/talks/thandie_newton_embracing_otherness_embracing_myself?language=en

NUS (National Union of Students) (2013) 'Race for equality: a report on the experiences of black students in further education'. Available at: http://www.nus.org.uk/PageFiles/12350/NUS_Race_for_Equality_web.pdf

Phillips, C. (2010) 'White, like who? Temporality, contextuality and anti-racist social work education and practice', *Critical Social Work*, 11(2): 71–88.

Robinson, L. (2009) 'Cross-cultural and black perspectives through the life course', in R. Adams, L. Dominelli and M. Payne (eds) *Critical practice in social work* (2nd edn), Basingstoke: Palgrave Macmillan.

Schon, D. (1987) *Educating the reflective practitioner*, San Francisco, CA: Jossey Bass.

Sedlacek, W.E. (1987) 'Blacks in white colleges and universities: twenty years of research', *Journal of College Student Personnel*, 28: 484–95.

Thomas, D.A. (2001) 'The truth about mentoring minorities', *Harvard Business Review*, 74(5): 99–105.

Thompson, N. (2005) *Anti discriminatory practice* (4th edn), Basingstoke: Palgrave.

Woodfield, R. (2012) 'Supporting black and minority ethnic student success in higher education – narrowing the attainment gap: feedback from the HEA, ECU and HEFCE sponsored summit'. Available at: https://intranet.birmingham.ac.uk/collaboration/equality/documents/students/presentation.pdf

FIVE

Men in social work education: building a gendered alliance

Peter Brown, Michael Cook, Christopher Higgins, Dean Matthews, Daniel Wilding and Andrew Whiteford

Introduction

Social work remains an occupation associated more with women than with men. Figures published in the UK in 2010 indicate that men are, indeed, numerically under-represented in both practice and training. Only 16% of the registrants for social work programmes in 2006 were men. This figure declined further in 2007, to 13%. Of the UK-registered social workers in 2009, 23% were male (GSCC, 2010).

Interest in this gender imbalance has been less concerned with equality of opportunity in employment than with exploring wider societal factors relating to why men choose social work as a career (Cree, 1996; Christie, 1998; Harlow, 2002; Holley and Young, 2005) and their potential roles within a profession where women represent the majority workforce (Scourfield, 2001; McLean, 2003; McPhail, 2004; Daniel et al, 2005; Gillingham, 2006). The literature remains largely a theoretical framework for practice but has begun to explore implications for social work education by investigating why once men have decided to apply, they are not selected for training (Perry and Cree, 2003), the likely causes and explanations for why men fail (Furness, 2011), and how they can succeed (Lloyd and Degenhardt, 2000; Cree, 2001).

Against this background, a small group of male practice educators, academics and service users involved with social work courses at Plymouth University began to notice how they differentiated their own assumptions about student motivation, capabilities and priorities as learners and potential future colleagues along gender lines. They seemed to be talking about men differently from their women colleagues. This interest in men's experience of social work education was further animated through informal contact with both individuals and small groups of male students. These encounters enabled an exchange of experience that revealed concerns and interests quite specific to our (male) gender. They encouraged us to take a more structured approach to exploring the notion of men in social work, creating space for men to meet outside of the timetabled curriculum and placements. As well as the opportunity to gather together, communicate with and relate to each other, we hoped that by creating a visible profile, wider consideration and dialogue might open up. We called this group 'Men in Social Work' (MiSW).

This chapter has given us the opportunity to explore how group support for us, as men engaged in social work, has shaped our experience of learning both in practice and in the classroom. Acknowledging in social work education that gender does matter and developing a politically informed personal awareness around gendered realities, identity and masculinity (Cree, 2001; Christie, 2006; McPhail, 2008), we have sought alliances with women colleagues and service users.

We have organised the chapter around our experiences of entering social work in the hope that it may inform, inspire or simply reassure other men considering a career in social work or those concerned with their continuing professional development. We discuss our experience of how wider social factors have shaped our desire and decision to do social work. We reflect upon our experience of learning in groups with women and each other in both practice and classroom settings. Finally, we explore the positive contribution that men can make to practice itself.

Other aspects of our identities have come to influence our story as much as, if not more than, just gender. Some of us are parents and grandparents, some are married or living with partners. We all recognise our class backgrounds and ethnicity as significant factors texturing our experience of being men. For all of us, the decision to get involved in social work was born from a desire for work that is more personally fulfilling.

Being men

Men and women are different. This difference comprises various elements, of which gender forms a significant part. Through MiSW, we have come to recognise that the question of gender requires a thorough examination if we are to gain a deeper understanding of the issues. Embarking on social work education has inevitably brought into focus societal stereotypes and generalised assumptions around gender, especially regarding historical power inequalities within the traditional Western cultures in which we are embedded (McLean, 2003; Parker and Crabtree, 2012). What has also become apparent to us is the unusual position of being in a minority group as men on a social work course. Being male in an environment that is traditionally a female-majority profession has raised some uncomfortable questions and challenges for us about our role, identity and behaviour in wider society (Miller and Bell, 1996; Christie, 1998; McPhail, 2004; Parker and Crabtree, 2012).

Here is an illustration:

> "My first real experience of discomfort was during a placement at a local children's centre. I was the only male in a large team working with parents and children under five. As part of my role, I was asked to help facilitate several groups. One in particular consisted of new mothers with infants up to six months. On entering the room, I became very self-conscious of my size and maleness, whispering almost, walking on tiptoe, feeling like a gorilla and avoiding the sight of women openly breastfeeding. I was asked by my colleague to just 'join in', but having little experience and no children of my own, I did not know what to do with myself. The incongruity of my position felt palpable. I did eventually sit with a young mother with twins who was glad of my help and thought it was beneficial for her children to socialise with a male worker. On reflection, my feelings were that I was an intruder in a group that I could never be a member of. No matter how hard I tried to empathise or intellectualise this particular situation, I would never truly understand the agony and ecstasy of childbirth or the bond created through breastfeeding my own flesh and blood. This experience really brought home the tangible differences that should be celebrated, encouraged and supported, rather than substituted."

Another example: "On the first day in placement, I was asked to 'deal with' an intoxicated service user whose behaviour was becoming threatening. I felt I was asked because of my size but did not feel able to refuse."

We shared at least three examples like this, of being asked to accompany social workers because the service user was judged to be 'difficult'. We speculated about asking for feedback about our 'empathic chokehold' if things got out of hand. One of us was challenged about the way he sat because it created a sense of his male power. He felt comfortable and thought he looked relaxed simply crossing his legs. Yet, every posture he adopted seemed to reinforce male power for his critics. One of us, who is well-built, spoke of the need to be aware of self, both verbal and non-verbal impressions, and of trying to "make myself smaller. I suppose I could be quite intimidating. This is really important".

It is argued that the social construction of masculinity, along with our understanding of gender identity, has been developing for millennia (Geddes and Thomson, 1889; Stoller, 1968; Fausto-Sterling, 1993; Butler, 1999). From the day we are born, the process of forming our identity along gendered lines begins and we are slowly conditioned into behaviours and thinking that are considered to have culturally appropriate sexual characteristics (Pavlov, 1927; Skinner, 1974; Zammuner, 1987; Brewer, 2001). It is with this conditioning that we all came into social work training to discover, somewhat abruptly, the concept of male privilege (Walby, 1990). It is difficult to deny that as men, we have inherited considerable benefits, improved life chances and freedoms that our female colleagues have had to struggle and fight for (De Beauvoir, 1972; Cott, 1987; Greer, 2006). We have come to recognise that male domination or patriarchal hegemony needs to be thoughtfully considered, understood, challenged and deconstructed on a personal level if we are to work in a profession where core values and practices are based on the promotion of social justice, equality, anti-discrimination and anti-oppression (Pease, 2011).

We have begun our social work education at a time when the profession is being subjected to neoliberal political criticism for overemphasising value-based ideals and social justice (Christie, 2001; Gove, 2013; Narey, 2014). We now appreciate how gender equality is one such ideal and are concerned that it should not be abandoned in a situation where political agendas masquerading as pragmatism trump these aspirations (Campbell, 2014). When considering the profession's core values and principles, it came as no surprise to us that gender inequality, female oppression and discrimination need to be openly challenged (BASW, 2012). In this regard, we have found ourselves considering the realities of practice after university and anticipate finding it particularly challenging, as Scourfield (2006) suggests, in respect of gender equality and identity. We want to ensure that our new-found and heightened awareness will support us, on the one hand, in challenging gendered stereotypes and oppressive behaviour while, on the other, acknowledging the deep cultural, religious and class contexts from which they emerge. While we feel better prepared not to construct potentially stereotyped images of masculinity, we have also spent time together exploring how we might approach working in a Muslim community, for example, and how working with secular, white, working-class individuals might also offer us challenges. Our ambition in this regard is to retain the respect and trust of the communities with which we may work and, in particular, to shape future behaviours through modelling, challenge and inclusion.

The social work profession has traditionally been viewed as female-oriented, with a strong alignment to feminist perspectives (Christie, 1998). It has been through considering our own social conditioning that we have begun to better appreciate how male privilege and patriarchal hegemony are not the sole causes of disharmony, conflict and inequality between the genders. In learning about anti-oppressive practice, we have come to appreciate how class, ethnicity, age, ability, religion and sexuality are equally relevant in providing a theoretical framework through which to view power, inequality and oppression. We would wish to argue that male, gender-biased privileges are slowly being addressed, but we appreciate that this is still far from universally true and, indeed, may never become so (Rosin, 2012; Campbell, 2014). We are, however, clearer about what we as individuals and together as men in social work can do.

Becoming a social worker

There are many reasons why men choose a career in social work. Perhaps a motivation is the desire to go against social norms (Perry and Cree, 2003) or that the profession affords men more opportunity to express themselves (Cree, 1996). Interestingly, in this regard, women are assumed to be making a more conventional career decision (Cree, 2001).

Conversely, these reasons may also explain why few men enter the occupation, and why, as Christie (2006) notes, they are more likely than women to end up in management roles when they do. Notwithstanding institutional discrimination and other restraints on career progression for women, Stevens et al (2012) highlight that male students were one-and-a-half times more likely to give career reasons for wanting to train in social work. As a group of men, we have found that we have in common many reasons for entering the profession. We all began the social work course as mature students with previous careers or jobs, yet, for the majority of us, this earlier work was not related to social work. A current or anticipated need to support a family financially was a significant factor for some of us in pursuing the relative security and tenure of professional status that social work can provide. Without exception, all of us have been motivated by the desire for improved job satisfaction, personal fulfilment and the opportunity to make a difference in the work we do. All of us acknowledge that previous personal experience of social workers was a defining factor in our choice, with this contact ranging from having been a care-leaver, through to being a carer or having a family member working in social work. One of us in particular identifies with a journey into social work that Jung (1951) refers to as the 'wounded healer', illustrating how individuals who have had contact with social workers at a young age become interested in becoming a social worker themselves (Hanson and McCullagh, 1995).

Despite having to respond to the surprise expressed by friends and families at our decision to consider social work (doubtless arising from the stereotypes explored earlier), our journey into social work education has been a positive experience overall. We have not encountered the discrimination and difficulties of entering a female-majority profession anticipated by Williams (2013). We all recognise how positive discrimination in recruitment campaigns for careers not traditionally associated with men, such as social work, nursing, early years teaching and administration (Simpson, 2004), have influenced us in choosing social work or even becoming aware of it as an option in the first instance. However, Pease (2011) believes that men should not be encouraged into social work just for the sake of simply having more men in social work. He argues that this will be a self-defeating exercise that will only serve to reinforce existing discrimination and inequality found in society, and, arguably, within the profession itself. One of us reflected: "Maybe I got on the course because they had to fill a quota. This thought stays in your consciousness."

Hanson and McCullagh (1995) also suggest the need to understand one's self as a drive to enter the social work profession. We all have come to better appreciate the general lack of fulfilment from the more traditional male work roles that we had previously occupied, particularly through employment. For us, engaging in a debate to challenge the identity and role of men in society has blurred the outdated post-war concept of the 'Beveridge family' (Christie, 2001; Simpson, 2004). We find traditional masculinities dissatisfying and search for newer, less stereotyped, roles in life. There is something more fulfilling about working with people to overcome adversity than working for people or having people work for you.

Learning with women

'Dominant', 'power-hungry', 'male superiority' (Parker and Crabtree, 2012), these are descriptors whose relevance we had not fully appreciated prior to our arrival in social work education, especially when it came to understanding our relationship with the women with whom we would be sharing a learning environment. Through the experience of working alongside women staff and students especially within practice settings and the classroom, we have come to identify how gender issues are a significant part of the experience of social work education. For many of us, this was our first experience in a female-majority environment.

Having collectively managed to negotiate our way within a perceived male-dominated sector for many years, entering a predominantly female profession was found to be stimulating. We note with interest a US study conducted by Wharton and Baron (1987), revealing that men who worked in a female-dominated setting compared to a mixed setting had greater job satisfaction and became less depressive. Compare this to a learning environment where one of us witnessed their male cohort population diminish from seven to one (themselves as the only male) over a two-and-a-half-year period. Another commented:

> "I was already aware that there were not going to be many men after being the only male during the interview process. It was not until the first day of lectures that it became apparent that so few men were actually participating on the course. There were eight in total out of over 80 students."

Gender suddenly mattered. Evans (1997) states that females hold traditional attitudes towards their male counterparts, with the expectation that men should undertake men's work and hold positions of power. Simpson (2004) reported that males in the teaching and health-care professions felt uncomfortable with the expectation that they would enter into management. We, too, are men who would rather do the one-to-one therapeutic work than be managers. Some of us found discomfort in having to resist, behave or act in these more traditional roles. We understand the privilege that comes with being a male but do not subscribe to these traditional attitudes of gender privilege. However, our practice was framed by university teaching, which we found undermined our efforts to reject the stereotype. Within the classroom, one of us recalled having heard a remark directed against males by a female peer. When challenged, she laughed it away, saying that she could not be sexist because she was a woman.

Hegemonic masculinity has fuelled feminist discourses that accentuate the notion that all men could potentially abuse women and children (Scourfield and Coffey, 2002; McLean, 2003; Gillingham, 2006). At the same time, there is an incongruity in traditional views of masculinity depicting men as potentially hostile towards, but simultaneously the protectors of, women and children (Cree, 1996; Scourfield, 2001). We feel that when the issue is explored within our formal teaching, the harm and unhappiness that men bring into individual, family and community relations is emphasised. At times in lectures we are told 'how men are' or 'this is what men do' to reveal male dominance, with no opportunity given for discussion or to explore stereotypes. In a subgroup, a female peer was talking about her own personal issues with men, and said "No offence to you." Afterwards, she deliberately struck up a conversation as if to say 'It's not about you personally.' When we are accounted for differently, it can be demeaning. As one of us observed: "I want women to be specific about their expectations of us, but to have positive expectations, not to reduce expectations because you are a man." The statement 'You *would* say that, you are a man' is quite demeaning and silencing. As men, we have also become aware, through discussion, of the negative impact that these assumptions have on us personally (Sobiraj et al, 2011) and how we might best seek support in dealing with the emotional impact. Our experience is that when negative stereotypes are reinforced, the potential for conflict increases and the capacity for both men and women to engage in the debate is diminished.

An example of this negative reinforcement occurred in a preparation for a placement session exploring the dynamic roles within a group and the impact that they might have on a hypothetical situation. The group comprised 13 females and one male. Two of the females picked the roles of the co-leader.

As the exercise ended – we miraculously managed to navigate ourselves off a desert island and to safety (An exciting day at university!) – we took some time to reflect on the performance of the group. The facilitator asked the two leaders how they felt working together as females. They explained that they felt comfortable as there were no power struggles within the working relationship. When asked how they would have felt working with the male within the group, they explained that they would not have felt as confident or comfortable working with the male as they did with females. This presented a great opportunity to explore the reasons behind the statement. However, the facilitator left these issues unexplored and unchallenged, which helped to reinforce negative assumptions and stereotypes about men in relation to power and control.

On the other hand, when we have been enabled to engage with pro-feminist ideas (as opposed to anti-male rhetoric) with our women colleagues and peers, we are more hopeful and inspired to create, with them, the alternative masculinities that Pease (2011) argues will change gender inequalities. Interestingly in this regard, Hyde and Deal (2003: 202) found that a significant number of women students (with a mean age of 27.6 years) 'did not view sexism or discrimination as a concern either in social work or in the society in general'. Speaking in practice settings and in class with colleagues, peers and service users has, we feel, instigated wider considerations of sexism and its relevance to social work. Indeed, Cree (2001) argues that it is the explicit acknowledgement of men wanting to engage in such a non-traditional occupation as social work that can lead to anti-sexist practice developing. As men, we are now thinking about ourselves, about the dynamics of a group and about how we might be seen 'as a man'. It feels like women have not questioned their gender in the same way or considered their footprint on gender. Women in this student cohort have not had the same opportunity as that provided by MiSW. *Both* genders have the responsibility to develop awareness, as we have on our footprint as a minority. If negative assumptions held by feminists are not challenged, they could be transferred onto male service users. It is so interesting that no one seems to want to talk about these issues.

McPhail (2008) explains that there has been a need to incorporate multi-gendered issues into the curriculum for several decades and we see real opportunity in building on our experience in this regard. We bring with us experiences that have arisen from what Rogers (2013: 910) refers to as 'gender role conflicts', which he suggests should be addressed in order to retain men in the profession. Social work education is well-placed to do this. We feel that teaching and learning around gender, whether in placement agencies or in the classroom, should, in the first instance, be more explicit. Second, it should expand to accommodate issues relating to masculine identity and male stereotyping. It should challenge stereotypical assumptions about the motivation of men to enter the social work profession (McLean, 2003) in order to fulfil gender-specific expectations and exert control over 'difficult' service user behaviours or to acquire managerial status. Our shared experience as men has revealed an alternate paradigm where caring for vulnerable people and professional alliance-building are valued more highly.

Working and studying with women

Social work education provides fantastic learning opportunities for developing self-awareness and an understanding of how we are perceived by others. We value this and acknowledge that it is a continual process enhanced via the thought-provoking moments that occur both in practice learning and in the university. We have previously observed that, as men, there are additional layers of complexity, such as age, class and race, to fathom as we navigate who we are and where we fit within the social work field. Here, we will discuss our experiences as students in the workplace, focusing on the positive contribution that men can offer to the profession.

Significant learning has occurred for us in working alongside staff and service users in both voluntary and local government agencies. We have observed particular expectations of men and have seen how they have fulfilled perceived stereotypical behaviours. An example of this was where a male manager created what might be regarded as a segregated working environment. Flanked by two senior male colleagues with a screen to divide them from the rest of the team, the office set up what could be construed as an advert for 'men in charge', reinforcing what Hogan (1998) describes as the social construction of masculinity. One of us reflected: "Having an opportunity to discuss this example with male colleagues allowed my perspective to be examined in a constructive non-collusive environment. This allowed me to explore my reactions, heightening awareness of male privilege." Being mindful of why we make the decisions we do can only serve to improve our contribution.

As men, we need to constantly challenge ourselves and each other to strive for the best possible concept of our male self if we are ever to be distanced from the old ideologies of patriarchy and hegemony. Social work education can lead the way in championing this, evolving new ways of being by utilising incidents drawn from practice by both male and female students to strengthen the understanding of future social workers regarding the role we men want to undertake within the profession.

So, what positive attributes do men bring to social work practice? Pragmatism, problem-solving and assertiveness are routinely cited in the literature. Our experiences in practice reveal that while these are traits commonly found in men, they cannot be exclusively owned by our gender in much the same way as multitasking and empathy are not exclusive to women. One of the greatest positives that we have observed in practice is that we are, indeed, not women: we think differently, act differently and push on with things differently. As a group of men, we are direct, solution-focused, practical, logical, task-oriented and directional. These traits can be both positive and negative in themselves. Nevertheless, as men, we try to celebrate difference and own our strengths just as we would assist a service user to do.

We spoke of the way in which men bond in groups, showing a particular type of loyalty. We also identified men's ability to deconstruct a situation, as well as to disconnect and therefore act more objectively. We recognised our social conditioning to disconnect from emotion, a form of distancing that, again, can be both positive in a crisis, for example, but less so in another situation. Men process differently. One of us observed: "since starting the course, I have had a culture-shift. Rather than thinking 'it shouldn't affect me, I'm a man', I've had different discussions with female peers, some more successful than others, as a way of processing".

We have observed a greater sense of confidence and comfort achieved by working alongside women in both practice settings and the classroom. For many of us, this has been a matter of adjustment both personally and professionally. In doing so, we have become more aware of gender difference in social work and in society more widely, and have gained the skill of challenging these issues appropriately. We feel the group process of meeting with the purpose of writing and reflecting together on this topic has been crucial in this. We view this new insight into ourselves as a powerful tool to change negative perceptions and stereotypes of men in the social world. Simply being men with the benefit of social work education, we feel empowered with the knowledge and skills to make a difference and effect positive change in the discourse pertaining to gender in society when working with men and women in practice.

When we do a piece of work with a client in practice or give feedback to a colleague on his or her work, it is vital to own it for ourselves. It strikes us that all people are created equal, then some learn to become social workers. We feel that for men and women alike, this is a fulfilling, transformative, fortunate and privileged place to be.

Warde's (2009) study suggests that the male alternative perspective strengthens the profession and that the gender difference can make social work practice more effective when applied in partnership. We have used group work tasks in both practice and the classroom to encourage and emphasise the importance of working together and we thus experience a microcosm of the wider world of social work. An example that illustrates this point arose during a placement, when the male student in a group of three was asked to take charge for a second time by the female project lead. When the women students pointed out that they were not asked to deputise on either occasion, two things happened. First, there was an epiphany for the male student in having a first-hand realisation of male privilege in action. Second, it opened up a discussion within the student group that allowed them all to gain a deeper insight into each other's standpoint in a way that they had never experienced before. We feel that having such opportunities to raise our awareness and learn to reflect together has provided us with a greater depth of perspective for future teamwork.

As part of writing this chapter, we have discussed ways in which we have built an intuitive and conscious alliance between ourselves and our female colleagues. Discussing and implementing strategies consciously with women colleagues have enabled us to establish boundaries while more instinctively making allowances for each other in an altruistic bid to complete the task. Trevithick (2014) purports that intuitive reasoning, used in conjunction with reflective practice, should have as equal importance as analytical thinking does in social work. One of our realisations has been that, as men, we do have the capacity for both schemes of thought.

Conclusion

The reaction of female peers to MiSW has been overwhelmingly positive. Women are recognising that men need this voice. They are really curious and interested in what we are talking about. They ask: 'Why haven't we got a group like this?' Social work education should pay equal attention to both genders. It rightly recognises the importance of feminist perspectives and its impact upon our practice as males. However, conversations need to take place around gender constructs and negative stereotypes in order to deconstruct masculinity and to discuss with women how it feels to be in a minority. Masculinity should not be abhorred or pathologised, but, rather, deconstructed into what is acceptable/unacceptable and helpful/unhelpful in order for it to be changed. We are living in a postmodern, globalised society in which the sociological 'grand narratives' and traditional dichotomous dualisms are giving way to subjective individualism. Logically, this should suit a profession that prides itself on treating people as individuals rather than as homogeneous categories (Bruckner, 2002; Simpson, 2004).

Only by partnering the gendered narratives through sharing, discussing and understanding the different perspectives from the beginning of a practitioner's career will students graduate with an informed personal awareness that gender does matter within social work. Second, as men, we must continually challenge ourselves and be open to constructive dialogue within the workplace and the classroom if we are not to undermine the contribution that we bring to practice. Patriarchal views and male privilege exist all around the world and it might be unrealistic to consider a worldwide gender balance. In the here and now, gender inequality positions men differently when it comes to employment within the helping professions. Yet, change can happen. The starting point is developing our self-awareness and how we are perceived by others; the epiphany moments during the practice experience of the social work programme have certainly allowed us to realise that men do have a positive contribution to make.

Recommendations to social work education

- Teaching about gender inequality cannot just be *delivered*. Men, in particular, need to be given opportunities to explore their position in relation to it: a space that is safe and offers trust and openness so that this is not a 'no-go area'.
- Keep offering a space for men to discuss their reaction whenever men's oppressive nature is talked about.
- A message for practice once we are qualified would be: we have been through the process of the MiSW group, we know what the issues are, we are aware, help us to continue with this work.
- The same opportunities should be available for women.
- Women and men need to expect behaviours from men that are atypically male.
- Do not set up dichotomies or oppositional thinking.
- Encourage the creation of a new masculinity.

References

BASW (British Association of Social Workers) (2012) 'The code of ethics for social work'. Available at: http://cdn.basw.co.uk/upload/basw_112315-7.pdf

Brewer, S. (2001) *A child's world: a unique insight into how children think*, London: Headline.

Bruckner, M. (2002) 'On social work and what gender has got to do with it', *European Journal of Social Work*, 5(3): 269–76.

Butler, J. (1999) *Gender trouble* (2nd edn), London: Routledge.

Campbell, B. (2014) *End of equality (manifestos for the 21st century)*, London: Seagull Books.

Christie, A. (ed) (2001) *Men and social work: theories and practices*, Basingstoke: Palgrave.

Christie, A. (2006) 'Negotiating the uncomfortable intersections between gender and professional identities in social work', *Critical Social Policy*, 26(2): 390–411.

Christie, R. (1998) 'Is social work a "non-traditional" occupation for men?', *British Journal of Social Work*, 35(8): 1343–55.

Cott, N.F. (1987) *The grounding of modern feminism*, New Haven, CT: Yale University Press.

Cree, V.E. (1996) 'Why do men care?', in K. Cavanagh and V.E. Cree (eds) *Working with men: feminism and social work*, London: Routledge, pp 65–86.

Cree, V.E. (2001) 'Men and masculinities in social work education', in A. Christie (ed) *Men and social work: theories and practices*, Basingstoke: Palgrave, pp 147–63.

Daniel, B., Featherstone, B., Hooper, C.A. and Scourfield, J. (2005) 'Why gender matters for every child matters', *British Journal of Social Work*, 35(8): 1343–55.

De Beauvoir, S. (1972) *The second sex*, Harmondsworth: Penguin.

Evans, J. (1997) 'Men in nursing: exploring the male nurse experience', *Nursing Enquiry*, 4(2): 142–45.

Fausto-Sterling, A. (1993) *Myths of gender: biological theories about women and men* (2nd edn), New York, NY: Basic Books.

Furness, S. (2011) 'Gender at work: characteristics of "failing" social work students', *British Journal of Social Work*, 42(3): 480–99.

Geddes, P. and Thomson, J.A. (1889) *The evolution of sex*, London: Walter Scott.

Gillingham, P. (2006) 'Male social workers in child and family welfare: new directions for research', *Social Work*, 51(1): 83–5.

Gove, M. (2013) 'Michael Gove speech to the NSPCC: getting it right for children in need'. Available at: https://www.gov.uk/government/speeches/getting-it-right-for-children-in-need-speech-to-the-nspcc

Greer, G. (2006) *The female eunuch*, London: Harper Perennial.

GSCC (General Social Care Council) (2010) 'General social care council annual report and accounts 2009–10'. Available at: https://www.gov.uk/government/uploads/system/uploads/attachment_data/file/247681/0201.pdf

Hanson, J.G. and McCullagh, J.G. (1995) 'Career choice factors for BSW students: a 10-year perspective', *Journal of Social Work Education*, 31(1): 28–36.

Harlow, E. (2002) 'Gender, parenting and managerial ambition in social work', *Journal of Social Work*, 2(1): 65–82.

Hogan, F. (1998) 'Reflections: on being a man in social work', *Irish Social Worker*, 16(3): 19–20.

Holley, L.C. and Young, D. (2005) 'Career decisions and experiences of social work faculty: a gender comparison', *Journal of Social Work Education*, 41(2): 297–313.

Hyde, C.A. and Deal, K.H. (2003) 'Does gender matter? Male and female participation in social work classrooms', *Affilia*, 18(2): 192–209.

Jung, C.C. (1951) *Fundamental questions of psychotherapy*, New Jersey, NJ: Princeton University Press.

Lloyd, S. and Degenhardt, D. (2000) 'Challenges in working with male social work students', in K. Cavanagh and V.E. Cree (eds) *Working with men: feminism and social work*, London: Routledge, pp 61–80.

McLean, J. (2003) 'Men as minority: men employed in statutory social care work', *Journal of Social Work*, 3(1): 45–68.

McPhail, B.A. (2004) 'Setting the record straight: social work is not a female-dominated profession', *Social Work*, 49(2): 323–6.

McPhail, B.A. (2008) 'Re-gendering the social work curriculum: new realities and complexities', *Journal of Social Work Education*, 44(2): 33–52.

Miller, J. and Bell, C. (1996) 'Mapping men's mental health', *Journal of Community and Applied Social Psychology*, 6(5): 317–27.

Narey, M. (2014) 'Making the education of social workers consistently effective'. Available at: https://www.gov.uk/government/uploads/system/uploads/attachment_data/file/287756/Making_the_education_of_social_workers_consistently_effective.pdf

Parker, J. and Crabtree, S.A. (2012) 'Fish need bicycles: an exploration of the perceptions of male social work students on a qualifying course', *British Journal of Social Work*, 44(8): 310–27.

Pavlov, I.P. (1927) *Conditioned reflexes: an investigation of the physiological activity of the cerebral cortex*, London: Oxford University Press/Humphrey Milford.

Pease, B. (2011) 'Men in social work: challenging or reproducing an unequal gender regime?', *Journal of Women and Social Work*, 26(4): 406–18.

Perry, R.W. and Cree, V.E. (2003) 'The changing gender profile of applicants to qualifying social work training in the UK', *Social Work Education*, 22(4): 375–84.

Rogers, L. (2013) 'Should there be mentoring efforts to help retain and recruit more males into baccalaureate and master's social work programs?', *Journal of Human Behavior in the Social Environment*, 23(8): 908–17.

Rosin, H. (2012) *The end of men*, London: Penguin.

Scourfield, J.B. (2001) 'Constructing men in child protection work', *Men and Masculinities*, 4(1): 70–89.

Scourfield, J.B. (2006) 'Placing gender in social work: the local and national dimensions of gender relations', *Social Work Education*, 25(7): 665–79.

Scourfield, J.B. and Coffey, A. (2002) 'Understanding gendered practice in child protection', *Qualitative Social Work*, 1(3): 319–40.

Simpson, R. (2004) 'Masculinity at work: the experiences of men in female dominated occupations', *Work, Employment and Society*, 18(2): 349–68.

Skinner, B.F. (1974) *About behaviourism*, New York, NY: Random House.

Sobiraj, S., Korek, S., Weseler, D. and Mohr, G. (2011) 'When male norms don't fit: do traditional attitudes of female colleagues challenge men in non-traditional occupations?', *Sex Roles*, 65: 798–812.

Stevens, M., Sharp, E., Moriarty, J., Manthorpe, J., Hussein, S., Orme, J., Mcyntyre, J., Cavanagh, K., Green-Lister, P. and Crist, B.R. (2012) 'Helping others or a rewarding career? Investigating student motivations to train as social workers in England', *Journal of Social Work*, 12(1): 16–36.

Stoller, R.J. (1968) *Sex and gender: on the development of masculinity and femininity*, New York, NY: Science House.

Trevithick, P. (2014) 'Humanising managerialism: reclaiming emotional reasoning, intuition, the relationship, and knowledge and skills in social work', *Journal of Social Work Practice*, 28(3): 287–311.

Walby, S. (1990) *Theorizing patriarchy*, Oxford: Blackwell.

Warde, B. (2009) 'Male social workers in child welfare: a qualitative analysis', *Child Welfare*, 88(4): 113–33.

Wharton, A.S. and Baron, J.N. (1987) 'So happy together? The impact of gender segregation at work', *American Sociological Review*, 52(October): 574–87.

Williams, L.C. (2013) 'The glass escalator, revisited: gender inequality in neoliberal times', *Gender and Society*, 27(5): 609–29.

Zammuner, V.L. (1987) 'Children's sex-role stereotypes: a cross-cultural analysis', in P. Shaver and C. Hendrick (eds) *Sex and gender*, London: Sage, pp 272–93.

SIX

Hidden in plain sight: use of an arts-based method for critical reflection

Annastasia Maksymluk

Introduction

This chapter explores the technique of employing imagery with students to support their development of critical reflection. My intention was to work productively with the frustration I perceived from students who appeared to find it difficult to understand that critical reflection demands the acknowledgement of the social location and embeddedness within particular social systems that influence our ability to act. I developed an accessible way of working with students in order to approach critical reflection in a non-textual way. The chapter draws on my work with nine social work, nursing and occupational therapy students undertaking placements in the health and social care statutory setting in which I was based.

As a practising social worker and educator, I am bound by time constraints and am aware of their impact on students. I therefore use images to stimulate discussion, reflection and learning at the end of a supervision session as part of a 'wind-down' and a retreat into a more interior, reflective space. I follow the same method in a responsive, ad hoc manner in an effort to overcome the 'stuck-ness' that students sometimes experience. For example, in response to a statement from a student such as 'I keep being told I need to show more critical analysis', I utilised a visual technique. In order to evaluate this use of an arts-based method to stimulate critical reflection by student social workers, I employed visual autoethnography as the principle way of monitoring responses and outcomes. What follows is a review of the literature, an account of the technique and student reactions, together with a summary of my learning for future use.

The case for an additional method

In her work around reflection, Fook (2002) has surmised that critical incident analysis is only productive when a person's thinking is not 'fixed' and resolved, but, rather, still open to movement. When I question students following statements such as the previous one, responses invariably fall into the following two types:

- 'I am able to undertake critical thinking but lack the time to do so and will utilise it properly when I have managed to read more'; and
- 'I don't yet fully grasp what critical thinking entails and therefore find it difficult to implement.'

Critical reflection is necessarily embedded in social work education (The College of Social Work, 2012; Croisdale-Appleby, 2014). To achieve this, I developed an arts-based technique to address students' fear and resistance in grappling with critical thinking. My motive was to devise a different method of showing students how critical reflection necessitates analyses of power relationships, but alongside this awareness, I aimed to show how analyses can be undertaken by simply engaging with all that is continuously played out before our eyes. Power relationships are not separate from casework and our everyday lives. They are not an adjunct. The goal I set myself was to make this awareness explicit in an accessible manner. I suggest that we can do this by training ourselves to take time to see. This involves making the distinction between vision and 'visuality'. Vision is presented as 'natural' and taken-for-granted, making sense of how we see and perceive the world around us, whereas visuality expands upon this to recognise how we process the richness of this as 'information'. It acknowledges 'knowingness' and conceptualisation as affected by constructor and viewer positioning. The relationships that exist within an image may not be immediately apparent. For example, how does an image that depicts a public space with an uncomfortable bench provoke a discussion about relationships? We have to go beyond simply seeing (vision) and registering the facility of the bench towards processing this information (visuality) – 'How is this public space being used?'; 'Which people are encouraged to use the space and which ones are not?'; 'Why would people be discouraged from spending time using the bench?'; 'How is this space organised and for the benefit of whom?' Questions such as these reference sets of relationships. The bench has not appeared out of nowhere. Its design has been produced following communication, interaction and decision-making, and people will be affected by these actions in different ways.

Why use arts-based methods to further critical reflection?

I chose to work with imagery because we are immersed in a taken-for-granted visuality within Western society. Our relationships, forms of communication and knowledges are constructed out of a constant interplay of fluid imagery. Richards (2006: 38, citing Rose, 2003) illuminates this:

> As a society steeped in popular culture, we rely on rapidly changing sensory images that present up-to-date information and instantaneous messages in mass media texts.... In fact, we are often told that we now live in a world where knowledge is visually constructed.

As educators, we can appreciate these facts and work with imagery as part of a multidimensional approach. This acknowledges multiple literacies as a way of extending methods that facilitate critical reflection. We know that social work education requires a graduate to be able to present as 'task-competent' alongside displaying a capacity for critical and independent thought. For this to occur, it seems pressingly important to work alongside students in a manner that stimulates recognition, deciphering and the deconstruction of the visual (Richards, 2006). We do not need to view visual forms of communication as disconnected from textual forms. Visual forms are wholly democratic inasmuch as we passively receive visual imagery via the act of looking. Bozalek and Biersteker (2010: 553) stress the democracy of visual learning methods, stating that they are 'accessible to people with different levels of literacy and the different types of representation themselves may act as a catalyst for different ways of thinking and knowing'. We do not have to decipher our response to visual imagery immediately. We can choose to simply experience and hold onto our initial sensory response. When we are teaching students about the complexity of social work, one of the facets of our work is to encourage students to hold onto that which they may not immediately understand and be able to process, to stay within the realm of the unfamiliar and not revert to simplistic classification responses. Furthermore, Bozalek and Biersteker (2010: 561) suggest that the distancing that can result from the act of representation can serve to ameliorate the resistance and anxiety that provokes classification. Distancing can alter the dynamic that produces stereotypical responses.

Working with visual imagery challenges us to move beyond a mechanistic stimulus–response analysis (Elfland, 2002) and acts to heighten awareness of our sensory responses. As art does not belong in the realm of the disembodied cognitive, it may serve to acknowledge the embodied experience, which draws upon touch, seeing and using the body to create. As Mullin (2003: 203) suggests: 'engaging with ... an artwork involves receptivity to asking oneself questions and entertaining different potential answers'.

However, apart from notable exceptions (Chambon, 2005; Phillips, 2007a, 2007b; Phillips and Bellinger, 2010) and a special issue of the journal *Social Work Education* in August 2012, visuality in social work education is largely conspicuous by its absence and so it may present as somehow detached and outside of social work. By disrupting the usual textual conventions of imparting and demonstrating social work knowledge, my hope was to demonstrate to students how relationships of power are part of the warp and weft of our everyday encounters. I also wondered whether working in a non-traditional manner would serve to challenge conventional ways of working, such as an expectation that critical reflection follows prescriptive, linear, textual formats. If a student can challenge one aspect of their practice, they may have the confidence to challenge other conventional practices that have been naturalised as 'normal' and therefore rendered less visible.

Critical reflection

Askeland and Fook (2009) provide a succinct overview of critical reflection using the work of Dewey (1933) within educational philosophy as a starting point. They remind us how reflective practice is both theory and process. Importantly, Brookfield (2009: 295) describes the process of reflection as being precipitated by a 'disorienting dilemma'. Critical reflection is presumed when analysis is extended to levels of meaning-making and is therefore disruptive of assumption.

Lymbery (2003: 107, citing Clark, 1995) maintains that 'the problems faced by social workers are sufficiently unfamiliar, complex and subtle to require the application of creativity and imagination to resolve them'. He suggests that social work practice should be located on a continuum encompassing both competence and creativity, and that while the competence model assists with the application of the technical aspects of social work, creativity is needed to develop existing knowledge to acquire new understandings (vertical transfer), and the application of existing knowledge to unusual contexts (lateral transfer) (Lymbery, 2003: 114).

Theorists have proffered various ways to assist educators to facilitate both the awareness of, and the ability to integrate, critical reflection. In fashioning my project, I was influenced by Parkes and Kadjer (2010), who suggest that four elements need to be in place to elicit reflective practice from students. First, students need 'to understand what reflective practice is or what it looks like' (Parkes and Kadjer, 2010: 226). I thought that the arts-based technique could suggest the differing forms that reflection can assume, and by extending our field of vision, we may seamlessly increase the breadth and depth we bring to reflection. Second, a safe and supportive environment is needed to convey trust and elicit gentle exposure to reflective practice. Third, 'adequate and strategic prompts' are needed, as well as, finally, opportunity and space for abilities and skills in reflection to be acknowledged and built upon (Parkes and Kadjer, 2010: 226).

Mandell (2008: 237) suggests that we need to focus on our personhood, recognising our 'emotions, cultural background, values, anxieties, self concept, social identities … with a critical analysis of one's role as a social worker in the relations of power that constitute our practice'. Building upon this, Mandell (2008: 239) also stresses how the reflective process should prioritise relational values: '[t]he identity of the social worker is constructed in terms of intersubjectivity'. These ideas validated an intuitive desire to conduct my exploration in an organic manner, working with my emotional responses, as well as those of the students I supervised.

The method

In order to engage with students, I asked them to produce collages made from images torn out of magazines and stimulated by an issue of interest to them. The collages were then used as a basis for discussion. At this point, it is important to state that this method of working is not an exercise in making art, using semiotics or employing psychological techniques. Neither educator nor student needs arts-based ability or experience. This method serves to integrate both our employment of visuality and our understandings of relationality as exercised within day-to-day living. As such, it forms part of a fuller response to experiencing social work practice and to working alongside students. I developed this way of working in order to create a safe space where the image is constructed as an object to be mutually explored in order to illuminate how and where relationships of power appear. These acts of 'looking and discussing' provide material that adds depth and complexity to analyses. They may also serve to gently illuminate the potential to reproduce oppression within interpretation, which may be especially useful when working alongside students to explore personal privilege.

I considered drawing and photography as methods to use but I discounted these as the former can appear threatening if students believe that they need to produce a realistic representation and hence need technical abilities. While photography has become extremely democratic via mobile phone usage, I feared that it may encourage too much distancing if, for example, a student went off alone to collate material (although I believe that photography offers an excellent medium for generating additional, practice-relevant discussions around issues such as identity, privacy and consent).

As a starting point, I encouraged students to generate their own image for discussion. I devised a simple method for doing this. I found the medium of collage proved to be a useful way of utilising an arts-based method in as non-threatening a manner as possible. I did not need to think ahead and plan too much; all I needed to do was ensure I had a small supply of newspapers or magazines, glue, and paper. I did not offer students scissors as I found that when I had done so previously, students responded in a seemingly technical manner by taking additional care to cut out their selections very carefully. This act, this way of responding to using a 'tool' via acts of distancing, can be used to generate discussion. Educators may choose to provide scissors in one session and not for the next in order to explore and review responses and make links with practice.

Students were invariably surprised within supervision when I changed the course of conversation and suggested that we undertake an activity together. I simply pulled a magazine out of my bag and asked the students to choose any image that 'spoke' to them. I gave few instructions other than:

> Let's create a quick image. Perhaps, think about a trigger – something that interests or niggles you that may have been milling around your head and that you may ordinarily choose to write or talk about. Use that trigger when you flick through the magazine. Rip anything out that catches your eye. Stick your selections on a sheet of paper in any way that feels suitable.

If a student appeared 'stuck' or anxious when endeavouring to search for an image that somehow displayed the 'correct' relevance for social work,

I gently suggested they pick an image at random. As previously stated, the intention was not to produce art or an 'accurate representation', but, rather, to produce a container that is replete with enacted choices. These can then be returned to, and 'mined' for the references they contain to relationality. Initially, students appeared perplexed as to how viewing imagery would extend their understanding of social work. I found that they derived reassurance when they recognised that within the realms of the visual, both student and facilitator have to seek points of illumination within murkiness. Once the students had made their choices and put a representation on paper, I worked to assist them to acknowledge that they had made particular visual choices. Of interest were the selection of images and their relative positioning, or relationality, rather than an image itself. These became the starting points for conversations. As a facilitator, I worked alongside the student to illuminate the questions and to emphasise the practice implications (Clemans, 2011). Relationships must be explicitly sought within a visual representation. These relationships may not be obvious. Crucially, right or wrong explanations do not exist. In this way, working with visual imagery leads to opening questions such as 'Where within the image are the relationships and what does the image tells us about those relationships?' As student and educator, we were, in a very organised manner, unravelling the choices that relate to occupying space – for example, the earlier example relating to the sets of relationships associated with a bench in public space. Additionally, images of females surround us but perhaps we need to consider the choices that are played out when a woman is presented within an image: 'How is the woman occupying the space?'; 'Who has the role of representing her?'; 'Who is assumed to be the viewer?'

Analyses become multilayered when they extend beyond the initial reading of the relationships conveyed by the producer of the image and towards a discussion of the relationships as experienced by the viewer(s). For example, a student undertaking a placement within an adult setting always chose to present imagery of children in relation to where she placed herself. Within discussion, she revealed that she was brought up in a household that fostered children and still did so. Within her role as a student social worker, she felt very responsible towards assisting her parents to undertake the role of foster carer, and conflicted that she wanted to work alongside adults. As educator and student, we explored this in individualistic terms. It also opened up discussion of the structural support offered to foster parents and the tensions inherent within relationships that are caring and also transactional. Thus, discussions serve to communicate 'the critical' within critical reflection as analyses of relationality address subjectivity, privilege and positioning. Working in an arts-based manner therefore places the onus upon the student to 'discover' the relationships stated and/or implied within a visual. In so doing, the student engages in analysis of their own social location. For example, one student chose to utilise many representations of 'self', that is, white males, within his collage. He was asked about the process of finding imagery of white males within UK-produced magazines. He replied by saying that the magazine was full of such representations in all poses with every imaginable expression. Following this, he was asked to replicate the process, looking for a similar amount of 'non-white' imagery with the same range of expression and pose.

Using an arts-based method in this manner is sufficiently startling to initiate the conversations necessary to make dominant discourses visible and to begin to acknowledge the critical element of critical reflection.

Using visual autoethnography for evaluation

In order to devise the most suitable methodology for evaluating this approach, I returned to my original trigger of pursuing an arts-based method of investigation reactive to the constraints of ordered and linear textual representation. Therefore, I utilised autoethnography as a methodology complementary to my project and chose to collect and present data visually. Autoethnography is a form of autobiographical reflection that explores personal experience and connects these observations to wider cultural, political and social meanings and understandings (Ellis et al, 2010).

I worked to produce a subjective, creative account of experiences and partly reproducible, contextualised understandings. I did not meticulously record research notes following a session alongside a student as this would have felt akin to following a mechanical and prescriptive linear route towards 'knowing' a phenomenon. Rather, I produced an image when I had a trigger I wanted to record and explore. As such, I followed the basic tenet of utilising critical reflection to explore that which is not already processed and resolved.

The images I created were not shown to students. I chose to informally check in at each stage of asking a student to create and use an image. In view of preconceived notions of strangeness that may accompany the use of a visual method within a pedagogical process, I had to ensure that the technique did not stimulate anxiety. Therefore, by gently questioning students to ascertain comfort levels, I received feedback that assisted my development of the technique and how I communicated it to students. I realised that I had to forefront the initial opening conversation with a request for the student to place to one side any assumptions they held about how social work knowledge is acquired.

Evaluation and learning for future practice

The purpose of the evaluation was to examine the utility of supporting student learning via the application of an image-based method within supervision and informal teaching moments. All the images I produced in the course of my evaluation conveyed multilayered levels of interpretation. The images served to convey the presence of complex multiple imprints arising from my statutory practice as a social worker alongside my work as an educator co-exploring visuality with students. They also exemplify the impossibility of aiming to separate these in a positivist search for objectivity.

My visual data served to demonstrate the difficulties of delineating clear-cut distinctions related to how we arrive at meaning-making. To illustrate, students initially appeared to react towards their visual material on an assumptive level. I wondered how far this resulted from wariness of the unfamiliar – that which is not immediately classifiable. Students appeared to strive to quickly arrive at plausible explanations. We became aware of how seductive and comforting it may appear to present interpretation in the form of sound bites in severance from the whole.

In the light of this, my data served to evaluate the main learning themes arising from using this method. The most recurrent theme of the evaluation was relationality, which was played out and explored throughout the time taken to work in a visual manner. In order to introduce this manner of working, I had to try to provide the necessary conditions for a student to feel safe, at ease and comfortable with the process, otherwise learning was likely to be impeded. My data revealed that it was necessary to act as a buffer between the student who is the focus of attention and who presents as not yet fully formed alongside any anxieties that a student may hold of themselves as needing to present as fully competent. This is pertinent to the fluid positioning that students hold while on placement as part of the process of becoming a professional social worker.

Processes of transition are usually not without accompanying anxieties. Within my evaluation, I noted how utilising a visual method, non-traditional to social work education, initially created or exacerbated these. The processes of countering and exploring anxieties became highly productive. When I suggested to students, prior to commencing a supervision session, that a small visual exercise could form part of the session, the response was invariably reactive to the anxiety related to performance, notably, 'I have not been expected to do this before as part of my social work training', or 'How do I prepare for it?' I interpreted these reactions as questioning expectations and relevance to social work: 'Are you wasting our time?' In response, I worked to ameliorate anxiety and provide a safe container, a visible thread between supervision and the project as an additional forum for exploratory conversation. I also connected this manner of working and social work: how the gathering of information, followed by rigorous inquiry and tentative interpretation, *is* social work. Thus, I was required to be transparent and explicit about the process that we were jointly undertaking.

Explicitness was a recurrent theme. I realised that working in a visual manner demanded overt framing and clear feedback loops, relating the activity to social work in order to maintain the comfort with ambiguity that visual interpretation demands. It entailed a shift away from calculable responses from students, perhaps the responses that students felt that they 'should' proffer to an educator rather than that which just came to mind. This was achieved surprisingly easily when the student and I both occupied a shared speculative space. There are no dualistic right or wrong responses to interpreting the image created by a student. Via the act of viewing, layers of inquiry and interpretation are added by the viewer. I noted that the lifting of notions of correct/incorrect responses from students served to open up dialogic space that could be acknowledged, potentially expanded into and occupied. When students were able to put anxieties aside, they appeared to experience this as a dynamic creative process.

Within many aspects of social work education, little room exists to play in terms of creative exploration (Weissman, 1990). Students may be required to list potential learning outcomes prior to commencing placement. Even from the outset, students may be required to follow formal linear lines of thinking that have the potential to be actualised as part of prescriptive, performative and 'tick-box' orientations. It can be productive to move away from the usual, the predictable route taken and the standardised format for problem-solving.

The evaluation addressed how working visually supported students to work with, and remain within, ambiguity. Students presented as engaging with ambiguity throughout the process of critical reflection conducted visually rather than textually. Being removed for a short period of time to undertake an activity concerned with visuality and, as part of this, to create a representation, served to assist students to connect with 'triggers' for learning that may or may not have been 'rational' and 'obvious'. For example, when critical reflection is asked of students as part of the formal assessment process, it can prove difficult for students to come up with something that is authentic, rather than something that serves to hit all the marking criteria. Working in a visual medium assisted students to generate material in an unforced manner that they could choose to return to and further explore later for assessment purposes should they want to. The generation of material worked to further student understanding of how the impetus, the trigger for a critical incident analysis and reflection, may initially present as minor. Students concurred that triggers for reflection that may appear to lie beneath rational processing mechanisms may yield much depth in terms of learning. This was actualised by the breadth and depth of dialogue generated from student imagery, which assisted students to recognise the complexity inherent in making choices and exploring relationships and connections. The process of producing a representation literally from fragments served to connect students to the seemingly insignificant.

My evaluation revealed the usefulness and strength of the emotional response within practice, and the need for students to appreciate and channel this appropriately. When students created an image or viewed the image of another, the initial response generated was invariably sensate and emotional. Significant learning moments were opened up during the exploration of these. Dialogue with students about emotional responses revealed the assumption that these may need to be sublimated as part of the process of becoming professional. This is played out within my data, which reference the removal of the body, and connects with the students' desire to reach a stage of being able to make 'objective judgements'. Students were aware of the requirement to develop their understanding of the identities they inhabit and, alongside this, resultant positioning and privileges, but believed, above all, that clear-cut, definitive answers were needed and appropriate. Incorporating a visual method served to acknowledge and honour these competing tensions as valid. Therefore, the project served to validate the legitimacy of remaining within ambiguity, with the caveat that we need to be connected with, and explicit about, these tensions.

Utilising a visual method necessitated the requirement to make connections clearly visible between interpreting a visual representation and social work. A recurrent theme from the evaluation alluded to earlier was student anxiety. I have already discussed student anxiety in relation to the method, but I now turn my attention to address the anxiety experienced by students generated from the need to situate disparate knowledges and add depth and criticality to their work. The evaluation revealed that the project was effective in assisting students to achieve this. The technique provided a space in which to explore these issues at a 'safe' distance via the process of distancing that takes place when the focus of discussion is a tangible object. Students did not appear to find it challenging to discuss the culture that they are immersed in, and form part of. Understanding was increased by considering how we construct our culture. These appeared to be comfortable processes. The leaps of understanding occurred when we moved beyond these processes towards deconstructing the everyday and the obvious that students chose to objectify within imagery. Students were startled to discover that when we discussed how space was negotiated, we were inherently having a conversation about relationships of power. Drawing from the method in this manner assisted students to embed understandings and move from narrow conceptualisations of power as structural, with power*ful* and power*less* participants. Engagement with the project was engagement with dynamic interpretations of power. For example, a student decided to represent her agency as she would like it to be. This provoked discussion about the differences she identified between her representation and the agency. The discussion was centred on the hands, presented in a nurturing manner within her image, which belied how the agency presented. The student conveyed how, prior to the exercise, she had accepted the environment and the practices emanating from her agency as imposed and just how it is, rather than manifestations of relationships of power that are open to change.

The project served as a successful vehicle to convey complex theorisations in a very accessible manner. It employed a method based upon mining the everyday and the taken-for-granted in order to draw out perceptions and cultivate expansive understandings. As the students and I illuminated relationships, we explored positioning. Doing this in a manner that was accessible, sensate and perceived as 'outside' conventional social work learning may have given students permission to explore deficits in their understanding. These occasionally presented as surprising gaps in knowledge of basic social work processes. From discussion, I realised that this was not attributable to gaps in teaching or a lack of commitment to learning from the student. Rather, it appeared to be the result of the student being so immersed within 'blocks' of newly acquired knowledges that the subsequent search for detail was leading to a blurring of focus on core processes. For example, I often asked students to describe what social workers do. Responses were either incredibly rambling or a student presented as completely unable to answer. However, when I asked a student the same question while we explored their visual 'production', they presented as able to answer far more confidently, probably because educator and student had to both look for visual triggers within an image. Our joint fumblings served to clarify core understandings in a very safe manner. To illustrate, on one occasion, a student noted how her image contained many representations of cameras and eyes, which she thought about and then said that this indicated assessment – how she was learning to assess others, alongside feelings of surveillance enacted over her by herself and by others, including me. I sought to consolidate these understandings via a constant reiteration and application of this awareness back to core social work. Thus, for example, when a visual representation was discussed, the student was encouraged to maintain a feedback loop between the acts of gathering information and employing tentative analysis and assessment. To illustrate, I asked a student to consider how their placement office had been decorated. He alluded to the magnolia walls and, after prompting, referred to the presence of a landscape on every publicly viewed wall. Much discussion was generated after I asked him if he thought that it was at all strange that the wall decor neither reflected the purpose of the agency nor the service users it served. Together, we made tentative hypotheses about the choices that had been made to present certain imagery and not others.

The potential of visual imagery for social work education

> ... our unexamined assumptions block our view. (Chambon et al, 1999: 266)

Phillips (2014) argues that social workers work in conditions where 'seeing' is a complex matter. Within her research, Phillips flags up how social workers may not 'see' that which is of crucial importance in the area of child protection: the actual body of the child. The technocratic measures that we draw on to help us assess what we see can actually obscure our view. Perhaps these measures act as a protective screen, a textual barrier that serves to distance us from the need to hold on to what we see? With this in mind, it seems imperative to work with the visual.

I have outlined a simple visual method where commonplace visual representations are torn into fragments, which serve to situate the everyday as 'practice' to be scrutinised and examined. Perhaps you may try out my visual method, or amend it to suit you, and arrive at additional effective ways of working in a non-textual manner alongside students.

This may serve to reiterate to students that social work is not conducted as discrete separate interventions, but, rather, occurs within a complex, permeable, sensate landscape. I have heard students make comments such as 'As I'm not in a statutory placement, how will I undertake assessment?' Such responses from students appear to feed into conceptualisations of a social work process such as assessment as legitimated and beginning and ending via and through a form headed with 'Assessment' (or related euphemism). A student's visual imagery may provide excellent material to co-explore where the connections may lie and to construct what we believe social work is into being. When students asked 'How is art relevant to social work?', I responded by asking 'What is social work?' After discussion, I hope we arrived at how art cannot be irrelevant to social work. As Foucault (1977) illuminated, images are not illustration; they are ways of telling and condensing patterns of relations.

Working in a statutory environment that values bureaucratic processing enacted within increasingly tight time frames, I find that little room is left for sharpening criticality. I nourish this through working alongside students and developing formats alongside the textual and linear to do so. This method has made me question how far social work education serves to restrict social work knowledge. Are we willing to enter unchartered waters alongside students to explore how their lived experiences and identified passions may be productively incorporated into their practice and how these may work to further social work knowledge? I have realised that it is therefore important to model all I have learned for the benefit of students, notably, that non-textual modes of communication are part of all that forms social work. Finally, I have consolidated my awareness that tightly categorised thinking can be limiting. It needs to be questioned and gently challenged in order to facilitate creative, productive possibilities.

References

Askeland, G.A. and Fook, J. (2009) 'Critical reflection in social work', *European Journal of Social Work*, 12(3): 287–92.

Bozalek, V. and Biersteker, L. (2010) 'Exploring power and privilege using participatory learning and action techniques', *Social Work Education*, 29(5): 557–72.

Brookfield, S. (2009) 'The concept of critical reflection: promises and contradictions', *European Journal of Social Work*, 12(3): 293–304.

Chambon, A. (2005) 'Social work practices of art', *Critical Social Work*, 6(1). Available at: http://www.criticalsocialwork.com

Chambon, A., Irving, A. and Epstein, L. (eds) (1999) *Reading Foucault for social work*, New York, NY: Columbia University Press.

Clark, C. (1995) 'Competence and discipline in professional formation', *British Journal of Social Work*, 25(5): 563–80.

Clemans, S. (2011) 'The purpose, benefits, and challenges of "check-in" in a group-work class', *Social Work with Groups*, 34(2): 121–40.

Croisdale-Appleby, D. (2014) 'Re-visioning social work education: an independent review', Department of Health, 27 February. Available at: https://www.gov.uk/government/uploads/system/uploads/attachment_data/file/285788/DCA_Accessible.pdf

Dewey, J. (1933) *How we think: a restatement of the relation of reflective thinking to the educative process*, Boston, MA: DC Health.

Elfland, A. (2002) *Art and cognition: integrating the visual arts in the curriculum*, New York, NY: Teachers College Press.

Ellis, C., Adams, T.E. and Bochner, A.P. (2010) 'Autoethnography: an overview', *Forum Qualitative Sozialforschung/Forum: Qualitative Social Research*, 12(1): Art 10. Available at: http://nbn-resolving.de/urn:nbn:de:0114-fqs1101108

Fook, J. (2002) *Social work: critical theory and practice*, London: Sage Publications.

Foucault, M. (1977) *Discipline and punish*, London: Allen Lane.

Lymbery, M. (2003) 'Negotiating the contradictions between competence and creativity in social work education', *Journal of Social Work*, 3: 99–117.

Mandell, D. (2008) 'Power, care and vulnerability: considering use of self in child welfare work', *Journal of Social Work Practice*, 22(2): 235–48.

Mullin, A. (2003) 'Feminist art and the political imagination', *Hypatia*, 18(4): 189–213.

Parkes, K.A. and Kadjer, S. (2010) 'Eliciting and assessing reflective practice: a case study in Web 2.0 technologies', *International Journal of Teaching and Learning in Higher Education*, 22(2): 218–28.

Phillips, C. (2007a) 'Pain(ful) subjects: regulated bodies in medicine and social work', *Qualitative Social Work*, 6(2): 197–212.

Phillips, C. (2007b) 'Untitled moments: theorizing incorporeal knowledge in social work practice', *Qualitative Social Work*, 6(4): 449–66.

Phillips, C. (2014) '"Seeing the child" beyond the literal: considering dance choreography and the body in child welfare and protection', *British Journal of Social Work*, 44(8): 2254–71.

Phillips, C. and Bellinger, A. (2010) 'Feeling the cut: exploring the use of photography in social work education', *Qualitative Social Work*, 10(1): 86–105.

Richards, J.C. (2006) 'Post modern image-based research: an innovative data collection method for illuminating preservice teachers' developing perceptions in field based courses', *The Qualitative Report*, 11(1): 37–54.

Rose, G. (2003) *Visual methodologies*, Thousand Oaks, CA: Sage Publications.

The College of Social Work (2012) 'Domains within the professional capabilities framework', version 01/05/2012. Available at: www.tcsw.org.uk/understanding-the-pcf/

Weissman, H. (1990) *Serious play: creativity and innovation in social work*, Silver Spring, MD: National Association of Social Workers Inc.

SEVEN

Getting our hands dirty: reconnecting social work education as if the earth matters

Andrew Whiteford

Introduction

I am a practice educator currently working in an undergraduate social work programme at Plymouth University. I have responsibility for developing and supporting practice learning arrangements and for working with students, both in placement and in the classroom, to facilitate their learning and professional development.

For the last seven years, I have been actively developing placements where students are directly involved in, and contributing to, a range of projects aiming to:

- improve and create access for people to natural green space;
- engage people more closely with food production;
- provide reparation or training opportunities benefitting the natural environment; and
- offer therapeutic benefit through horticultural or recreational activity.

My efforts have been located within first-year individual and group placements. My aims are to:

- reveal the benefits of closer alliance with the natural environment;
- advance an appreciation in students of the interdependence between social and environmental justice;
- develop awareness of how environmental conditions affect well-being; and
- identify approaches that they may apply to their practice.

In this chapter, I will explore the work that I have undertaken regarding sustainability and social work. It will reflect my own personal, transformational experiences and how my practice as a social work educator has developed more broadly as a result. I will first locate my work in wider global and vocational contexts and discuss some of the strategies that I have developed in response to the challenges and opportunities that the work has presented. I will also consider the impact that my work has had on student learning, as well as my own, with a view to establishing future directions in advancing environmental social work.

The inspiration for the initiatives described in this chapter came from my attendance at Schumacher College's 'Roots of Learning' course in early 2007, supported and funded by the Centre for Sustainable Futures (a Centre of Excellence for Teaching and Learning financed by the Higher Education Funding Council for England to promote Education for Sustainable Development) based at Plymouth University (see Schumacher College, no date). Subtitled 'Education as a Springboard for Transformation', the course was specifically designed for teachers and academics who were interested in introducing sustainability into schools and higher education. A significant aspect of my work since that time has involved exploring the multidimensional and contested meanings associated with the term 'sustainability'. Literature relating to social work and sustainability reveals diverse perspectives. A recurring theme, however, is the link between sustainability and broader considerations of the green or natural environment. Emerging from this is a discourse concerning environmental social work, supported by a growing theoretical and research base. As Blake (2009: 99) identifies: 'sustainability themes have multifarious implications for social work including societal resilience to future ecological and economic shocks'. Locating my educational practice within definable parameters in this regard has been an emergent and critical process.

The earth matters

> To forget how to dig the earth and to tend the soil is to forget ourselves. (Gandhi, 1946: 282)

Social work has a long-standing declared focus on 'person-in-environment' and 'engages people and structures to address life challenges and enhance wellbeing' (IFSW, 2014). For the Global North, where food and water security are not yet a primary concern, the focus is almost exclusively on social, cultural and economic structures, restricting consideration of 'environment' to the interpersonal and denuding it of any natural connotation. By acknowledging the extent to which nature is also a provider of, and a constraint on, social relationships, individual opportunity and personal well-being, environmental social work looks to expand this established framework by revealing the need for social work to broaden its understanding of environment to include the biological.

Similarly, with 'principles of social justice, human rights, collective responsibility and respect for diversities central to social work' (IFSW, 2014), the primary focus remains on the need for social, ideological and political change. Social work has a strong tradition of working with the most marginalised and least well-resourced individuals and communities, where the consequences of environmental and resource disruption are experienced first and most harshly. Environmental social work seeks to embrace the principles of environmental sustainability and to bind them to those of social justice, arguing that environmental awareness and action in social work practice are critical to its pursuit.

Lastly, as a profession, social work enjoys a unique combination of values, knowledge and skills that make it well placed to work with the interconnections between people and environment. Acknowledged as a 'practice-based profession', as well as an academic discipline, social work 'promotes social change and development, social cohesion, and the empowerment and liberation of people' (IFSW, 2014). Environmental social work encourages the consideration of our relationship with lifestyles and values that either positively or adversely impact the environment (our habitat). We can, through our practice and in our lives, advocate for sustainable and healthy ecosystems that ultimately provide us with nutritious food, fresh water, clean air, shelter and relative climatic constancy.

Professional reconnection

> We have to learn our way out of current social and environmental problems and learn to live sustainably. (UNESCO, 2005)

In 2010, the International Association of Schools of Social Work, the International Council on Social Welfare and the International Federation of Social Workers (IFSW) proposed a framework for the Global Agenda for Social Work and Social Development. Their vision was to create a basis for developments in professional education, research and action, acknowledging the need for social work 'to organise around major and relevant social issues that connect within and across our profession' (IFSW, 2012). Environmental sustainability (alongside social and economic inequalities, the dignity and worth of the person, and the importance of human relationships) was one of four areas on which the agenda was based.

More recently, in relation to its position on 'Globalisation and the environment', the IFSW (2014) acknowledges that people need 'supportive circumstances to give expression to most of their rights and to realise their human potential'. It is argued that these circumstances must include the 'confidence in a sustainable natural environment which supports life [alongside] the importance of peace [and] the avoidance of violent conflict and the existence of an equitable social order' (IFSW, 2014). Furthermore, as one of nine policy principles, the IFSW (2014) recognises 'that the natural and built environments have a direct impact on people's potential to develop and achieve their potential, that the earth's resources should be shared in a sustainable way'. The IFSW (2014) also makes the commitment that we, the social work profession, 'will conduct our own business to ensure that our concept of human rights includes the natural and built environment, with special focus on the needs of ethnic minority and indigenous people'.

Here, for the first time, is an internationally framed mandate supporting a practice paradigm that accounts for the interconnections between people and the natural environment. Social work is needed with disenfranchised communities, where the consequences of disconnection are most severe and where the task of regenerating interdependence is most urgent.

The literature relating to the environment and social work tends towards envisioning the ecological imperatives that social work practice can, and should, respond to (Molyneux, 2010). While asserting that social work should adapt its educational model to equip students to respond to these challenges, it has nevertheless only just begun to explore the implications for social work education. Kemp (2011: 1025) identifies the latter as the 'missing link' in the profession's effort to revision itself in the light of emerging global environmental concerns.

Writers encourage the application of social work values (Besthorn and Canda, 2002; Coates, 2003), knowledge (Soine, 1987, Kauffman et al, 1994) and skills (Rogge, 1994; Muldoon, 2006) to understand how environmental degradation, climate change and resource depletion impact on social relationships, individual opportunity and personal well-being. Social work education has thus acquired a set of organising principles around which curriculum development is being discussed.

Personal reconnection

> The personal is ecological. (McMain-Park, 1996)

It is only with hindsight that I better appreciate the formative influence of the Schumacher College course described earlier. It was through this experience that crucial learning and ideas were drawn out that are now woven into the fabric of my approach. Most significant is that early exposure to sustainability can be critical in guiding further learning (Sterling, 2007). It is important to be mindful of this when planning and supporting practice learning arrangements so as to maximise their transformative potential and to not disengage learners (Jones, 2007). This was something that I did not appreciate at the time, however, and that reflection and research have only just revealed to me.

In many ways, I have come to understand my current practice and study as a kind of *reconnection* through reflecting on an earlier career in outdoor education, working primarily in 'Small School' and community-based settings, where I first explored the place and meaning of the outdoors in education. This early work centred on personal development, skills acquisition and curriculum enhancement with young people experiencing a range of social, emotional and educational challenges. I was particularly interested in 'wilderness' experience and sail training as a means to build individual confidence, enhance interpersonal skills and develop relationships.

Through this work, I became increasingly concerned for the social, economic and psychological environments of the young people that I worked with, and I went on to train in social work in order to pursue this concern more fully. My interest in the natural environment was suspended, however, as I focused on what I considered to be a new set of priorities. I worked with adults and young people in a variety of settings involving outreach, detached, educational and casework approaches. Nevertheless, my interest in learning prevailed and I began to work with students on placement in these settings, moving eventually into my current role as a social work educator.

Prior to this, some of my earliest formal learning occurred within the progressive US public education system in the mid-1960s. I remember these formative years as happy ones and recall huge amounts of time playing (both in and out of doors) and talking (with teachers and other children), as well as achievements (both mine and others').

Upon my return to the UK, I recall with some trauma a very different experience – rote learning, inkwells and being bullied by teachers and other children. Like most children, I developed ways to cope and adapt, keeping a low profile and nursing my defiance. I failed to learn my times tables, could not spell and my handwriting was, and still is, illegible, but I knew that I could work most things out (given enough time), find most things out (given enough resources), try most things out (given enough opportunity) and explain myself (given someone to listen). I learnt pretty quickly, by necessity, how not to let school interfere with my education!

The experience at Schumacher College recovered my sense of bewilderment, creative uncertainty and hope for the way I might be in the world and how I might, more specifically, be with my work. I began to understand this personal change as akin to what the literature describes as 'transformative learning' (Mezirow, 1991; Cranton, 1996; Jones, 2003). The course at Schumacher expressly aimed to 'help teachers to transform their classrooms and curricula'. Other participants arrived on the course with a diverse combination of interests and motivations. Some were specifically involved in environmental education, with a focus on how to teach about sustainability as a discipline. There were also people involved in secondary and higher education who were interested in how to make education, in its broadest sense, more sustainable. The third sector, comprising development workers, health workers and environmental activists, were interested in supporting more sustainable, environmentally engaged living arrangements through direct work with people and communities.

While excited about the course, I remember feeling disoriented by the diversity of interests and knowledge of other participants. I was not confident that I had a sufficient grasp of the links between sustainability and social work. I was clearer about my own position regarding sustainability. Interestingly, this became my entry point into the debate. Being encouraged and given the space to articulate personal perspectives enabled my own thinking to evolve regarding social work and sustainability. Most critically, it led me to recognise how interdisciplinary dialogue is a real strength in this regard (Schmitz et al, 2013). I experienced how important it is to initially frame sustainability-related work with learners through the attitudinal positions that they personally occupy (Jones, 2007).

The following extract from guided reflection work at Schumacher reflects some of the early aspects of transformation that I now understand as essential in terms of (re-)engaging on a meaningful level with environmental issues:

> For me, the first and most significant event was the re-engagement of my feelings for the natural environment and

> how we are relating to it. I was surprised and somewhat taken aback by my response to this reawakening. Surprised because I had forgotten so much about myself, and taken aback because of the intensity with which the feelings returned. This was time for reflection!! I do not think this aspect of learning can be overemphasised. It was a moment when I was able to experience the issue fully and provided the basis and connection to it. I began to think about the way we teach social work in its broadest sense. I began to know why the imperative needs to be about engaging with students at the earliest possible opportunity ... on thinking about social justice and human rights ... and planetary well-being!

I emerged from Schumacher transformed, yet unsure what to do next. I felt that I needed to engage with environmental politics more fully, become more active in reconnecting people (myself included) with nature and take on further study and research. I was encouraged and reassured by writers such as Lysack (2009), whose own journey in politicising his environmental 'despair and grief' led to an 'ecological self' emerging and a foundation for action. Keefe's (2003: 5) discussion on the 'bio-psycho-social-spiritual origins of environmental justice' suggests that:

> only when the social world is re-joined, when words try to describe the experience does it take a particular form and meaning. So the ineffable experience is soon structured or refuted for the person having the experience by his or her social context.

A challenge has been to retain and reflect the 'profound empathy' that now motivates and informs my practice in working with students around the meaning of environmental considerations in social work. Sterling (2007: 72) describes third-order learning where 'an expansion of consciousness and a more relational or ecological way of seeing arises, inspiring different sets of values and practices'. This is learning that arises from what Cotton and Winter (2010: 34) identify as 'education for the environment', which 'conceptualises the transformative (and contentious) component of environmental education'. Sterling (2007: 73) suggests that individuals at this level can, and should, 'advance intentional learning' related to sustainability. The next section of this chapter explores my efforts to do so.

Getting down to earth

> All education is environmental education. By what is included or excluded, students are taught that they are part of or apart from the natural world. (Orr, 2004: 12)

It was encouraging to understand at Schumacher that social, rather than technological, questions are considered the 'key leverage points' (Cook, 2004: 46). While the social is clearly the domain of individuals and organisations concerned with humanitarian issues, including social work, the course tutors also talked in general terms about 'change agency' and encouraged participants to view themselves as 'agents for change', a concept not unfamiliar to social work (Pincus and Minahan, 1973).

It was while trying to contribute my ideas at Schumacher that I made my earliest attempts to theorise the need for social work practice to adopt sustainability as a core organising principle. I came to appreciate that these early connections were about social work's concern with social justice. Its knowledge and values relate to people being experts in their own lives and I saw the need to broaden its person-in-environment perspective to include the natural environment. Furthermore, while being taught about an educational approach to sustainability espousing reflection, critical analysis and action, I was reminded that this 'transformed educational paradigm', advocated by Sterling (2001: 22) as essential for learning about sustainability, finds expression throughout social work pedagogy (Jones, 2010).

As I embarked on this project and began to absorb ideas from permaculture, ecology and sustainability, I had to establish new frameworks and perspectives around which to organise and articulate my practice. Latterly, it has become equally apparent that working across disciplines significantly strengthens learning (Hayward et al, 2012; Schmitz et al, 2013; Tighe et al, 2013).

I quickly came to appreciate the extent to which I was already immersed in a teaching and learning culture where some of the factors outlined earlier already existed and where I was able to create conditions in which they might develop. The undergraduate social work programme at Plymouth was, at the time, moving away from a conventional modular approach towards a practice-led curriculum integrating theory and practice in a critically aware manner (Bellinger and Kagawa, 2010; Adamson, 2011). It was well placed to advocate for environmental thinking and action through a 'social learning' process that Tilbury (2007) argues is the context for sustainability itself. Practice learning and especially community-based field education have been identified as significant for the development of environmental social work (Bartlett, 2003; Whiteford et al, 2010; Lucas-Darby, 2011). It is my role as a social work practice educator to which I will now turn.

Connecting with issues of sustainability such as resource depletion, environmental degradation and biodiversity has been challenging. With the continued and accelerated restructuring of the profession, along with reductions in public spending in the UK, it is hard to imagine how the consideration of the natural environment can address the immediate concerns of social work practitioners or be regarded as relevant to everyday practice. Within social work education, the focus has almost exclusively centred on the social realm, with considerations of the environment restricted to the interpersonal (Besthorn, 2003; Keefe, 2003), denuded of its natural connotations (Marlow and Van Royen, 2001; Coates, 2003). A lack of precedence in locating field placements within agencies that explicitly address sustainability issues necessitated innovation. Initially, my efforts were focused on developing existing placements to pilot the idea of a sustainability-oriented placement, aiming to minimise unnecessary disruption or risk to student expectations. I was also supported by a sustainability activist who partnered me as a consultant. In the first year, I set up three group projects, one of which was to support the growth of a women's mental health self-help network. A second was to engage students in enabling a new community centre to reach out to local residents. A third project was for students to canvass colleagues and the public on what sustainability means. We provided a series of four, one-hour workshops for the nine students involved and their supervisors. Topics included: 'What is sustainability?'; sharing and reflection on the individual projects; and an open workshop for the students to present their projects, together with their learning.

Despite hopes that these early placements would generate more sustainability-oriented opportunities, their impact was minimal. Although the workshops had enhanced student learning and introduced the notion of sustainability-oriented placements for social work, they did not warrant continuation. Instead, I decided to integrate such placements into mainstream placement provision.

A more significant outcome was the networks developed through Plymouth's Centre for Sustainable Futures, with, for example, a permaculture consultant involved in community work and an urban growing project. Additionally, through personal volunteering, I identified opportunities with community allotments. By actively following up these possibilities, I was able to establish them as placements that, in turn, led to further possibilities opening up. Being open to opportunities at all times is common to all placement finders. I found that I became alert to the potential for social work learning in environmentally oriented projects where students would spend most of their time outdoors. This process has continued, with new placements being generated every year, such as developing access to a garden for people with dementia, working with offenders to restore a walled garden and return it to production, and supporting access to a community allotment for people seeking asylum. Placements have involved 64 students across 18 different work settings spanning seven academic years. In this regard, the process of developing placements has been no different from any other, but at this point, largely due to my own re-engagement, arrangements gravitated towards settings where students encountered issues relating to environmental aspects of sustainability. I found myself increasingly immersed in local environmental networks, in establishing new and interesting professional relationships. Alongside my work to encourage other team members to be confident in supporting these placements, I have been able to facilitate conventional placements to move towards environmental activity. An example of this was a centre for people with learning disabilities that used a student placement to create an outdoor growing space alongside service users.

While presenting students as a resource to these projects, it is inevitable that some arrangements require more support and oversight than the project staff can afford. This has also led to us not being able to continue working with some projects.

Experience has shown that the more robust arrangements tend to involve one or two students engaging in the routine, established work of the project. Less successful, even with additional support, have been instances where students work as a group to develop an area of work for the project. Many of the projects are, by their very nature, highly developmental, with staff time and resources committed to managing this while also having to accommodate a new perspective – that of social work – into their agency. Group-based community development work is also demanding of students, regardless of setting. Working outdoors and in less conventional social care settings requires different things of them. Overall, I have found that the added complexities of placing groups of students distract from the potential for students to learn and make a net contribution to any project that they work with. I have also found that the more robust and enduring arrangements are with projects that have a culture and established protocols relating to volunteering through which I can negotiate and contract placements.

In the field of environmental-based community work, this is, thankfully, quite common.

It has been while preparing placements that I have encountered further challenges and some welcome opportunities. There is a tendency in projects to view the offer of a student as simply another volunteer working to improve or conserve the environment. Agencies should be encouraged to regard the student as a resource. It is imperative, therefore, to emphasise the skills, interests and motivations that social work students, in particular, bring. Furthermore, being prepared to negotiate and reconcile social work and environmental politics has been necessary at times to maintain the profession's commitment to social justice, equality and human rights. These discussions are invaluable as they test and develop a project's capacity to link their work, social work and, most critically, learners' needs. I have come to value this dialogue not only as a means to assure quality, but also as an opportunity to support the projects themselves to develop their work by making good use of students to engage with, and support, their service users. It is equally challenging and formative to explain what social work *is* on such a regular and fundamental basis.

While early placements contributed to the students' progress and learning, it was noticeable that some students were more at ease with the reflective approach that learning for sustainability requires while others preferred a more task-focused method (Blake, 2009). Essentially, this has meant ensuring that direct work with people is available for students and that the aim of any work is primarily for the benefit of people. In this regard, students are enabled to identify where the social work is in what they are doing while developing generic, foundational practice skills.

Support from the programme lead was crucial to the success of these placements. Moreover, having established and prepared practice learning arrangements, I was less inclined to offer any formal input to interpret these new arrangements for colleagues. I preferred instead to rely on standard practice in sharing responsibility for their management with colleagues so that an appreciation of the issues involved might develop by absorption through everyday practice. I found sufficient opportunity to raise awareness and contextualise the placements through routine allocation and team meetings. While, on the whole, colleagues welcomed the opportunity to work with students in a new context and embraced the opportunity to do so, there were occasions when I felt disappointed by an apparent lack of investment. I had not fully appreciated that people's engagement with the nuances and tensions involved in bringing social work together with environmental work would be different from mine. The routine expectations we have of social care agencies to provide work for students need to be modified, as does the level and style of support we provide to these emergent and tentative arrangements. Anticipating the need to pay equal attention to preparing colleagues in this regard is vital if responsibility for arrangements is to be shared.

A small-scale evaluation of student learning that I undertook as part of a master's module revealed an active engagement with the practice learning experiences, on both a personal level and in terms of students' emerging understanding of what sustainability for social work is, or could be. Students acknowledged the significance of the natural environment and responses indicated a balanced perception of it in relation to human well-being. There was general support for the argument that social workers should support projects and campaigns aiming to protect green spaces. It was also recognised that this responsibility should be held more widely than just within social work. While on the whole agreeing that being in a natural environment with people has a positive effect on relationship-building, students remained person-centred in that they were mindful that responses also depend upon other factors. With few exceptions, it would appear that students appreciated the benefits for themselves of accessing the natural environment. These included, notably, improved mental and physical health, along with opportunities to reflect and develop relationships. There was some indication that direct contact through practice learning has shaped student perceptions of the relevance of green space to social work practice (Mind, 2013).

Conclusion

As I move towards a new level of engagement with sustainability as a social work educator, I am presented with some challenges in terms of objectively evaluating the development both of my practice and of student learning. I acknowledge my own immersion in the subject matter of sustainability and the potential subjectivity related to this. Having made some radical changes in my own lifestyle and consequently in my relationship with the green environment, I am engaged with the subject at a deep level and I acknowledge that I am passionate about the importance of sustainability, not just in my professional social work role, but in the way I am in the world.

It was McMain-Park (1996: 320) who, while arguing that the 'personal is ecological', asserted that 'environmental relationship, justice and integrity must occupy a position of utmost priority for the profession'. She began to discuss environmental justice alongside social justice and introduced activism and alliance-building to the professional repertoire of approaches that may link the two. The experience of developing these placements for me has been about relationships, with ideas, with nature and, above all else, with people. My conclusions are framed by the concept of alliance-building in this regard and might be summarised thus:

- Professional alliance
  - commit yourself to a dynamic theory and practice exploration;
  - reconcile and link social justice with environmental justice (curriculum); and
  - create transformative teaching and learning strategies (pedagogy).
- Personal alliance
  - personal positioning is critical for both educator and student;
  - be prepared to (re)consider your own position to the environment; and
  - do not expect others to share and appreciate your position.
- New alliance
  - develop networks with 'non-traditional' partners;
  - embrace new ideologies and outdoor activity; and
  - integrate issues across both work-based and classroom-based learning.
- Unlikely alliance
  - look initially to where placements already exist;
  - be prepared to interpret and explain what social work is; and
  - maintain focus on the professional role and purpose within the setting.

Professional leadership has been identified as one of nine domains of the professional standards framework developed by the Social Work Reform Board in the UK (TCSW, 2012). With a concern for 'human protection and empowerment' (Muldoon, 2006: 7), its claim to a 'uniquely preserved wisdom about the radical potential of human beings to recreate themselves' (Weick, 1987: 228) and a 'historical and explicit focus on person-in-environment' (Zapf, 2009: 30), social work might be expected to offer such leadership within an interdisciplinary effort to reconnect people and their environment.

A profession such as social work requires education and training that develops a mixture of knowledge, values and skills appropriate to its vocational task. It needs continually to anticipate the rapidly changing social, ideological *and* environmental forces that demand personal, as well as professional, adaptations. I believe that the work I have undertaken makes a contribution towards this by developing an educational culture within social work that is fit for such a 'postmodern ecological view' (Sterling, 2007: 67) that is recognisable and replicable by others.

References

Adamson, C.E. (2011) 'Getting the balance right: critical reflection, knowledge and the social work curriculum', *Advances in Social Work and Welfare Education*, 13(1: Special Issue: Critical Reflection: Method and Practice): 29–48.

Bartlett, M. (2003) 'Two movements that have shaped a nation: a course in the convergence of professional values and environmental Struggles', *Critical Social Work*, 4(1). Available at: http://www.uwindsor.ca/criticalsocialwork

Bellinger, A. and Kagawa, F. (2010) 'Learning beyond compliance: a comparative analysis of two cohorts undertaking a first year social work module', *Journal of Pedagogic Development*, 2(1): 40–50. Available at: http://www.beds.ac.uk/jpd

Besthorn, F.H. (2003) 'Radical ecologisms: insights for educating social workers in ecological activism and social justice', *Critical Social Work*, 4(1). Available at: www.uwindsor.ca/criticalsocialwork/

Besthorn, F.H. and Canda, E.H. (2002) 'Revisioning environment', *Journal of Teaching in Social Work*, 22(1/2): 79–101.

Blake, J. (2009) 'Sustainable communities and social work practice learning: reflections on emergent, learning partnerships', *Journal of Practice Teaching and Learning*, 10(2): 93–114.

Coates, J. (2003) *Ecology and social work: toward a new paradigm*, Halifax, NS: Fernwood.

Cook, D. (2004) *The natural step: towards a sustainable society*, Totnes, Devon: Green Books Ltd.

Cotton, D.R.E. and Winter, J. (2010) '"It's not just bits of paper and light bulbs": a review of sustainability pedagogies and their potential for use in higher education', in D. Selby, S. Sterling and P. Jones (eds) *Green infusions: embedding sustainability across the higher education curriculum*, London: Earthscan.

Cranton, P. (1996) *Professional development as transformative learning: new perspectives for teachers of adults*, San Francisco, CA: Jossey-Bass.

Gandhi, M.K. (1946) *Harijan*, 25 August, p 282.

Hayward, R.A., Miller, S.E. and Shaw, T.V. (2012) 'Social work education on the environment in contemporary curricula in the USA', in M. Gray, J. Coates and T. Hetherington (eds) *Environmental social work*, Abingdon: Routledge, pp 248–59.

IFSW (International Federation of Social Workers) (2012) 'Global definition of social work and social development'. Available at: http://ifsw.org/get-involved/agenda-for-social-work/

IFSW (2014) 'Global definition of the social work profession'. Available at: http://ifsw.org/policies/definition-of-social-work/

Jones, P. (2003) 'Educating for change: transformative learning and progressive social work education', *Advances in Social Work and Welfare Education*, 5(1): 72–85.

Jones, P. (2007) 'Engaging for transformation: the challenge of bringing the environment into social welfare and community development education', *New Community Quarterly*, 5(2): 37–39.

Jones, P. (2010) 'Responding to the ecological crisis: transformative pathways for social work education', *Journal of Social Work Education*, 46(1): 67–84.

Kauffman, S., Walter, C., Nissly, J. and Walker, J. (1994) 'Putting the environment into the human behaviour and the social environment curriculum', in M. Hoff and J. McNutt (eds) *The global environmental crisis: implications for social welfare and social work*, Brookfield, VT: Avebury, pp 277–96.

Keefe, T.W. (2003) 'The bio-psycho-social-spiritual origins of environmental justice', *Critical Social Work*, 4(1). Available at: www.uwindsor.ca/criticalsocialwork/

Kemp, S.W. (2011) 'Re-centring environment in social work practice: necessity, opportunity, challenge', *British Journal of Social Work*, 41: 1198–210.

Lucas-Darby, E.T. (2011) 'The new color is green: social work practice and service-learning', *Advances in Social Work*, 12(1): 113–25.

Lysack, M. (2009) 'Practices and skills for building social and ecological resiliency with individuals and communities', in S. Hick, H. Peters, T. Corner and T. London (eds) *Structural social work in action: examples from practice*, Toronto, ON: Canadian Scholars Press, pp 211–28.

Marlow, C. and Van Royen, C.A.J. (2001) 'How green is the environment in social work?', *International Social Work*, 44(2): 241–54.

McMain-Park, K. (1996) 'The personal is ecological: environmentalism of social work', *Social Work*, 41(3): 320–3.

Mezirow, J. (1991) *Transformative dimensions of adult learning*, San Francisco, CA: Jossey-Bass.

Mind (2013) 'Feel better outside, feel better inside: eco therapy for mental wellbeing, resilience and recovery'. Available at: http://www.mind.org.uk/media/336359/Feel-better-outside-feel-better-inside-report.pdf

Molyneux, R. (2010) 'The practical realities of eco-social work: a review of the literature', *Critical Social Work*, 11(2): 61–9.

Muldoon, A. (2006) 'Environmental efforts: the next challenge for social work', *Critical Social Work*, 7(2). Available at: http://www1.uwindsor.ca/criticalsocialwork/2006-volume-7-no-2

Orr, D. (2004) *Earth in mind: on education, environment, and the human prospect*, Washington, DC: Island Press.

Pincus, A. and Minahan, A. (1973) *Social work practice: model and method*, Itasca, IL: Peacock.

Rogge, M. (1994) 'Field education for environmental hazards: expanding the person-in-environment perspective', in M. Hoff and J. McNutt (eds) *The environmental crisis: implications for social welfare and social work*, Brookfield, VT: Avebury, pp 258–76.

Schmitz, C.L., Matyók, T., Sloan, L.M. and James, C. (2013) 'Environmental sustainability: educating social workers for interdisciplinary practice', in M. Gray, J. Coates and T. Hetherington (eds) *Environmental social work*, Abingdon: Routledge, pp 260–79.

Schumacher College (no date) 'Roots of learning: strategies for creative social change'. Available at: https://www.schumachercollege.org.uk/courses/short-courses/roots-of-learning%3A-strategies-for-creative-social-change

Soine, L. (1987) 'Expanding the environment in social work: the case for including environmental hazards content', *Journal of Social Work Education*, 23(2): 40–6.

Sterling, S. (2001) *Sustainable education: re-visioning learning and change*, Dartington, Devon: Green Books.

Sterling, S. (2007) 'Riding the storm: towards a connective cultural consciousness', in A.E.J. Wals (ed) *Social learning towards a sustainable world: principle, perspectives and praxis*, Wageningen, The Netherlands: Wageningen Academic, pp 68–82.

TCSW (The College of Social Work) (2012) 'Professional capabilities framework'. Available at: http://www.tcsw.org.uk/pcf.aspx

Tighe, M., Whiteford, A. and Richardson, J. (2013) '"Stepping out": enabling community access to green space through inter-disciplinary practice learning in Plymouth, UK', *International Journal of Practice-based Learning in Health and Social Care*, 1(2): 8–22.

Tilbury, D. (2007) 'Learning based change for sustainability: perspectives and pathways', in A.E.J. Wals (ed) *Social learning towards a sustainable world: principle, perspectives and praxis*, Wageningen, The Netherlands: Wageningen Academic, pp 117–31.

UNESCO (United Nations Educational, Scientific, and Cultural Organization) (2005) 'Snippet: goals of the UN DESD'. Available at: http://www.gdrc.org/sustdev/un-desd/desd_goal.html

Weick, A. (1987) 'Reconceptualizing the philosophical perspective of social work', *The Social Service Review*, 61(2): 218–30.

Whiteford, A., Horton, V., Garrard, D., Ford, D. and Butler, A. (2010) 'Sustaining communities: sustainability in the social work curriculum', in D. Selby, S. Sterling and P. Jones (eds) *Green infusions: embedding sustainability across the higher education curriculum*, London: Earthscan, pp 241–56.

Zapf, M.K. (2009) *Social work and the environment: understanding people and place*, Calgary, Alberta: Canadian Scholars' Press, University of Windsor.

EIGHT

Social media for students in practice

Joanne Westwood

Introduction

This chapter examines social media in social work practice contexts and settings and explores how agencies, organisations and practitioners can ensure that it is used safely. In social work practice, the barriers to engagement with social media and, in particular, the concerns about practitioner, service user and carer privacy and confidentiality are amplified. This chapter explores the opportunities that social media presents in practice contexts, as well as the possible threats. New communication technologies have the potential to contribute a great deal to social work practice benefitting service users, and practitioners, adding novel dimensions to practice, but only as long as they are used ethically by practitioners who are aware of the importance of professional boundaries. This chapter draws on a small piece of research with practice educators about their use of social media with students. Reflective questions are posed throughout to encourage the reader to consider the use of social media in their own practice.

Definitions

As with any new development in social work, a range of terms start to appear that need deciphering. Included here is a very brief definition of some of the most popular terms used in this chapter and their relevance to social work practice:

- *Social media*. Social media is a publishing and broadcasting medium (BASW, 2012). Social media is part of Web 2.0 technology, which is designed around user interaction. Social media users can connect and interact with Web-based content. Social media has the potential to promote and communicate news, information and ideas. It is potentially a powerful mechanism for raising awareness of social work issues and social justice.

- *Social networking sites*. A social networking site (SNS) is an online space where people can build their own profile, share content (eg photographs or films) and connect with others. An example here is Facebook, which is used as both a social networking tool by individuals and as a marketing tool by businesses. It has also been used to explore values and ethical dilemmas related to social work practice, as will be discussed in this chapter. LinkedIn is another SNS that connects professionals with each other, and allows them to share information, interact and post comments.
- *Blog*. A blog is a personalised website where you can 'blog' (write) about your opinions, ideas, views, thoughts or reflections. Blogs can be made private or available to only certain individuals, or, like all forms of social media, they can be made public. As such, they are also global and permanent once published. 'Micro-blogging' also includes ideas and opinions but in a condensed and limited form. Twitter is an example of a micro-blog, as it is limited to using 140 characters. Twitter users may have personal and/or private profiles. In any case, for social workers, what they post on Twitter is publicly available (unless privacy settings are in place) and so care must be taken to ensure that posts are appropriate and in keeping with the professional value base of social work.
- *E-professionalism*. E-professionalism is a term that has emerged more recently and it describes the ways in which users of social networking sites understand, manage and respond to social media. It is of particular significance in social work because of the daily interface with vulnerable people, and because of the need for confidentiality and trust between service users and practitioners.

Background

Emerging in the early part of the 21st century, social media develops, promotes and improves online networking between individuals and is used by industry and commercial organisations to market their businesses. As a relatively new development, the primary and allied health and social work professions are still grappling with its forms. Social media encompasses a broad range of tools, networks and mediums that people use to communicate in different ways and formats. People share content, opinions, information, their thoughts and ideas. These may be in text, image, audio or video format, or a combination of each. There are SNSs where people can create their own profiles, such as Facebook (which has 1.3 billion users) (Statistic Brain, 2014a), Google+, Bebo, LinkedIn and MySpace. Other SNSs allow people to blog or micro-blog, write articles, share their opinions and provide updates on projects they are working on, or simply provide a status update. These include Twitter, Blogger, Whatsapp and Tumblr. Latest figures suggest that, globally, there are 645,750,000 registered Twitter users and, on average, 58 million 'tweets' per day (Statistic Brain, 2014b). There are SNSs that are mainly visual/audio and allow people to share photographs, films, videos and music, for example, Instagram, Flickr and Youtube.

Social media and social work practice

Social media has the potential to raise awareness and promote issues relevant to social work practice (Kimball and Kim, 2013). Whose Shoes? (see: http://nutshellcomms.co.uk/) is a good example of how an organisation has used social media to promote and encourage collaboration and co-production between service users, carers, commissioners, social workers and academics. Originally designed as a board game, Whose Shoes? is now also an interactive tool that is used to facilitate policy and practice development in regard to personalisation and self-directed support for adults. The organisation behind this initiative uses social media to promote and market the online and real-time game-based planning tool, raising awareness of the personalisation agenda (Needham and Glasby, 2014) and supporting individuals and communities of practice while learning to bring about local changes in how adults are cared for.

In another example, a report published by the international accountancy firm Binder Dijker Otte (BDO, 2012) illustrated a range of developments, using case studies from across the UK to illustrate how social media had been used to engage with the public and raise awareness of important social issues. For example, a social media campaign in Leicester was launched to encourage teenage girls to carry condoms. The pre-campaign survey showed that 53% of students thought that it was positive that girls carried condoms, the post-campaign survey found that 78% thought so (BDO, 2012: 9). BDO, however, also report that many local authorities have punitive social media policies when it comes to staff accessing social media, based on the view that social networking at work distracts employees from their work. However, the benefits of encouraging social media, and the opportunities that it presents to engage with local people and promote awareness of important local issues, are missed with this stance.

Reflective questions

- What is your agency's/organisation's social media policy?
- Are you able to use social media during work hours?

Practice educators and work-based supervisors who support the fieldwork practice aspects of social work education all play an important role in enabling student social workers to develop professional accountability and practice that is ethical and safe. Yet, little is known about the role that social media plays in this training despite its growing significance in our everyday lives and in the lives of service users. The issues about remaining professional and a potential disregard for confidentiality were highlighted in a well-reported case involving a social worker who posted a comment on Facebook expressing her delight that a judge had removed children from their parents, describing this as a 'career high' (BBC News Essex, 2013). This social worker clearly breached professional boundaries and the British Association of Social Workers (BASW) code of ethics; however, it is unlikely that most breaches of confidentiality on SNSs will be as explicit as this. Nevertheless, it is incumbent upon practice educators to engage with questions about SNSs and how students use these, as there is continual growth in the use of technology more generally by agencies and organisations to provide services. There is also a normalisation of people using online resources to seek help and support where this would have once been provided face to face.

There is a lack of published research that examines social work practitioners' use of social media, although this is an emerging area of study. Rosenthal Gelman and Tosone (2010) bemoan the lack of training and education available to social workers to use technology to generally advocate for social work service users or to inform their interventions. In the UK, Rafferty (2011) describes an example from social work practice in a care leavers project that followed up the young people who had left care by checking their Facebook pages. The ethical issues here are clear: did the care leavers know that they were being 'followed up' in this way? Did the agency have a policy that was shared with the student who was tasked with the follow-up activity? In a recent Australian study of 935 health professionals' use of social media, Usher (2012) found that the majority (83%) did not use social media in their professional roles and that this was primarily related to their lack of knowledge of the technology. Only 19% used social media in their private lives. While this may not tell us about the uptake of social media by social workers, Usher's study reveals a lack of engagement by practitioners in an environment where there is unprecedented and uncharted growth in new and emerging forms of communication, of relating and practising in social work. It is well established that, in the UK, social work practice educators use the Internet and online sources to support their continuing professional development and to keep up to date with practice knowledge, policy and legislative changes (Horder, 2007). This engagement by practice educators with online resources might be enhanced by their engagement with SNSs, where materials can be accessed, archived and shared quickly. This is a useful social media activity that can also be easily shared with students.

Reflective questions

- Can you communicate about work issues with colleagues and/or your students using social media?
- What professional activities do you carry out using social media?
- How do you keep up to date with professional/practice issues and developments?

The British Association of Social Workers' code of practice for social media

In 2012, BASW published their 'Social media policy', recognising the potential that social media has to promote the values of social work across a global stage and with international partners. BASW also foresaw that social workers would need to be proficient and literate in their use of social media. The policy aims to 'clarify what BASW considers to be the professional responsibilities of social workers and social work students, in relation to the increasing use of social media' (BASW, 2012: 4). BASW illustrates the potential dilemmas that practitioners may come across in relation to the use of social media by service users, for example, where a looked-after child might be contacting their birth family, or where a service user posts abusive messages about a practitioner on a social media site. It is likely that practice educators will come across both the negative and positive aspects of social media in practice.

The BASW policy states that:

> social workers need to be aware of and knowledgeable about technological developments and understand the impact, use and advantages as well as possible ethical concerns and risks in relation to themselves, the people they are working with and their employers. (BASW, 2012: 5)

BASW states that there is a real need to reflect on the changes in the way we communicate and consider how this impacts on practice. In particular, BASW (2012: 5) refers to the 'collection and use of information about and by individuals and how to maintain the service users' right to a relationship of mutual trust, privacy, and confidentiality'. The 'Social media policy' is designed to apply to social workers in the UK, including employers and education and training providers. BASW recommends that social media policies and codes of practice for staff are proactive and support professional development and e-professionalism. In developing social media policies, Kimball and Kim (2013) suggest that agencies should be proactive in establishing these and involve social media users, legal representatives and human resources departments. In a spirit of participation, collaboration and transparency, it would also be considered good practice to include service users and carers in designing such policies.

Reflective questions

- What are your own concerns about using social media in your practice with social work students?
- What advice would you give to a service user about using social media to communicate with your agency?
- How can you model e-professionalism with social work students in practice placements?

Social media in social work practice education

The use of SNSs in social work education to complement existing teaching and learning strategies has been a recent development (Westwood, 2014a). The obstacles to engagement with social media are discussed by Thackray (2014), who describes four issues that determine how we engage with social media: technological barriers that impact on the adoption of new technology; developing an online identity and the boundaries that determine how an online identity is shared; privacy and being exposed online; and the adoption of a new online culture. For those who are new to social media and technology, and may perceive themselves to be digital 'visitors', starting off slowly and building up knowledge is recommended. Many social work students are already digital 'residents', familiar with, and active users of, new communication technologies. They might be willing to share their expertise and know-how with their practice educators.

While there is a range of concerns about using social media in social work education, there is also great potential for SNSs to enhance the students' learning experience in relation to skill development and understanding values issues for practice, as illustrated by Iverson-Hitchcock and Battista (2013), Singh Cooner (2013, 2014) in his work on using closed Facebook groups with student social workers, and Taylor (2014), who uses Twitter to promote membership of a national online social work book group that involves students, academic and practitioners. Social work educators who integrate social media into their teaching argue that it supports students to develop a professional online identity commensurate with social work values. In addition, social media provides a wealth of opportunities to the profession in terms of future practitioners being advocates for social justice. For students, developing e-literacy helps them to stay updated on policy and legislative changes that affect their practice (Iverson-Hitchcock and Battista, 2013). How social media might enhance practice education when students are on fieldwork placements, however, relies on organisations', practice educators' and agencies' familiarisation with, and adoption of, social media as a learning and development strategy. As outlined earlier, while there is some evidence of it being used in this way, there is limited empirical work available and so we are entering uncharted areas of practice learning.

People who use social work services are among the growing numbers of those who use social media, taking advantage of new technology and changing the way in which they seek support. Also, from a worker's and an organisation's perspective, new ways of intervening are being delivered and developed (Mishna et al, 2012). In their study, Mishna et al (2012) found that service users were initiating contact using a range of technology, although younger service users were more likely to use texting. For some of the practitioners involved in the study, the online interaction potentially complemented the face-to-face work and service users were able to give feedback using email for example. However, one participant described how a service user had posted a blog criticising the social worker and the intervention that they had received, which was public and, crucially, permanent. Thus, for all of its potential and opportunities, the privacy and confidentiality that characterise social work interventions are potentially threatened by the advent of social media.

While there are real concerns among practitioners and students about the use of social media in practice, Rafferty (2011) argues that this should encourage real *engagement* with social media rather than avoidance. This position was adopted by Singh Cooner (2013) for a research study with social work students using closed Facebook groups and real-life social work practice scenarios. In the study, students were invited to set up a Facebook account, which enabled them to work together on tasks outside of the classroom environment. Even though students were not always comfortable using this medium, they did report that the exercises they were tasked with enabled them to engage with real-life practice dilemmas and consider the potential consequences.

Ethical approval was granted by the University of Central Lancashire Research Ethics Committee for a small-scale online survey that asked respondents questions about their use of social media with social work students. Initially, 14 practice educators agreed to participate; however, only three responses were submitted.

Those practice educators who did respond expressed concerns about the blurring of professional boundaries, breaches of confidentiality and the possibility that engagement with service users using social media might also lead to conflicts and misunderstandings. The responses to the consultation also revealed that agencies and organisations were using social media to market and publicise their services and activities, as well as to advise their followers of new developments, to communicate broadly (not individually) with service users and to share relevant local and national news. The practice educators were invited to describe what support they might need to help them to use social media. As well as robust guidance and monitoring, they suggested ongoing training and support in terms of safeguarding and boundaries and easy access to resources to enable their engagement. In relation to how service users might benefit from social media, they suggested that it has the potential to reduce isolation for service users, who might gain from online peer support networks. Also, they mentioned that social media could be used as a tool to celebrate the work of unpaid carers, to provide a more positive image of social work generally and to provide updates about activities. In essence, there was an emphasis on embracing aspects of social media that were seen as being able to meet some of the needs, some of the time, for service users who are isolated. Social media was not perceived as being able to replace, but only to complement, social work and what social workers can offer. Albeit only a small-scale consultation, this study suggests that practice educators do have a role to play in supporting student social workers to develop their understanding of how SNSs can be used appropriately and ethically.

Reflective questions

- What barriers are there for you in using social media in your professional role?
- How would you advise a student social worker to respond to a 'friend' request from a service user on Facebook?
- What advice would you give to a student who has a Twitter account that they use for both work and for their social life?

Professional boundaries

In their discussion of ethical issues regarding social media and social work, Kimball and Kim (2013: 186) describe how online networks that include colleagues, friends, old school friends and family are separate in real life, whereas 'these worlds collide' online. Thus, it is important when designing policies that the personal and the professional are distinguished (TCSW, 2012). Professional boundaries are defined as 'the boundary between what is acceptable and unacceptable for a professional to do, both at work and outside it and also the boundaries of a professional's practice' (Doel et al, 2010: 1867).

Doel et al (2010) argue that ethical engagement is essential for the development of ethical social work practice. As discussed in this chapter, social media provides opportunities for ethical engagement; it presents real-time ethical issues that move students and practitioners away from a 'tick-box' ethical checklist approach and into a public, global forum where conversations and discussions about practice take place and involve service users, carers and professionals. This public forum potentially dissolves or blurs the boundaries that more formal situations dictate. However, this blurring is not always appropriate. In their discussion of how digital technology 'crept in', Mishna et al (2012) discuss how social workers experienced and responded to the influx of new technology and the ethical issues that resulted from this. In their article, Mishna et al (2012) remind us that the Internet generally allows service users to access information about practitioners and vice versa. However, does being *able* to access information about a service user mean that a practitioner *should* access this? These ethical questions are presented in the Social Work and Social Media (SWSM) app designed by Singh Cooner (2013) and reviewed in Westwood (2014b). The activities included in the SWSM app are designed to trigger discussion, reflection and debate about the ethical issues of using social media in social work using several practice-based case studies. The case studies illustrate: how service users seek advice about using social media; how staff can benefit from advice shared on social media; and how it presents opportunities for service users to give feedback about their experiences.

The tasks deal with issues related to looking at service users' social media sites, for example, Facebook or Twitter, when preparing for a visit, and are suitable for team discussion, individual supervision sessions with students and between practitioners and their managers.

Reflective questions

- How does your team currently deal with queries from service users or carers about using social media?
- What do you think are the main barriers or facilitators to your team engaging with questions regarding social media?
- What ethical issues related to social media have you or your team responded to?

Summary

This chapter has examined some of the key issues related to the use of social media in social work practice education. The developments in technology during the early part of the 21st century show no signs of slowing down; indeed, they are more likely to speed up as new technologies are introduced. These developments present vital opportunities to engage with service users at an organisational level to develop social media policies and codes of conduct when using social media generally and, to a certain extent, to engage with individual service users if this is appropriate. However, the risks and potential for blurred boundaries and concerns about misconduct might detract from, or even prevent, social work students and practice educators embracing these opportunities. Student social workers may be keen users of social media in their private lives, and may wish to avoid using social media with service users for fear of breaching professional boundaries or putting themselves or service users at risk of harm. Practice educators play an important role in working with students to express and reflect upon these concerns and to develop an understanding of how social media interactions can lead to conflict and tension between practitioners and service users, and how it has the potential to strengthen relationships and communication. Practice educators can contribute to the development of students' professional identity and ethical practice by engaging in social media activities and familiarising themselves with the key policy frameworks and codes of conduct related to social media in their agencies and organisations.

References

BASW (British Association of Social Workers) (2012) 'BASW social media policy'. Available at: http://cdn.basw.co.uk/upload/basw_34634-1.pdf

BBC News Essex (2013) 'Essex social worker: children put in care "career high"'. Available at: http://www.bbc.co.uk/news/uk-england-essex-22651876

BDO (Binder Dijker Otte) (2012) 'From housing and litter to Facebook and Twitter'. Available at: http://www.bdo.co.uk/__data/assets/pdf_file/0008/186524/BDO_Local_Government_Team_-_Updating_your_status_social_media_report.pdf

Doel, M., Allmark, P., Conway, P., Cowburn, M., Flynn, M., Nelson, P. and Tod, A. (2010) 'Professional boundaries: crossing a line or entering the shadows', *British Journal of Social Work*, 40(6): 1866–89.

Horder, W. (2007) '"Reading" in professional practice: how social work practice assessors access knowledge and information', *British Journal of Social Work*, 37: 1079–94.

Iverson-Hitchcock, L. and Battista, A. (2013) 'Social media for professional practice: integrating Twitter with social work pedagogy', *Journal of Baccalaureate Social Work*, 18: 33–45.

Kimball, E. and Kim, J. (2013) 'Virtual boundaries: ethical considerations for use of social media in social work', *Social Work*, 58(2): 185–8.

Mishna, F., Bogo, M., Root, J., Sawyer, J. and Khoury-Kassabri, M. (2012) '"It just crept in": the digital age and implications for social work practice', *Clinical Social Work Journal*, 40: 277–86.

Needham, C. and Glasby, J. (2014) *Debates in personalisation*, Bristol: The Policy Press.

Rafferty, J. (2011) 'Use and application of social media in social work and social care education'. Available at: http://swscmedia.wordpress.com/2011/11/27/use-and-application-of-social-media-in-social-work-and-social-care-education-2/

Rosenthal Gelman, C. and Tosone, C. (2010) 'Teaching social workers to harness technology and inter-disciplinary collaboration for community service', *British Journal of Social Work*, 40(1): 226–38.

Singh Cooner, T. (2013) 'Using Facebook to explore boundary issues for social workers in a networked society: perceptions of learning', *British Journal of Social Work*, 44(4): 1063–80.

Singh Cooner, T. (2014) 'Using closed Facebook groups to teach social work skills, values, and approaches for social media', in J. Westwood (ed) *Social media in social work education*, Northwich: Critical Publishing, pp 29–39.

Statistic Brain (2014a) 'Facebook statistics'. Available at: http://www.statisticbrain.com/facebook-statistics/

Statistic Brain (2014b) 'Twitter statistics'. Available at: http://www.statisticbrain.com/twitter-statistics/

Taylor, A. (2014) 'When actual meets virtual: social work book groups as a teaching and learning medium in social work education', in J. Westwood (ed) *Social media in social work education*, Northwich: Critical Publishing, pp 40–52.

TCSW (The College of Social Work) (2012) 'Professional capabilities framework'. Available at: http://www.tcsw.org.uk/pcf.aspx

Thackray, L. (2014) 'Obstacles to and engagement with social media', in J. Westwood (ed) *Social media in social work education*, Northwich: Critical Publishing, pp 7–16.

Usher, W. (2012) 'Australian health professionals' social media (Web 2.0) adoption trends: early 21st century health care delivery and practice promotion', *Australian Journal of Primary Health*, 18(1): 31–41.

Westwood, J. (ed) (2014a) 'Introduction', in J. Westwood (ed) *Social media in social work education*, Northwich: Critical Publishing, pp 1–6.

Westwood, J. (2014b) 'Social work and social media: an introduction to applying social work principles to social media', *Social Work Education: The International Journal*, 33(4): 551–3.

NINE

Developing placement capacity in the third sector

Sallie Allison, Dawn Clarke, Hannah Jago and Margaret Jelley

Introduction

This chapter explores the principles that underpin the development of agency capacity to provide high-quality practice learning in third-sector agencies even when there is no qualified social worker on site. It is a reasonable expectation that students of any profession will learn to practise alongside an experienced and skilled practitioner. Indeed, the most recent Practice Educator Professional Standards (PEPS) issued by the UK College of Social Work emphasise the importance of practice educators being qualified and registered social workers. Furthermore, while there is some flexibility for students in their first placements, these standards state that for final placements with an off-site practice educator, 'the student will work alongside a social worker who must be in a post requiring registration' (TCSW, 2013: 16). However, in an environment of austerity, the reduction of state functions and the commissioning of statutory services from private and voluntary agencies, this standard may prove aspirational. There is evidence of regional diversity in placement provision (GSCC, 2012), revealing that some programmes are unable to obtain sufficient statutory placements for their students. Increasingly, the mixed economy of care means that many social workers are in posts that do not require registration, even within the state sector. Despite these seismic changes, the illusion persists that statutory placements are the gold standard and always fully available. In contrast, this chapter offers an alternative perspective through the voices of students, supervisors and practice educators to illustrate the quality of third-sector placements.

Partnership working is a key concept in this area of work and can have significant benefits for service users, the course, the students' developing professional practice and for agencies themselves. We will share our experiences of working with students who have become ambassadors for the programme and, indeed, co-constructors of social work within voluntary, independent and private agencies, which, together, comprise the third sector. We will explore the benefits of taking students for all placement providers, both in the third sector and local authorities, that offer placements and post-qualifying employment (McGregor, 2013). Agency and student perspectives are central to the narrative, providing examples of best practice. Before exploring the underlying principles and our own learning, we set the local context within the current provision of social work placements in the UK. We explain how this impacts on the need to develop agency capacity to offer quality practice learning, which, we believe, has wider global application, not only for social work, but for other professions as well.

As noted elsewhere in this text, the current UK economic and political context within social care has created a reduction in placement offers from local authorities in the south-west of England. This has led the BA (Hons) Social Work programme at Plymouth University to work increasingly with the third sector. Bellinger (2010a) charts the historical and political changes within practice learning over the last two decades, which have prompted debates about the core purpose of practice learning itself. Is it a training ground for jobs rather than education for a profession? Bellinger (2010a: 601) suggests that 'A shift in resources from a professional council to an employer-led body (HMSO, 2000) raises the stakes in the debate about who "owns" social work in England and the extent to which it is defined by local authority practice.'

The irony of this situation is played out locally each summer as practice learning teams endeavour to secure placements. Although local authorities seek graduates who have had local authority placements, the number of such placement offers has steadily reduced. In addition, students often feel that they have a substandard opportunity if they are matched to a third-sector placement. At Plymouth University, we value and seek to support practice learning in all sectors, knowing that statutory interventions and legal frameworks are central to agency practice throughout social care, not just within local authorities (Bellinger, 2010b; Lavalette, 2011). Figure 9.1 illustrates the shift in the provision of practice learning placements between 2005 and 2012 in Plymouth.

So, what is the impact of this trend for those of us responsible for practice learning? It has led to the team at Plymouth seeking to develop more placements in third-sector settings, including those without a qualified social worker presence. We believe that we have been successful in securing high-quality placements that meet national requirements and include the need for students to undertake complex work. What follows is an example of best practice written from student, agency and practice educator perspectives.

Figure 9.1: Distribution of placements for the Plymouth site undergraduate programme

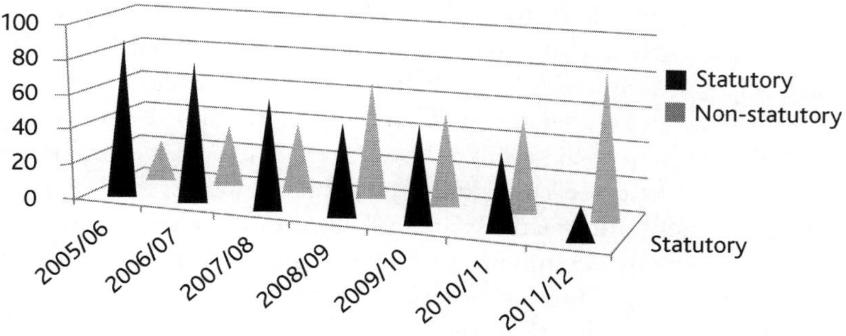

A student perspective

In order to determine what makes a positive social work placement, we must critically explore the dynamics that exist between the service user, student, university, placement setting and the experience that each brings to that collaboration. Being a student on placement presents a chapter of opportunity for growth, self-reflection and insight into social work practice. It can lay the core foundations of ideas and reflective thinking that shape the developing practitioner to work creatively and sensitively with service users in years to come. This statement, true as it may be for many students, and positive as it may sound, is not the case for all. For some students, placement can feel like a lonely environment, one where they feel out of their depth and unsupported while working hard to honour the learning from their university. From talking to my peers throughout our training, it was clear that we all had our 'ups and downs' while on placement.

My own personal experience draws upon two settings in my final year. The first setting was a third-sector agency where cohesive dynamics were lacking for many reasons. The agency and I did not maintain good communication or clarity regarding the purpose of the work, which unfortunately led to my decision to request the termination of the placement. At the time, I was unhappy with this outcome and was disappointed with my own practice. That said, with the support from my practice educator and a new agency supervisor, I was able to reflect both upon my time spent at the first placement as an excellent learning experience and on my practice, values and determination. This experience taught me that positive placement experiences develop and grow when four elements (the student, the university, the agency and the service users) work collaboratively and communicate well to achieve a common goal. In a way, all four elements have their own and shared agendas.

The student wants to do well, to learn and feel ready to practise social work in 'the real world', but they also need to pass their degree and this can, at times, cause conflict in practice. The service user wants to, or has to, access a service that can help them with the identified needs they present to the agency. The university has a responsibility to ensure the student is learning and also that the teaching enables them to practise safely and effectively and pass their exams and assignments. The placement agency might use students as a spare pair of hands or as another member of staff when resources are stretched, as they often are. They have to ensure, however, that the student is practising in a safe way with the service users. The agency wants to be recognised as an organisation that can use students in a positive way to develop their service. If students are given responsibility for meaningful work and are supported in doing it, then the placement becomes more desirable for future students. This not only raises the profile of the agency, but also ensures student placements for the future.

As student social workers, we are trained to look upon situations in a critical way, challenging what we see and questioning our role in the work we do and the services the agency delivers. At the beginning of my university career, I saw social work practice as belonging to the local authority and felt that my learning at university would prepare me for the world of social work. The knowledge and skills learnt at university did support me to achieve in my degree; however, it was my final placement in a third-sector agency that provided me with the space, flexibility and environment to think critically about what social work is and how to be an active member of this community. This final, third-year placement had the capacity and resources to let me practise safely, independently and creatively, allowing me to finally reach the stage of feeling confident and ready to graduate. My agency supervisor, practice educator and I communicated regularly and in a positive way, which enabled us to discuss critically where the learning opportunities were and where there could be some development.

There were many identifiable similarities in the social work I was practising with service users and my position in the dynamics between the four elements of service user, student, university and placement agency. One example can be seen when the agency supporting the service users seeks feedback about what is working for them and what could improve their lives through the service they are receiving. This was very similar to the meetings between my practice educator, the placement supervisor and I, although I must be clear that I am not comparing my student situation to that of service users – I respect the position many people are in, and the challenges and inequalities they face. Mirroring good practice with service users often resembled the support I got from my practice educator and placement supervisor.

My practice educator and supervisor were both clear about the purpose and focus of the placement, and their commitment to making it a success was at the centre of their approaches to the work. Each offered me an understanding of who she was and where she came from, which enabled me to understand their previous experiences and how they had supported their own practice with people. Both talked about their professional histories and offered practice examples of people they had worked with. This gave me confidence in them and the support they could offer me while I was on placement. The supervisor helped me to understand who I was working with, and to learn from the experiences she shared with me. She challenged my thinking in a supportive, safe way and made me feel like a valued member of her team, openly welcoming my own experiences and thinking. The social work values that the practice educator was instilling in me, in terms of encouraging me to believe in my abilities, were actively shaping my practice with service users.

Their encouragement for my achievements on placement made me feel extremely well supported. This collaborative, supportive network acted as a safe base for reflection and analysis. The working relationship and values exchanged between the practice educator, placement supervisor and myself were absorbed into my practice with service users. For example, I felt as though the practice educator had faith in me to do well and achieve in the final placement, after a less than smooth start to the year. This mirrored a strengths perspective, together with the values I hold of self-efficacy regarding the service user's ability and potential to achieve and make positive changes in their lives. The trust and value I felt from the supervisor increased my own practice confidence and I maintained a high level of enthusiasm for the work. This positive energy was channelled into the work I was doing with service users and may have enabled them to feel more confident with me as a student practitioner. I felt part of a team and experienced partnership working in a professional way. It reinforced the learning around inclusion that I had received during university teaching, and, in turn, I hoped that the service users I was working with also felt included. I worked hard to ensure a partnership approach with service users where possible.

It was this reflection that helped me to see the full circle that evolves between the student, the university, the placement supervisor and, most importantly, the service users. If the student's practice makes a positive change in a service user's life, this can be fed back to the agency, which feeds back to the university and back to the student. It displays the joined-up working between all four elements, supporting what the university is teaching, what the student is able to practise, the learning that comes from contact and work with the service users, and the agency that enables this interaction to happen. This positive circle of events comes from effective communication, a supportive environment and core values, keeping each element's expertise and experience at the centre of the work. This promotes the idea that no one single element can work without the others, and all members of this interaction are valued, active agents.

Figure 9.2: The Jago model

Notes: S = Student; SU = Service User; P = Placement; U = University.

Figure 9.2 (the 'Jago model') shows the collaboration that can exist between all units during a social work placement. It illustrates all units moving in a similar direction, highlighting the collaboration when shared goals and purpose of work exist together during a piece of work. There are a number of factors that affect the success and outcome of a placement. Placements are complex experiences for all involved and, as mentioned, there are ups and downs for everyone.

There are clear identifiable factors that contribute to a placement experience being positive. The following list that we have devised can be used as a checklist to support others in improving and understanding their placement experiences and how to make improvements and adjustments.

Supportive factors include:

- effective communication with all;
- sharing common goals/purpose of work;
- being valued and respected;
- a safe environment to explore social work practice;
- understanding the expectations of everyone involved;
- being encouraged to be a co-constructor of the work being done;
- partnership working and feeling trusted;
- core values of non-judgemental, anti-discriminatory, anti-oppressive, human rights-based practice;
- exploring the potential of everyone involved;
- analysing power dynamics for all units involved; and
- reflection of learning and progress, mirroring supervision and support.

Challenging factors include:

- poor communication;
- lack of agency preparation;
- lack of student preparation;
- not understanding the purpose of the work;
- difficulties in identifying the learning for the student appropriate to their stage of university;
- unsafe practice;
- misconceptions;
- absence of power analysis;
- poor boundary management; and
- personal problems affecting work, including difficulties with academic work.

The success of a social work placement for all involved is important in ensuring learning and skills development for the student and positive outcomes for services users. My final-year placement provided me with the opportunity to step out of my comfort zone and assess who I was becoming as a social worker. From a student perspective, what made this placement a success were the cohesive working relationships that I developed. They were instrumental in shaping my practice with service users. My placement experiences with service users further reinforced my understanding and application of core social work values and approaches.

A placement supervisor perspective

The Disability Information and Advice Centre (DIAC) provides information, advice and advocacy to people with impairments and/or health issues and carers. Service delivery is person-centred, underpinned by the social model of disability (Oliver, 1990), a commitment to secure the rights of the individual and a clearly defined quality framework. Deliberately broad and holistic, this brief ensures that people with a range of issues feel at ease approaching the service for help and support.

I managed DIAC for 10 years from 1992, and after two years of intense development, approached Plymouth University to offer placements to social work students. I felt that the work undertaken by DIAC could support practice learning and provide the challenges and opportunities that students needed to qualify. I also saw an opportunity to build capacity in an overstretched service and help future social workers better understand the non-statutory sector – and if I am honest, the chance to influence future practitioners! Plymouth Guild is a well-established and well-known local charity with a clear structure and policy framework. DIAC had an excellent reputation in the city. I am not a qualified social worker, but I felt that my degree in Social Policy and Administration and my many years' experience in managing statutory resource centres for older people and services in the voluntary sector would stand me in good stead. I have personal childhood and adult experiences of poverty, domestic violence, trauma and loss that I draw on to help students to connect with service users' lives when appropriate. Interestingly, although these were beneficial, it was my commitment to developing people and to justice that served me best in my role as placement supervisor.

Initially, the team needed convincing that we could accommodate students. The collective experience of social work within the team had been negative and local authority staff were frequently disrespectful to voluntary-sector personnel. The team view of students was negative; we were all overloaded and the general feeling was that students would create more work. I ploughed ahead and was offered first-year undergraduate students. There were difficulties in the first year of this initiative. The students were helpful at the very 'front end' of the service – their taking telephone and 'drop in' enquiries and researching queries were beneficial to us and met students' learning needs. However, the length of placement (20 days) and the students' skills and abilities ruled out more complex work. I was disappointed but determined to develop it further. The service needed 'more hands on deck' and I felt very strongly that the complexity of the work would meet students' learning needs. I was determined to link the work carried out by our agency to social work education; in my opinion, future practitioners should work with injustice and inequality outside of the statutory sector to truly see the barriers and impact on people. Our work needed second- or third-year students who, with effective supervision and support, could carry a caseload, properly complete benefit claim forms and provide advocacy.

Over time, students were given the opportunity to practise in partnership with service users within a framework that values everyone's expertise. Learning in the third sector gives students insight into 'being on the outside', with decisions that need challenging and no 'insider information' or networks to fall back on. This places them firmly alongside the service user, experiencing at first hand the barriers and attitudes that collude to maintain exclusion and prevent personal development and independence.

Students learnt to value partnership and were able to shine a light on the variable and tenuous nature of partnerships in the third sector; for example, strategic relationships carved out to secure funding are not always welcome or workable at the sharp end. Competitive relationships with other providers impact negatively on potential collaboration. The role of critical friend, frequently built into contracts with the local authority, for example, can bring tensions and conflicts. Many service users do not trust 'the council', social services, social workers or council-funded service providers. Challenging statutory decisions about care plans or service provision, however carefully crafted, can result in punitive action or the loss of local authority reputation. Students learnt to mirror the evidence about service user need with their rights when presenting cases professionally. Identifying statutory-prescribed channels for consultation and feedback ensured that good relations were maintained with commissioners. In this way, working with colleagues and other professionals to achieve positive outcomes with service users gave students the opportunity to mirror and model effective working relationships.

Students were taught to complete benefit claim forms, giving them the opportunity to explore and further understand service users' lives. The issues arising from this work ensured that they used and developed their assessment and casework skills. The completion of complex social insurance claim forms was, on most occasions, the starting point for casework. Access to benefits, which underpin independence, is fraught with barriers and this work gives students an insight into poverty, housing, carers' issues and the impact of ill-health and impairments. Students were frequently shocked at the circumstances that people were experiencing and the responses that they received from statutory organisations. They researched rights and opportunities and presented these to service users, supporting choice and control.

DIAC provided the opportunity to work with a diverse range of colleagues – volunteers and staff. In particular, the diversity around disability gave students a taste for what could work. Someone they may have viewed as a service user became a colleague they relied on for expert benefit advice. Talking through issues around mental health became different conversations when students discovered that team members had bipolar disorder. Seeing the social model in practice and working with service users experiencing discrimination or poor-quality health care gave students who struggled with the concept some tangible examples. Students were encouraged to make connections between policy, practice and service-user experience. Social policy issues were discussed within the team and linked to campaigning activities.

DIAC provides a safe environment to learn – the pressure of 'having to know the answer' does not exist because the team culture recognises the potential complexity inherent in the individual's identity and the range of influences on their circumstances. In-house procedures to manage complex enquiries ensure that routes to expertise and duties of care are clearly defined. Safety is also assured, with procedures in place to minimise and manage risk. Students learn to assess risk, that risk is inevitable, that it can be managed up to a point, but that it is not always predictable.

Practice educator perspectives

As the landscape of practice learning has changed nationally and locally over the last decade, our focus has needed to shift from supporting practice learning in all sectors to seeking practice opportunities predominantly in the third sector. The changing nature of the third sector means that this work is never-ending (TSO, 2007; Dickinson et al, 2012). Organisations merge, close or reconfigure (Alcock, 2010; Rose, 2013). Individuals change role, move on or have different priorities. Services are beset by funding targets and have to deliver different outcomes (McEwen et al, 2010). This has also involved us in finding a substantial number of placements in agencies without a social work presence (Bellinger, 2010b). This process moves away from the notion of an apprenticeship model of learning towards one similar to the 'role emerging' model that occupational therapy has championed (Thew et al, 2011). When we are looking for opportunities, we seek agencies that will value the student, not just provide a placement. Our view is: 'We have these really great students that you won't get from anywhere else.' We work hard to promote how agencies can benefit from students' expertise, up-to-date knowledge and enthusiasm. In addition, as Dawn (supervisor) reflected earlier, placements provide an opportunity to shape future professionals for those who want to have students with them and who also understand that students are learners.

Students are the next generation of social workers. We have a responsibility to give them a good and realistic understanding of the profession for which they are training. They are our future colleagues and possibly our families' social workers one day. We must ensure that every student is exposed to the demands of social work: managing power constructively, and developing clarity about role identity and function so that unsuitable students can recognise that the profession is not for them. Safeguarding service users, however, does not require us to relinquish the position of respectful partnership. Our approach to practice education is underpinned by the belief that every student should have an individualised set of arrangements to support their learning and that the third sector can provide this (Scholar et al, 2012). In order to learn, students need: the right people around them; knowledge and academic foundations for the profession of social work; and practice experiences that challenge them, make them think and question their ideas, assumptions and views. They need service users willing to share their lives, and they need to be able to understand their own learning needs and be motivated to meet them. Practice educators' knowledge of individual differences, strengths and needs enables good matching to take place.

In some instances, it is the specific skills of the supervisor that may be key to an arrangement, particularly if the student has specific learning needs. Some require a more nurturing set of arrangements, for example, with a supervisor who is fully available on site, as in (the student) Hannah's experience. In other circumstances, it may be the particular type of learning environment in terms of the service-user group and ways of working that the agency can offer that are relevant, as in the example given later. In both instances, knowledge of the available learning opportunities and predictions about how the student may make sense of the learning are key to a successful arrangement. As Hannah observes, the opportunity to model good social work practice with service users arises from the dynamic relationship between student, supervisor and practice educator. This can be as important as the opportunities within the placement itself. Students are fully aware that information is shared between everybody, which maintains a level of open communication for the purpose of learning. A named practice educator for both the student and the supervisor provides a consistent link between student, agency and university. As Dawn comments, this provides 'a safe environment to learn', enabling any issues or difficulties to be highlighted and addressed without delay.

Over time, relationships with supervisors and agencies allow us to build capacity together. Where this works most successfully is where students actively share responsibility for the placement's success, as seen in Hannah's account. Additionally, they may themselves identify further service areas within agencies that could be developed for future student learning, or work that would be suitable for students at more advanced stages. An experience of working with a local prison illustrates this. The previous experience of agency personnel working with a student from another discipline was that of being left unsupported by a university. What convinced them to take a social work student was the level of support available to supervisor and students. We had to invest a lot of time before the prison would be confident about students doing work they deemed 'specialist and potentially dangerous'. By reframing their 'specialist work' as social work, we aligned agency thinking with student learning needs. We chose a student who could be an ambassador, who could reassure the agency that they were capable, who would self-brief in terms of relevant research and who could confidently engage in social work even without a social worker on site. The student's proactive approach in networking with different departments within the prison generated interest in social work students. Through her work with service users, the student built relationships with other services in the prison, such as those addressing drug and alcohol use, resettlement, signposting, and support for people when they are released.

This resulted in the other services actively requesting student placements themselves the following year, having witnessed the benefits. (It is worth noting that the student subsequently gained employment in this setting on graduation and is now a supervisor.)

Regrettably, such initiatives that place final-year students as the only social work presence in the agency will no longer be possible within the current UK standards (TCSW, 2013).

Graduates generally remember their practice experience more clearly than any other aspect of the course (Lam et al, 2007). Students may have preconceptions about where they want to go that placements can reverse. Being given very different experiences can be uncomfortable at the time but students frequently say how pleased they are to have been given the opportunity to broaden their perspectives. Practice learning is designed to give new experiences, to challenge and change their ideas; it is not about 'being comfortable'. There is a subtle difference between preferences and learning needs. The professional work of practice educators is to negotiate with students to help them identify what their student learning needs really are and to find the environments in which they might be met. This is similar to what Shulman (2011: 186) terms 'making a demand for work' through 'challenge with support'. If professionally we work from a place that service users and carers are experts about their own needs (Beresford and Croft, 2001), then as practice educators, we need to use an approach that models this with students. This is complex to negotiate when learning outcomes for qualifying practitioners need to be met and student preferences negotiated. However, this is similar to good social work practice, working in partnership with service users and carers while safeguarding vulnerable adults and children. In this way, practice educators seek to demonstrate relationship-based social work approaches throughout their practice (Jordan, 2007; Ruch et al, 2010).

Maintaining good-quality placement capacity requires constant attention. As a dynamic activity, it cannot be reduced to a formulaic or procedural approach. It is both administratively complex and pedagogically driven, requiring the same skills as professional social work. High-quality practice learning that is well organised and supported is essential for social work education. Moreover, developing capacity for student learning with local third-sector agencies creates both diversity of opportunity and a depth of understanding about the important work undertaken by these services.

Conclusion

The chapter has aimed to give positive examples of how it is possible to work within the third sector to develop agency capacity for valuable placement opportunities. In the absence of a qualified social worker on site, the off-site practice educator is key in supporting and monitoring the learning opportunities available. The narratives presented earlier highlight the benefits for all elements identified in the Jago model of working within a principled framework congruent with our own social work identities.

Bill Jordan (1991) argues that the remit of social work education should be that of developing professionalism underpinned by values. A future challenge rests with the response from educational providers to recent reviews of social work education in the UK by Narey (2014) and Croisdale-Appleby (2014). The underlying assumption of such reports privileges social work placements with local authorities, specifically children's services, over others. Ironically, however, statutory functions are increasingly located within the third sector. Moreover, as educators, we must be vigilant to the threats to holistic, rights-based practice commonly found in the third sector (Lavalette, 2011). We have demonstrated the capacity of placements within the third sector, including those without social workers on site, to develop professional practitioners at all stages of their learning.

Not all organisations are appropriate for practice learning, however, and even within suitable agencies, it is important to find the right person to work alongside. Individuals can either obstruct or facilitate. A committed supervisor who is familiar with the programme and can dedicate time to the student does not appear by chance. As this chapter has illustrated, they are the product of partnership working between service users, students, supervisors and practice educators.

In conclusion, we offer some key learning points for practice educators:

- know and be able to articulate your own professional identity;
- commit to the notion of partnership working, and the relationship between student, supervisor, service user and practice educator;
- maintain open communication;
- model good social work practice in all aspects of the work;
- maintain trust;
- know the student, know the placement;
- if a placement match does not work, reflect on the interaction of elements identified in the Jago model;
- promote the notion that students are experts of their own learning needs;
- maintain mutual respect for each other's roles and responsibilities; and
- maintain an inclusive approach to the way that social work is defined.

We know that the context for social work will continue to change with changing political agendas. We would argue that we need graduates who: are not only ready for mainstream employment, but also creative and adaptable; derive confidence from professional values; take initiative and assume responsibility; can engage with adults and children who are vulnerable in our society; and can seek services and support across all the social care sectors.

References

Alcock, P. (2010) 'Building the big society: a new policy environment for the third sector in England', *Voluntary Sector Review*, 1(3): 379–89.

Bellinger, A. (2010a) 'Studying the landscape: practice learning for social work reconsidered', *Social Work Education*, 29(6): 599–615.

Bellinger, A. (2010b) 'Talking about (re)generation: practice learning as a site of renewal for social work', *British Journal of Social Work*, 40: 2450–66.

Beresford, P. and Croft, S. (2001) 'Service users' knowledges and the social construction of social work', *Journal of Social Work*, 1(3): 295–316.

Croisdale-Appleby, D. (2014) *Re-visioning social work education: an independent review*, London: Department of Health.

Dickinson, H., Allen, K., Alcock, P., Macmillan, R. and Glasby, J. (2012) *The role of the third sector in delivering social care*, London: NIHR School for Social Care Research.

GSCC (General Social Care Council) (2012) 'The supply of social work practice placements: employers' views'. Available at: http://cdn.basw.co.uk/upload/basw_114123-7.pdf

HMSO (Her Majesty's Stationery Office) (2000) *The Care Standards Act 2000*, London: Her Majesty's Stationery Office.

Jordan, B. (1991) 'Competencies and values', *Social Work Education*, 10(1): 5–11.

Jordan, B. (2007) *Social work and wellbeing*, Lyme Regis: Russell House Publishing.

Lam, C.M., Wong, H. and Leung, T.T.F. (2007) 'An unfinished reflexive journey: social work students' reflection on their placement experiences', *British Journal of Social Work*, 37: 91–105.

Lavalette, M. (2011) 'Social work in extremis – disaster capitalism, "social shocks" and "popular social work"', in M. Lavalette and V. Ioakimidis (eds) *Social work in extremis: lessons for social work internationally*, Bristol: The Policy Press, pp 1–14.

McEwen, J., Shoesmith, M. and Allen, R. (2010) 'Embedding outcomes recording in Barnardo's performance management approach', *International Journal of Productivity and Performance Management*, 59(6): 586–98.

McGregor, K. (2013) 'Why we need more voluntary sector placements for social work students', *Community Care*, August. Available at: http://www.communitycare.co.uk/blogs/social-work-blog/2013/08/why-we-need-more-third-sector-placements-for-social-work-students/

Narey, M. (2014) 'Making the education of social workers consistently effective', Department for Education, HM Government. Available at: www.gov.uk/government/publications

Oliver, M. (1990) *The politics of disablement: critical texts in social work and the welfare state*, London: St. Martin's Press.

Rose, L. (2013) 'Exploring local hotspots and deserts: investigating the local distribution of charitable resources', *Voluntary Sector Review*, 4(1): 95–116.

Ruch, G., Turney, D. and Ward, A. (eds) (2010) *Relationship-based social work: getting to the heart of practice*, London: Jessica Kingsley Publishers.

Scholar, H., McCaughan, S., McLaughlin, H. and Coleman, A. (2012) '"Why is this not social work?" The contribution of "non-traditional" placements in preparing social work students for practice', *Social Work Education: The International Journal*, 31(7): 932–50.

Shulman, L. (2011) *The skills of helping individuals, families, groups and communities*, Belmont, CA: Brooks/Cole.

TCSW (The College of Social Work) (2013) 'Practice educator professional standards (PEPS) and guidance'. Available at: http://www.tcsw.org.uk/Educators/

Thew, M., Edwards, M., Baptiste, S. and Molineux, M. (eds) (2011) *Role emerging occupational therapy: maximising occupation-focussed practice*, Chichester: Wiley-Blackwell.

TSO (The Stationery Office) (2007) *The future role of the third sector in social and economic regeneration: final report*, London: The Stationery Office@Blackwell. Available at: www.gov.uk/government/publications/the-future-role-of-the-third-sector-in-social-and-economic-regeneration-final-report

TEN

Observations of student practice: what difference does observer qualification make?

David Neal and Angie Regan

Introduction

Practice observations can be pivotal to students' transformational learning and the formation of a professional identity. We suggest that key elements underpinning the process of transformation might be the qualifications and the independence of the person observing the student.

In this chapter, we explore the impact of practice observations on students' learning and the formation of their professional identity. Based on findings from a pilot study, we consider the importance of both the professional qualifications and the independence of the person observing the student in practice. As social work educators, we are increasingly concerned about the potential erosion of standards in practice education. An emphasis on practice educator qualifications has been particular to the UK, although national aspirations to have all students taught and assessed by someone with an additional pedagogic qualification could not be realised (Parker, 2007; Bellinger, 2010a). The requirement for practice educators to reach a particular standard has disappeared entirely as the current practice educator framework has no links to academic accreditation. Students can now be assessed by almost anyone, or any agency. Accordingly, the importance of pedagogy in the supervision and assessment of learners in practice is no longer supported by a national framework or through resource provision (Bellinger, 2010a). Instead, in the UK, the College of Social Work (TCSW, 2012b) emphasises the need for students to be supported by qualified social workers, whose post requires them to be registered with the Health and Care Professions Council (HCPC).

Unusually, the undergraduate programme where the authors work had, since 2001, retained a requirement that all students must be observed and assessed in practice by social workers holding the Practice Teacher Award (CCETSW, 1991a) or equivalent. The move towards more conventional arrangements provided an opportunity to explore the impact of observer qualification and relationship on the student experience.

Context for the study

In the UK, the principle of observing a student's 'live' practice as a mode of assessment was formally introduced in the Diploma in Social Work (CCETSW, 1991b). The primary purpose of the observation was to assess the student against national core competencies and a range of value requirements. Alongside this, the Central Council for Education and Training in Social Work (CCETSW, 1991a) invested in a new infrastructure to support practice learning, recognising a need to address inadequacies in the teaching and assessment of students in practice. Bellinger (2010a) highlights that prior to this initiative, there were very few requirements for those involved in practice education, the majority of whom were agency-based supervisors. Bellinger notes that, as a result, student assessment reports were often of variable quality and were regularly overturned by universities, and that this contributed to the poor status of practice education.

CCETSW's goal to assure quality was predominantly realised through the Practice Teacher Award (CCETSW, 1991a), which recognised that pedagogy in practice learning was equally important to that in the classroom. Within this context, practice observations were not just about measuring competency, they involved substantial pedagogic intervention. Teaching, learning and assessment aspects of the observation process were directed at improving the overall standard of emerging professionals and of social work practice more generally. CCETSW's aspirations, however, were never fully achieved. Bellinger (2010a) provides an in-depth analysis of the factors that contributed to a lack of investment in this new infrastructure and an erosion of quality standards associated with the practice teacher role. Specifically, placement shortages and a high turnover of practice teachers ultimately led to a lack of consistency in who could practice teach, while progressive deregulation removed many requirements. Among these was the need for second opinion practice teachers for students who were failing and the requirement for direct observation of all students' practice.

In 2012, TCSW (2012a) reintroduced the principle that a student's direct work with service users should be embedded within the overall assessment of their practice. There is a comprehensive set of expectations for the qualifying level of social work in England. These are published within the HCPC's proficiency standards and TCSW's Professional Capability Framework (PCF). It should be noted that professional standard requirements in Scotland, Wales and Northern Ireland continue to be expressed in the national occupational standards for social work. TCSW recommends that the assessment of students should foster the integration of practice and academic learning and be based on the PCF for the student's respective stage of learning. Their guidelines specify that modes of assessment should include direct observation and incorporate feedback from professionals and service users. The observation is underpinned by the principle that significant weight must be given to the assessment made by the person observing the student, who will make a judgement about the student's capability to work at the required level. However, TCSW provides little guidance about who is competent to undertake observations or what pedagogic knowledge and skills might be required.

The new Practice Educator Professional Standards (PEPS) for Social Work (TCSW, 2012b) identify minimum requirements, which are expressed through guidance statements. These detail what a practice educator should be able to demonstrate at two levels of responsibility, namely, Practice Educator Level 1 and Level 2. We would argue that these current arrangements lack the necessary rigour and consistency in relation to the training and assessment of practice educators. For example, there appears to be no national curriculum, assessment framework or quality assurance mechanisms, while the approval of who has met the PEPS has no formal ties to academic accreditation and appears discretionary across multiple social work organisations.

In common with many UK programmes, assessment of students' practice through observation is an integral aspect of the undergraduate programme structure at Plymouth University. Students are required to undertake observations throughout their practice learning, ensuring that each observation is representative of their practice with service users in the agency where they are placed. These observations are 'free-standing' and draw on a range of experienced and qualified observers who are not the student's supervisor.

Students are encouraged to embrace each observation as an opportunity to be critically reflective of their own practice. Practice observations are not summative (pass/fail) events, but intended to promote learning from reflection, facilitated by the pedagogic intervention of the observer and through the provision of independent, high-quality, formative feedback.

Both in the UK and internationally, there have been debates about the status of practice education in relation to the academic component (Ryan et al, 1996; Bellinger, 2010b). We know that students are as able to build specific knowledge and theoretical understanding through practice learning as they are through academic learning, and that these sites of learning should be seen as symbiotic. Practice learning is greatly valued by students (Lam et al, 2007), who cite this to be a transformative aspect of their education and professional development. Research evidence also validates practice as the pivotal mechanism that enables students to apply, transform and integrate academic knowledge within their practice realities (Nixon and Murr, 2006).

The undergraduate programme at Plymouth University has a practice-led curriculum (Adamson, 2011) and students are encouraged to learn how to negotiate their own meanings from practice experience rather than uncritically assimilating meaning from others. Learning that arises from constructing new and revised interpretations of an experience can be transformative for students, and is more likely to foster the autonomy, critical self-awareness and accountability that professional social work requires (Ford et al, 2005; Ferguson and Lavalette, 2007).

Critical reflection is widely recognised as fundamental to effective practice, both in social work and in allied health and social care professions (Taylor and White, 2006). Gardner et al (2006) argue that critical reflection is integral to the development of a professional identity that values uncertainty and can be reflexive to the concept of multiple explanations and possibilities. Fook et al (1997) and Parker (2007) have argued that the practice learning context is influential in determining whether students are supported and challenged to develop their capacity for reflective practice and transformative learning.

From a critical theory perspective, reflection focuses on uncovering power dynamics and detecting the creation and maintenance of hegemony (Brookfield, 2009). The role of social work education is not only to help students to work productively and effectively within existing systems, but also to call the foundations and practices of those systems into question in order to seek improvement. As critical theory regards the mainstream majority as ideologically manipulated to conform, critical reflection involves taking perspectives on socio-political structures or personal and collective actions that may be alternative to those held by the majority (Benjamin, 2007). The role and status of those undertaking practice observations may, therefore, be significant in maintaining the transformative nature of practice education.

Practice observation

Currently, social work education in the UK requires students to undertake 170 days' experiential learning in a social care setting. Their practice is directly and systematically observed and assessed against a framework, with feedback provided from a range of sources (TCSW, 2012a). Within the authors' programme, the observer is a qualified social worker who holds an additional pedagogic qualification. This requirement is based on the centrality of critical reflection and on the recognition that a social work qualification alone does not automatically equip practitioners to support the learning of others (Gardner et al, 2006). As noted, the educational discourse, facilitated and encouraged by the observer, can create the conditions for transformational learning. In order to minimise the power differential and promote learning in a safe, non-hierarchical environment, each observer is independent of the student and has no other supervisory or assessment role in relation to them. The role of the observer is one of facilitator of the student's professional learning. Independent of the agency and accountable to the programme, the observer is well placed to model and encourage the student to adopt a critically reflective position. This is not only in relation to the agency and its established practices, but also towards social work more broadly in its national, international and historical contexts.

Here, we outline the practice observation process in order to provide a context for the pilot study and its findings. In the Plymouth undergraduate programme, this begins with the student identifying work with a service user that they consider is representative of their practice. The student takes into account and manages issues relating to: the service user's context, situation and consent to the observation; the student's role within the agency and purpose of the work; and the capabilities they hope to demonstrate and would like feedback on. The student provides the independent observer, who they might not have met before, with reference material showing how they have prepared. This provides a starting point for the student, prior to the observation, to elaborate their thinking in discussion with the observer, and for the observer to begin to form an assessment of the student.

During the practice observation, the observer collates evidence of the student's practice. The service user is told that the observer will take no active role in the work that the student is undertaking so that their presence impacts minimally on the interaction between the student and service user. After the observation, the observer gathers feedback from the service user and relevant agency staff on the student's practice and the extent to which what they have observed is typical. Those views are integrated into the observer's feedback report and improve the validity of the assessment of the student.

The student provides the observer with a written, critically reflective evaluation of their observed practice in which they consider what they did well and areas for development. On receipt of this, the observer writes a report to the student on their progress towards the national capabilities, drawing from all aspects of their contact with the student, the observation itself, the student's self-evaluation and feedback from others. The student responds to the observer, revising their statement of progression and their developmental needs, thereby ensuring continuity and consistency across all aspects of their learning.

A core element of practice observations is that they are student-led and closely based on the 'York model' (University of York, 1999). As noted, the student selects the focus of the work that they would like to be observed, and identifies their learning goals and what they would specifically like feedback on. This can be empowering for the student and enables them to take risks in learning in a safe, supportive environment. The process provides opportunities for students to develop their ability to be self-directed and self-aware, enhancing their confidence, use of initiative and decision-making skills. The student's active use of reflective skills in critical self-assessment encourages them to take responsibility for their ongoing learning while promoting the impetus for their continuing professional development.

The pilot study

In 2011, programme staff agreed to undertake a trial period whereby practitioners without a specific pedagogic qualification would undertake students' practice observations. For the purpose of this chapter, in order to distinguish them from the qualified practice educators, we will refer to these individuals as 'agency supervisors'. Those with the additional qualification will be referred to as 'practice educators'.

The proposal made by the programme's local authority placement providers indicated that they would increase the number of placements if a broader range of their practitioners were able to undertake practice observations. Their argument was influential in a context where there is a growing expectation nationally on universities to provide local authority placements to students and where the number offered to the programme locally had significantly reduced since 2005. The subsequent pilot study aimed to undertake a comparative evaluation to examine whether the pedagogic qualification made any difference to the students' experiences. A particularly significant aspect of the proposal was that the practitioners identified by those agencies to undertake practice observations would also be the supervisors of the students they were to observe. While this is a model commonly used within social work programmes, as previously explained, it represented a change for this programme. This presented an opportunity to make a comparison in relation to the students' experience.

A review group was convened comprising five stakeholders, each with considerable experience of observing students in practice. These were one independent freelance practice educator, two practice educators employed by local authorities, and two university-employed practice educators. A total of 15 feedback reports were examined by the review group; five had been completed by agency supervisors and 10 were completed by practice educators. Identifying features were removed from all reports within the sample and an identification number was randomly allocated so that the reviewers did not know the authors' qualifications. Reviewers each read three reports, a mix of those written by agency supervisors and practice educators. Reviewers were asked to respond to specific questions about each report in order to elicit their views on the following areas:

- the clarity of the feedback to the student;
- the balance of student strengths and learning needs identified;
- the proportion of attention given to student learning and to agency function; and
- the overall quality of the feedback report.

In addition, views were sought from students individually and through a focus group. The students, eight in total, had significant experience of being observed by pedagogically qualified practice educators and were therefore well placed to offer an informed view on the quality of their experiences. The majority of the students also had experience of being observed by their agency supervisor. Students were asked open and neutral questions designed to enable them to share their experiences of being observed. Key themes arising were collated and reported to programme stakeholders with student views incorporated to enrich the findings.

Findings

Key themes arising from the review are outlined in the following. The analysis of feedback reports concluded that only 20% of agency supervisors gave students clear and balanced feedback about their strengths and learning needs compared to 80% of practice educators. The review group found that agency supervisors tended to overemphasise the student's strengths, particularly where this related to the discharge of agency function. Student views included a concern that an agency supervisor might, depending on their relationship, be 'too harsh or too lenient'. Balanced feedback to students was greatly valued by them as it enhanced confidence in their progress and development plans, as expressed in the following quote: "The big difference, change for me is … now believing in my practice."

The review group found that 40% of reports written by agency supervisors provided balance in their consideration of student learning and agency function, while the remaining 60% focused on agency function. This compared to 30% of practice educator reports providing a balance of student learning and agency function, with the remaining 70% focusing more on student learning.

The review found that 60% of reports provided by agency supervisors emphasised the student's performance according to their agency's expectations of their ability to discharge relevant policy and procedure. The apparent expectation of compliance by the agency supervisor is also reflected in student comment: "The agency supervisor referred constantly to what they themselves would have done."

In comparison, the majority of practice educator reports gave more attention to the learning goals expressed by the student and their performance in relation to generic and international concepts of social work:

> "With the practice educator, I unpicked and explored all around identity, gender, feelings, language … really made me think more broadly."

> "The practice educator helped me to critique my position, my practice … helped me bring it all out, move on and develop."

Students who had been observed by their agency supervisor noted how their anxiety was considerably heightened in comparison to their experience of being observed by a practice educator. There were two aspects in particular that resulted in this: first, the power dynamic within the student–supervisor relationship; and, second, how equipped they felt the agency supervisor was to undertake the observation. A recurring theme was that students felt unable to question their agency supervisor safely without it impacting on the remainder of the placement and jeopardising the agency supervisor's assessment of them. An example offered was how, when asked by the supervisor to change the timing of her planned work with a service user (to fit with the schedule of the supervisor), the student did not feel able to question this even though she believed it reflected poor practice, which she feared might impact on her relationship with the service user. The student noted how she had felt compromised by the power dynamic inherent in the student–supervisor relationship: "I felt unable to challenge it … worried it might impact on the rest of the placement."

In addition, students commonly undertook work with service users whose previous practitioner was the agency supervisor. This raised concerns for them about the potential impact of the supervisor's presence as observer. They noted how this might lead to distractions during the observed session, and, in addition, that service users might draw comparisons between the practice of the student and the agency supervisor.

Students expressed concerns about how equipped they felt their agency supervisor was to complete the practice observation process effectively. They were anxious that the supervisor was 'too busy' and that the observation would be an 'additional pressure' that might not be given the attention it required. In addition, they raised questions related to the supervisors' knowledge and experience of the observation process, and also the particular skills needed for gathering and providing verbal and written feedback to the standard required by the programme. In contrast, "I felt confident the practice educator would include honest, critical feedback from the service user and agency supervisor as they can see … explore any disconnect between what is said and what is meant."

However, students generally appreciated that agency supervisors were familiar with the work of their agency and so they were not expected to describe and explore it. While this may have been easier for a student, it can also be seen as a missed opportunity for the student to engage in a dialogue in which they are encouraged fully and critically to explore their own practice, that of the agency and the nature of the work they are engaged in.

The review of the pilot study indicates greater inconsistency in the quality of the students' experience when the agency supervisor completed their observations compared with those provided by a practice educator. The qualifications of the observer and their relationship to students and their placement agencies are identified as highly influential. We recognise that some agency supervisors are able to complete practice observations with students very effectively.

However, pilot study findings suggest that there is no guarantee that this will always be the case. While the pilot study shows that there was also some inconsistency in the standard of observations completed by practice educators, the evidence suggests that they were *more likely* to be focused on students' ongoing learning. Significantly, when working with practice educators, students noted how they felt more able to be openly critical of their own practice and agency processes in the context of a broader, international conceptualisation of social work activity. Agency supervisors were found to be more likely to engage with the student as an apprentice or trainee, thereby risking a 'surface' approach to learning, where students are encouraged to reproduce limited models of practice without meaningful understanding, transformative learning or global contextualisation (Marton, 1975, cited in Fry et al, 2003).

Discussion

Transformative learning through critical reflection should not be seen as an add-on. Rather, it is the essence of social work practice education. With this in mind, the goal of practice observations is to help students become autonomous practitioners by learning to negotiate their own meanings, rather than uncritically acting on those of others. Educational interventions are necessary to ensure that students acquire the understanding and disposition essential for transformative learning in their professional development. The theory of transformative learning (Mezirow, 1991) is rooted in educational discourse and we would argue that enabling students to achieve this within the process of practice observations requires the knowledge and capacity to teach and assess with reference to substantive pedagogical theory. Student testimony indicates that this teaching intervention promotes new knowledge and skills, a deeper understanding of self, and a sense of empowerment through an epistemological change to the way they make meaning.

Critical reflection is central to transformative learning. Within the practice observation process, it is primarily the student's discussion with their observer that provides the medium for an explicit reassessment of their experience and the understandings they derive from it. Such dialogue can enable a student to explore beliefs and assumptions, both their own and others', by reflecting upon evidence that may support their understanding. They can test the validity of their beliefs through exposure to the differing viewpoints offered by the observer. The theory of transformative learning arises from a reappraisal of prior understanding in order to create new interpretations of an experience that can guide future actions. The transformative process begins with the assumptions that frame the student's point of view and influence their thinking, beliefs and actions in a given practice situation. It is the revision of this frame of reference that creates a profound shift in the student's professional capability and identity. Brookfield (2009) argues that it is this 'perspective-transformation' that leads to a more developed and functional frame of reference, one that is critically reflective and open to further revision. In essence, this comprises meta-learning, or learning to learn.

Promoting a student's ability for critical reflection enables them to develop an awareness of their own power to transform their practice (Ruch, 2002). When students are critical in questioning assumptions, they are more able to challenge frames of reference and paradigms, imagine alternatives, and retain a perspective on their own influence and its limitations. Dialogue with the observer can promote a student's efficacy in working with others to evaluate their practice. Social work is a contested discipline where legislation, service users' needs and rights, agency resources, and local and national demands to meet prescribed targets all combine to make daily practice a sea of competing priorities. The need for students to view practice from multiple perspectives therefore becomes crucial.

It is important to adopt a liberating approach to teaching, one that promotes the development of an independent professional identity and values autonomous thinking rather than an unquestioning acceptance and application of knowledge (Bernstein, 2000; Miller, 2000). Here, autonomy refers to the understanding, skills and disposition necessary for students to become critically reflective and to engage in discourse that tests their assumptions against the experiences of other professionals who share the knowledge, skills and values of the profession. The communicative aspect of this process involves student, observer and others, notably, service users and carers who are involved in the student's learning, striving to reach an understanding of any given aspect of their practice. This dialogue seeks to deepen the student's understanding of self, and the more interpretations of an event that are available, the greater likelihood there is of finding a more dependable interpretation or synthesis. Here, discourse is a dialogue between student and observer that is devoted to assessing and evaluating evidence, exploring alternative points of view, and fostering deep and sustainable learning in the process.

Related to this is the importance of fostering a non-hierarchical student–educator relationship where the observer places themselves alongside the student. In fostering a safe learning environment, the observer functions as a facilitator rather than an authority, thereby modelling the critically reflective approach expected of the student. We believe that the mutuality inherent in this approach serves to enhance the criticality in the student's written and verbal dialogue with the observer and helps to create a shared sense of ownership and community of learning (Wenger, 1998). This would be difficult where actual or perceived power creates hierarchy, for instance, where the observer is an integral part of the student's placement agency, or where agency culture leads to restrictive learning (Fuller and Unwin, 2003; Clapton et al, 2006). This latter principle assumes even greater significance given the rise of managerialist approaches to social work practice (Jordan and Jordan, 2000; Lymbery, 2001; Jones, 2008). Hugman (2009) identifies a growing trend in the UK towards producing compliant social workers who are process-oriented. Preston-Shoot (2000) argues that such environments undermine the capacity of social work education to produce creative autonomous practitioners. Hierarchical arrangements favour training for compliance, bureaucratic efficiency and the uncritical acceptance of established practice.

Learning through principles of apprenticeship in narrow fields of statutory social work, for instance, may result in a smoother, more efficient operationalisation of the agency's desired outcomes (Fuller and Unwin, 2003). While this may appear beneficial in the short term, the consequence of social work becoming defined by statutory employers is that it can potentially align social work activity as purely techno-managerial (Bellinger, 2010b) and constrained by current political imperatives and dominant ideology (Ferguson and Woodward, 2009; White et al, 2009).

Ideas and actions that may be regarded as common sense are often based on assumptions regarding the credibility and authority of the source. The assumptions accepted unquestioningly are therefore often those that have been constructed by a dominant group or class for political gain. This is what Gramsci (2005) describes as hegemony. Contemporary social work practice has a pivotal role to play in the promotion of social justice and human rights. A goal of social work education should, therefore, be to liberate students from the influence of hegemony, which may mask sociological and political dimensions by pathologising particular groups or individuals.

Through a mutual dialogue, the practice educator promotes a real integration of what the student is doing in practice with the knowledge that informs that practice. Laurillard (2002) recognised the importance of engaging students in an active and participatory way, a 'conversational' approach, so that deeper learning can occur. In addition, the practice educator uses their social work and their educator skills to elicit meaningful feedback from the service user and relevant agency staff, thereby ensuring a triangulation of perspectives and increasing the potential for transformational learning for the student.

Conclusion

This chapter has questioned the received wisdom that students learn best and develop their professional identity by working alongside experienced social workers. Without a pedagogical framework, the student experience may be reduced to one of skills-transmission rather than holistic learning for the profession, producing compliant uncritical practitioners with attention to organisational efficiency rather than professionals committed to meeting the needs of people and to social justice (Hugman, 2009).

The practice teacher role established in 1989 in the UK was accompanied by definitions of eligibility and function embedded within regulatory frameworks and grounded in substantial pedagogic activity. In contrast, the latter development of the practice educator role contains no real redefinition of the term. What is more, reviewing the learning outcomes reveals that the functions of enabling learning have shifted to focus more on measuring the outcome. Practice educator training has no formal or mandatory ties to academic accreditation and can therefore be provided by almost anyone. In addition, the practice educator learning outcomes can be seen as ambiguous and ill-defined, and therefore likely to result in an inconsistency in quality standards that will pervade the practice educator workforce.

Practice observations occupy a pivotal role in social work education as a teaching, learning and assessment intervention. They directly promote a student's ability to learn from the process of critical reflection, fostering transformational and sustainable learning and development:

> "A big surprise for me ... the practice educator pointed out how I used agency jargon and [uncritically] took a position of agency representative, no dialogue with the service user, just parroting. I'd been taught by the agency and stuck to their agenda. I thought I was doing great. I wouldn't have known if not pointed out by the practice educator, wasn't aware of how I'd been."

Social work has traditionally recognised that there are no absolute truths and that the way in which professionals construct meaning is likely to be in a continuous state of flux (Fook et al, 1997). It is therefore imperative that social work education supports students to develop a critical world view and an understanding of themselves, their practice context and the paradigms underpinning it.

Acknowledgements

With acknowledgement and special thanks to students Keryl Hebson, Ellen Brettelle and Byran Driver, and to other students whose experiences are included in this chapter.

References

Adamson, C. (2011) 'Getting the balance right: critical reflection, knowledge and the social work curriculum', *Advances in Social Work and Welfare Education*, 13(1): 29–48.

Bellinger, A. (2010a) 'Studying the landscape: practice learning for social work reconsidered', *Social Work Education*, 29(6): 599–615.

Bellinger, A. (2010b) 'Talking about (re)generation: practice learning as a site of renewal for social work', *British Journal of Social Work*, 40(8): 2450–66.

Benjamin, A. (2007) 'Afterword – doing anti-oppressive social work: the importance of resistance, history and strategy', in D. Baines (ed) *Doing anti-oppressive practice: building transformative politicized social work*, Halifax: Fernwood Publishing, pp 191–204.

Bernstein, B. (2000) *Pedagogy, symbolic control and identity: theory, research and critique*, Oxford: Rowman and Littlefield.

Brookfield, S. (2009) 'The concept of critical reflection: promises and contradictions', *European Journal of Social Work*, 12(3): 293–304.

CCETSW (Central Council for Education and Training in Social Work) (1991a) *Improving standards in practice learning: regulations and guidance for the approval of agencies and the accreditation and training of practice teachers*, Paper 26.3, London: CCETSW.

CCETSW (1991b) *DipSW: rules and requirements for the diploma in social work* (2nd edn), Paper 30, London: CCETSW.

Clapton, G., Cree, V.E., Allan, M., Edwards, R., Forbes, R., Irwin, M. and Perry, R. (2006) 'Grasping the nettle: integrating learning and practice revisited and re-imagined', *Social Work Education: The International Journal*, 25(6): 645–56.

Ferguson, I. and Lavalette, M. (2007) 'Democratic language and neo-liberal practice: the problem with civil society', *International Social Work*, 50(4): 447–59.

Ferguson, I. and Woodward, R. (2009) *Radical social work in practice: making a difference*, Bristol: The Policy Press.

Fook, J., Ryan, M. and Hawkins, L. (1997) *Professional expertise: practice, theory and education for working with uncertainty*, London: Whiting and Birch.

Ford, P., Johnstone, B., Brumfit, C., Mitchell, R. and Myles, F. (2005) 'Practice learning and the development of students as critical practitioners: some findings from research', *Social Work Education*, 24(4): 391–407.

Fry, H., Ketteridge, S. and Marshall, S. (2003) *Teaching and learning in higher education* (2nd edn), London: Routledge.

Fuller, A. and Unwin, L. (2003) 'Learning as apprentices in the contemporary UK workplace: creating and managing expansive and restrictive participation', *Journal of Education and Work*, 16(4): 407–26.

Gardner, S., Fook, J. and White, S. (2006) 'Critical reflection: possibilities for developing effectiveness in conditions of uncertainty', in S. White, J. Fook and S. Gardnerm (eds) *Critical reflection in health and social care*, Maidenhead: Open University, pp 228–41.

Gramsci, A. (2005) *Selections from the prison notebooks*, London: Lawrence and Wishart.

Hugman, R. (2009) 'But is it social work? Some reflections on mistaken identities', *British Journal of Social Work*, 39(6): 1138–53.

Jones, R. (2008) 'Social work and management', in A. Barnard, N. Horner and J. Wild (eds) *The value base of social work and social care: an active learning handbook*, Maidenhead: Open University Press.

Jordan, B. and Jordan, C. (2000) *Social work and the third way: tough love and social policy*, London: Sage.

Lam, C.M., Wong, H. and Leung, T.T.F. (2007) 'An unfinished reflexive journey: social work students' reflection on their placement experiences', *British Journal of Social Work*, 37: 91–105.

Laurillard, D. (2002) *Rethinking university teaching: a conversational framework for the effective use of learning technologies* (2nd edn), London: Routledge-Falmer.

Lymbery, M. (2001) 'Social work at the crossroads', *British Journal of Social Work*, 31(3): 369–84.

Marton, F. (1975) 'On non-verbatim learning -1: Level of processing and level of outcome', *Scandinavian Journal of Psychology*, 16: 273–79.

Mezirow, J. (1991) *Transformative dimensions of adult learning*, San Francisco, CA: Jossey-Bass.

Miller, J. (2000) *Holistic learning*, Toronto: OISE.

Nixon, S. and Murr, A. (2006) 'Practice learning and the development of professional practice', *Social Work Education*, 25(8): 798–811.

Parker, J. (2007) 'Developing effective practice learning for tomorrow's social workers', *Social Work Education*, 26(8): 263–79.

Preston-Shoot, M. (2000) 'Stumbling towards oblivion or discovering new horizons? Observations on the relationship between social work education and practice', *Journal of Social Work Practice*, 14(2): 87–98.

Ruch, G. (2002) 'From triangle to spiral: reflective practice in social work education, practice and research', *Social Work Education: The International Journal*, 21(2): 199–216.

Ryan, G., Toohey, S. and Hughes, C. (1996) 'The purpose, value and structure of the practicum in higher education: a literature review', *Higher Education*, 31(3): 355–77.

Taylor, C. and White, S. (2006) 'Knowledge and reasoning in social work: educating for humane judgement', *British Journal of Social Work*, 36(6): 937–54.

TCSW (The College of Social Work) (2012a) 'Practice learning guidance: use of the PCF and assessment criteria for practice learning'. Available at: http://www.tcsw.org.uk/uploadedFiles/TheCollege/_CollegeLibrary/Reform_resources/Practice-Learning-Guidance%28edref8%29.pdf

TCSW (2012b) 'Practice educator professional standards for social work'. Available at: http://www.tcsw.org.uk/pcf.aspx

University of York (1999) 'Facts, feelings and feedback: a collaborative model for direct observation', Interviewing Skills and Direct Observation Project Team. Available at: http://www.york.ac.uk/spsw/research/themes/communication-skills/interviewing-skills/

Wenger, E. (1998) *Communities of practice: learning, meaning and identity*, Cambridge: Cambridge University Press.

White, S., Wastell, D., Peckover, S., Hall, C. and Broadhurst, K. (2009) 'Managing risk in a high blame environment: tales from the "front door" in contemporary children's social care', in *Risk and public services*, London and Oxford: ESRC Centre for Analysis of Risk and Regulation, pp 12–14.

ELEVEN

Filling the gap: constructive responses to the erosion of training standards for practice educators

Julie Mann

Introduction

Learning in practice settings is a common component of all professional courses in health and social care in the UK, for example, nursing, social work, physiotherapy and speech and language therapy (Doel and Shardlow, 2009). It is seen as an essential feature in supporting the development of a competent practitioner and plays a central role in professional identity formation (Walker et al, 2008). For students on placement, there is the opportunity not only to 'carry out' practice, but critically to improve and extend their professional knowledge and process skills (Eraut, 1994). It must be recognised, however, that students experience varying degrees of quality in the practice learning experiences offered to them (Lefevre, 2005; Wilson et al, 2008). There is also a wide divergence of views on what constitutes 'professional practice learning'. Some would see it as 'practice experience' – an opportunity to be in an agency and see others at work (Brennan and Little, 1996). Others see it as an apprenticeship (Field, 2004) or, developed further, as a reflective apprenticeship (Evans, 1999), while still others see it as an environment in which transformative learning can take place (Mezirow, 2003; Jones, 2009) through 'disorientating' dilemmas and creativity. These models of learning are not mutually exclusive.

Underpinning this chapter is the belief that transformative learning will afford students and those wishing to be engaged in their practice education the opportunity to develop their abilities as effective, self-aware and critical practitioners. It may even bring them to make a contribution to social transformation rather than maintaining and reproducing the existing social system (Jones, 2003). This chapter seeks to examine the gaps that have occurred in social work practice education, and to make the case for robust practice educator standards for practice outcomes.

Those who work with learners in practice have an array of titles depending on the profession, the country, the tasks undertaken and even, in some cases, the stage that the learner has reached, for example, field instructor, preceptor or mentor (nursing), practice teacher/assessor/educator (social work), practice educator (nursing), supervisor (physiotherapy, clinical psychology), and associate tutor (teaching). While a number of these terms are used by some interchangeably and as if they carry the same meaning, it is important to notice the differences in terminology, and the gaps and erosions in standards that they may be masking.

To identify these gaps, I will offer a brief overview and critique of practice education developments from the introduction of a national qualification in 1989 to the publication of new standards in 2013, and the political and historical context in which these new standards were deemed to be necessary. This chapter comprises a critically reflective account of how one institution met the challenges posed by these changes. Although the focus is on UK regulation, the principles that emerge have wider application for any profession concerned with the quality of its new entrants.

Historical context

Prior to 1987, there was very little regulation of practice learning. Students were placed with 'student supervisors', who offered variable opportunities for learning on placement and whose reports at the end of the placement were inconsistent in quality. Due to the ad hoc nature of practice learning for, and assessment of, students, the reports that student supervisors submitted were routinely dismissed or overturned by academic staff (Bellinger, 2010b). Practice learning was very much the 'poor relation' (Ford and Jones, 1987) in social work qualifying programmes.

In 1987, the Central Council for Education and Training in Social Work (CCETSW) commissioned a number of 'demonstration programmes' for training practice teachers. Once evaluated, these programmes formed the basis for the Practice Teaching Award (PTA) (CCETSW, 1992). Alongside this, with the introduction of the Diploma in Social Work in 1991, students had to provide evidence for the first time that they were meeting a set of published core competencies. Also, and crucially, the practice teacher's report stood in its own right in the assessment of students (CCETSW, 1991: 26).

This meant that practice learning and the assessment of it were given equal value to classroom-based learning (Bellinger, 2010b). The PTA also brought with it an emphasis on fostering criticality and reflexivity in students (Evans, 1999; Brookfield, 2009).

In response to the introduction of this trailblazing award (Slater, 2007), the Far South West Practice Learning Consortium was set up to deliver and assess the PTA locally by the practice learning coordinator at Plymouth University. The consortium comprised practice teachers, agency representatives concerned with practice learning and academic staff from Plymouth University. In line with national imperatives, service users and carers also sat on the management committee of the consortium in its last three years. The consortium ensured a steady supply of practice teachers to support and assess social work students in the south-west region over many years.

However, the social work profession and therefore social work education nationally were thrown into crisis in the first decade of the new century, prompted by a number of factors, not least, one child's death (Laming, 2009). Within practice education, reduction in the funding available for practice teaching, together with a national recruitment and retention crisis in social work, put intense pressure on PTA programmes. In addition, there was an ever-widening gap in the supply of award-holder placement provision (Slater, 2007). Regional research had also found that only 27% of PTA-holders were practice teaching regularly, and that a quarter had not offered any placements to students at all since gaining their award (Slater, 2007). A number of PTA programmes were forced to close and when the General Social Care Council (GSCC) launched its review of the post-qualifying framework, the writing was on the wall for the PTA. Even prior to this, it had ceased to have currency as a nationally agreed standard. This gap was to be filled by the new Post-Qualifying (PQ) framework.

A commitment to transformative learning

The PTA ended nationally in 2007, and with it came the closure of the consortium in our region. The GSCC's PQ framework of Specialist and Higher Specialist awards came into existence in 2005 and was expected to fill the gap in training practice educators. However, the mandatory training to 'enable others' now included within 'Specialist' PQ programmes offered only a very basic level of practice education training for those seeking the specialist awards, most usually in childcare. This short-lived qualification was intended to solve the placement problem but actually placed unrealistic demands on often recently qualified practitioners to manage a caseload, study for the childcare award and supervise a student. The Practice Education pathway itself was available only at Higher Specialist and Advanced Award levels (GSCC, 2008). Notice the shift in terminology here from 'practice teaching' to 'practice education'. At the same time, 'practice assessor' became the common term for those who worked with and assessed learners in practice, thus again moving the function from enabling the process of learning to measuring the outcome (Bellinger, 2010b). These and other subtle changes in terminology have led to a lack of clarity and to considerable confusion for those working with learners in practice. Further, these changes meant that a gulf was created between the 'Enabling Others' requirement within specialist awards and the two higher tiers of the Practice Education PQ framework.

As Bellinger (2010a, 2010b) makes clear, the concomitant reduction in practice learning standards was subtle and well disguised. There were changes to funding arrangements. Monies specifically designated for practice learning were time-limited and thereafter no longer ring-fenced for social work education alone. A Practice Learning Task Force (PLTF) had been set up in 2002 to act as a 'short-term change agency' to increase the quantity and quality of practice learning opportunities. While it raised the profile of some new practice learning opportunities, it diverted attention away from the lack of agreement about what good support for practice learning comprised and how people should be equipped to provide it. Short-term funding was made available for non-assessed two-day training. Although many welcomed the opening up of new and rich sites of learning, the requirement for practice assessors to meet a particular standard had disappeared almost entirely, and with it, so did the space for 'critically reflective learning' (Brookfield, 2009).

Locally, very aware that these erosions were taking place, our main concern was to ensure that the standards set through the PTA as a way of assuring quality in the social work programmes were maintained. The choice was between developing the lower-level 'Enabling Others' requirement into a viable training course or moving up to a master's-level qualification. Precious lessons had been learned in delivering our PTA programme over 15 years. At the same time, this was an opportunity to be innovative and creative in our design of a new pathway. One principle was that it should be open to anyone working with professional learners, not only social work educators, but also a range of professional disciplines where support and assessment of learners' practice are a requirement. Equally, service users and carers were encouraged to participate.

Another principle was to ensure that those who undertook the pathway would bring to their work the self-awareness and reflexivity that had been such a hallmark of the PTA (Slater, 1996). The aim was to develop proactive, flexible and open-minded practitioners who would be able to grapple with complexity, work autonomously and, through their practice with learners, co-create new knowledge (Bellinger et al, 2014). Students need to be given permission and encouragement to explore, to think and to reflect critically, and practice educators should be able to facilitate this (Fook et al, 1997; Parker, 2007; Brookfield, 2009). We came from a position of recognising the complexity of professional practice learning and the diversity of learners engaged in it, set within a shifting political and social landscape where the erosion of standards for practice learning was dressed up in the 'language of improvement' (Bellinger, 2010b).

The modules that were developed, named 'Supporting Adult Learners in Professional Practice Settings' and 'Assessing Adult Learners in Their Practice', respectively, mapped across to the Southern England Consortium (SEEC) Level 7 descriptors (master's level, equating to GSCC PQ Higher Specialist and Advanced levels). These descriptors are nationally recognised descriptors for generic academic standards in higher education (SEEC, 2010). Level 7 requires a high degree of autonomy and independent thinking, a highly developed ability to deal with complex and unpredictable situations, an ability to apply knowledge flexibly and creatively in unfamiliar contexts, and an ability to generate transformative solutions. It also incorporates a critical, ethical dimension to the resolution of practice dilemmas and an ability to work proactively with others to formulate solutions. The higher academic level emphasises criticality and reflexivity. Level 6 (third-year undergraduate level, equating to GSCC PQ Specialist level), by contrast, does not require the same degree of autonomy, flexibility or creativity on the part of the participant.[1] It focuses instead on individual responsibility, drawing on largely standard techniques and information sources to solve problems.

We had hoped to locate the modules in a health-run master's programme at Plymouth University but found responses to our approaches problematic, highlighting the different culture and value base that can exist between health and social work disciplines (Itzhaky et al, 2004). As the modules were to be open to a range of professional disciplines, service users and carers, we looked further afield to the Integrated Master's Programme (IMP) in Education within the Faculty of Education. Initial advances were greeted with interest and encouragement. As we learned more about the IMP, we were pleased to find a pedagogical approach and value base congruent with our own, a flexible programme with financially affordable modules, and a core team who were welcoming and enthusiastic to engage with us.

The IMP at Plymouth offered a portfolio of taught modules, as well as the opportunity to undertake independent study modules. It had an innovative design in that participants did not have to follow a set curriculum. Instead, the pedagogical structure was one that allowed participants to determine their own focus of study while having to adopt a range of academic approaches or modes of learning specified by the assessment criteria. These modes, three of which were 'Critical Review of a Body of Knowledge', 'Understanding the Use of Data' and 'Making an Argument', were designed to provide IMP participants with the building blocks for writing a master's dissertation. Each module assignment had to meet the 'deep criteria' and also the criteria for one of the five assessment modes specified by the programme.

There were a number of pathways within the IMP, many of which carried a named award. In order to attract professional accreditation, the module assessments for the practice education pathway had to incorporate practice. This restricted the choice of assessment modes to the remaining two, 'Critical Reflection on Practice' and 'Developing Practice Through a Project', with participants being able to choose which mode they would use for each of the modules we had developed. The two modules together made up the IMP named award PG Cert: Education (Professional Practice Learning Pathway). Professional accreditation at PQ Higher Specialist level was obtained in August 2007 and accreditation at PQ Advanced level a year later.

Participants on this pathway could step off the programme after successful completion of the two modules as they then met the requirements of Plymouth University's social work qualifying programmes for supporting and assessing learners in practice. (These requirements were intended to ensure the provision of a strong practice learning framework for all students.) Those wishing to obtain the GSCC Higher Specialist Award had to complete these two modules plus two others linked to professional practice learning, either from the IMP portfolio of taught modules or through undertaking independent study modules. Successful completion of a dissertation would bring with it the now-discontinued GSCC PQ Advanced Award. All participants were required to be supported by a suitably qualified mentor.

The modules

The aims for both required modules stated that developing criticality and reflexivity was central, as was the ability to transfer professional practice knowledge, values and skills into creative work with a wide range of learners in practice. More emphasis was placed on the ability to draw critically on theories of organisational structures, management, adult learning and teaching in the aims for 'Supporting Adult Learners in Professional Practice Settings', whereas the aims for 'Assessing Adult Learners in Their Practice' focused on developing a critical capacity to judge a learner's performance in practice and to analyse one's own performance and development as an assessor of the practice of others. In both, developing confident, reflective and proficient practice educators/assessors capable of maintaining professional values in complex situations was the priority given the need to protect the safety and well-being of members of the public in any situation involving learners (GSCC, 2010).

The pathway team members operated from a strengths perspective and sought to develop communities of practice (Wenger, 1998) with participants. Locally produced Standards for the Promotion of Race Equality, Social Justice and Human Rights (Boyce et al, 2008) underpinned the delivery of the modules. All were committed to an approach to learning as emancipation (Friere, 1970) and were acutely conscious of the power of modelling (Fook and Askeland, 2007). The aim was to deliver the modules in a manner that modelled consistently good practice within practice education. The team also sought to demonstrate our value base from the outset by employing basic communication skills such as showing respect to participants on arrival and, at all other times, checking the environment, listening attentively to all contributions, managing the dynamics of the group carefully and offering individual time, as necessary. We were aware of the power dynamics of tutors–participants and assessors–assessees – not only would we be looking with participants at issues surrounding 'failing students', but we would also be marking the participants' work.

While providing participants with a safe space within which to explore ideas about practice education, our intention was also to encourage criticality as a means of learning how to think differently, rather than simply offering opportunities to reflect (Ford et al, 2004; Brookfield, 2009). We deliberately had no template to give participants of the correct way to support and assess learners; instead, we sought to offer them the tools and materials to think independently and creatively, to critically engage with literature, and to be proactive in finding ways through tricky and 'disorientating' practice education dilemmas (Mezirow, 2003). Furthermore, it was important for participants to have an understanding of the wider political context within which professional education takes place and to learn to recognise 'erosions' (Bellinger, 2010b). The course aimed to develop participants' skills in acting strategically to minimise their effects. We therefore included sessions on, for example, 'The political context of practice education', 'How do we construct our identity as assessors?' and 'Organisational theory and its implications for promoting and managing learning'.

Delivery

Each module was to be delivered over six workshop days – two consecutive days per month, over three months. The rationale for this was to enable busy professionals to negotiate release time on this monthly basis. A mixture of delivery methods was employed, such as formal presentations, interactive exercises and discussions, and guest speakers, including service user and student input, with tasks set between the pairs of workshop days.

The first intake of participants was in September 2007. We were excited and not a little apprehensive (Agazarian, 2004), filled with feelings similar to those when meeting a student social worker in practice for the first time. Would the group engage? Would they 'get' what we were trying to deliver? Would they baulk at not being offered that template for how to work with learners? There were 13 in that first group, 12 of whom were social workers; the 13th was a service user.

The two modules were delivered concurrently that first year, which proved somewhat confusing for the participants, so in subsequent years, these were delivered sequentially. Despite this confusion, the participants did, indeed, engage with the module content, although some said that it was challenging (As we wanted it to be!) and one participant asked for 'the textbook' that would set out how to work with learners.

Delivery of the modules continued for the next five years, with an average of 10 participants in each cohort. The mix of formal input, practice exercises, role play by tutors, in-depth discussion of ethical dilemmas when working with learners, managing student failure and presentations by cohort members has been well received by participants. Guest speakers have included: service users presenting how they support and assess students; a social work student talking about experiences of being assessed; a former participant offering tips on assignment writing for the two modules; and a member of the university's Disability

Assist Team giving advice on working with learners with disabilities. Crucially, teaching has focused on criticality, organisational theory, education issues, well-being, stress and self-care.

While there have been substantial numbers of social workers undertaking the modules each year (overall, 25 from the statutory sector, 15 from voluntary, independent and private organisations, and five university-employed practice educators), there have also been professionals from a range of other disciplines: five military personnel, four teachers, three health service workers, one probation officer and one fire-service worker. A small but significant number of service users have also participated, most of whom have also successfully completed the module assessments. This mix of disciplines and backgrounds contributed to lively debate on the taught days. It enabled participants to appreciate a context wider than their own within which professional practice education takes place, and held teachers to the generic approach.

Assessment

Assessment for the modules was by submission of a 5,000-word assignment, using either the 'Critical Reflection on Practice' or 'Developing Practice Through a Project' assessment modes. The former gave participants the opportunity to reflect on work they had done with a learner, the latter offered them the chance to undertake a small piece of research of their own choosing related to practice education that they were keen to investigate, which would further their own development as a practice educator and contribute to practice educator practice generally. Two examples of assignment titles students chose are 'A critical evaluation of my assessment practice when failing a student nurse' (Critical Reflection on Practice mode) and 'Social work students: identifying stress and supporting coping in practice learning settings' (Developing Practice Through a Project mode).

Group tutorials were offered after the workshop days had ended to support participants in thinking about and planning their assignments. Most submissions demonstrated a well-developed degree of criticality and reflexivity. They reflected an ability to think independently and to be creative in dealing with complex practice learning situations. However, some participants failed the module assessment at their first attempt. There appear to have been a number of possible reasons for this, among them the leap to master's-level study or simply having been away from formal assignment writing for a substantial period, pressures from work, most notably, a lack of release time, or personal circumstances, or a combination of all of these. We offered these students additional tutorial support on a one-to-one basis. All but a few of those who had failed initially passed the assignment at their second attempt.

Feedback

Feedback from participants and from the external examiner was generally positive. Comments from social worker participants bear this out, for example: "I found the sessions generally inspiring and thought-provoking, especially when innovative and fresh ideas were presented. The tutors and all staff are very supportive"; "It has been informative, challenging, varied and thought-provoking. It has enabled me to consider my own practice within a wider context and through a critical lens." The following quote from a service user participant also points to the effectiveness of the modules: "As a result of undertaking these Practice Education modules, it is with more confidence that I have been able to contribute to innovative projects with the BA Social Work'.

Formal feedback from the external examiner to the university states that 'they [the modules] are tailored to the situations of the participants.... It is clear from the participants' work that they are able to use their learning directly in their practice' and on assignment feedback to participants, that 'the manner of the feedback ... is exemplary, well structured and succinct'.

In the light of feedback received both at the end of each workshop day and from formal module evaluation by students and the external examiner, we have reviewed our delivery on an ongoing basis and have modified and updated the content of the modules accordingly year on year.

Analysis

We have been pleased and proud to have been able to offer a high-quality programme to those wishing to engage in practice education over the years, first through the PTA and then through the Professional Practice Learning Pathway within the IMP. This has created a community of critically aware and reflexive practice educators who have consistently demonstrated careful, considered practice in their work with social work learners.

However, this pathway has already been forced to mutate into something less substantial, as described in the following. This illustrates well how the erosions that Bellinger exposed in 2010 are already fully formed landslips. Nationally, there is no longer any infrastructure to support practice education in social work. At a time when the complexities of practice should demand higher practice educator standards, many practice education programmes in England are set at a lower academic level; some have no formal assessment attached at all. There is increasing demand from statutory agencies locally to reduce our academic level to Level 6 or lower. The cost of master's modules has risen considerably due to changes in government funding for higher education, putting the pathway out of reach for many, particularly where they have to self-fund. This is increasingly the case as funding sources, particularly in the voluntary, independent and private sectors, where many local practice learning opportunities lie, have dried up. There is no clear assessment framework within the new Practice Educator Professional Standards (PEPS) developed by the College of Social Work (TCSW, 2013). These factors all contributed to the undermining of the IMP. Ironically, the same College of Social Work endorsed the IMP Professional Practice Learning Pathway as fully meeting these new practice educator standards.

If practice educators are no longer required to bring a high degree of criticality, creativity and independent thinking to their work, and student social workers are offered what amounts to 'apprenticeships', where 'compliance, bureaucratic efficiency and uncritical acceptance of an approved evidence base' (Bellinger, 2010a) become the markers for qualification, this could threaten the very existence of social work as a profession. The Professional Capabilities Framework (PCF) (TCSW, 2012a) is the overarching framework of standards and professional development in social work. Practice educators are now required to help learners work towards meeting these at the appropriate level. Extensive recommendations for changes to the profession called for the need to develop professional expertise through taking time to stand back and think about what has been experienced (Munro, 2011; Croisdale-Appleby, 2014). However, it is very hard to see how such changes will be brought about effectively if the professional development requirements for practice educators are diminished. As occurs so often, the rhetoric does not match the reality and PQ training remains confused, fragmented and disjointed.

New initiatives

While mourning the loss of the IMP Professional Practice Learning Pathway, and recognising that practice education resources are depleted, we are already finding creative ways to modify the two practice education modules, retaining as much of their quality as possible despite the current reductionist climate. Due to faculty reorganisation, the modules have been moved to an MSc Advanced Professional Practice programme within the university. Each will be delivered over four workshop days and each carry 20, not 30, master's credits, thus being more affordable. With the PEPS and PCF now being in full swing, it has not been difficult for us to map our learning outcomes onto their respective domains. Indeed, from the outset, the modules have required participants to evidence these capabilities and values. We have been able to retain the principle that the modules should be available across disciplines. The modules remain open to anyone responsible for supporting and assessing professional learners.

As practice settings increasingly employ a number of different professionals, the modules are well equipped to deliver inter-professional training for practice educators built on past experience (Doel and Shardlow, 2009). A contract with a local statutory agency to deliver the modules has recently been negotiated, thus demonstrating that we are working to meet local workforce development needs. However, it does not escape our notice that while local agendas are important, tailored local responses should not be at the expense of a consistent national standard (Plenty and Gower, 2013). We stand by our principle of developing proactive, flexible and open-minded practitioners able to grapple with complexity, to work autonomously and to co-create new knowledge (Bellinger et al, 2014). Feedback from participants, students and stakeholders, together with our own evaluation and reflections, will inform us as to whether we have been able to achieve this.

Although we, and others around the country, have created new routes into practice education in response to the frameworks of PEPS and the PCF, the challenges we face do not end there. Our ability to maintain the capacity to provide high-quality practice education, 'based on creativity and innovation juxtaposed against a turbulent political and economic climate' (Plenty and Gower, 2013: 64), is likely to be increasingly threatened. The situation feels precarious and not unlike the gap left when the PTA ended. We managed to fill that gap successfully in 2007. We will soon be able to evaluate whether our latest model for the training of practice educators is able to uphold the standards that we have set ourselves in the face of ongoing financial constraints and increased prescription.

Conclusion

This chapter has reviewed the recent history of practice education in the UK and the initiatives taken in practice educator preparation at Plymouth University. Our journey has been challenging and difficult, but also affirming and positive. The learning has been deep and has confirmed for us some crucial factors that we believe must be taken into account when designing a practice education course of quality. These are:

- pay attention to the political and economic climate for practice and education;
- look beyond the narrow disciplinary boundaries and 'usual alliances';
- promote and safeguard space for critical reflection;
- resist instructional, reductionist, 'how to' approaches that fail to prepare social workers for the complexities of practice; and
- ensure that practice educators are equipped to respond to the academic level and needs of students.

The challenge is to spot the gaps and erosions as they appear and act to contest and resist them in the ways suggested earlier. This will ensure, as far as possible, that future practice educators and the learners they work with will be sufficiently critically aware, innovative and creative to be the new standard-bearers for the health, education and social care professions in the future.

Note

[1] Please note, the term 'participant' is used for those undertaking training to teach and/or assess students on placement, whatever their profession.

References

Agazarian, Y.M. (2004) *Systems-centered therapy for groups*, London: Karnac.

Bellinger, A. (2010a) 'Talking about (re)generation: practice learning as a site of renewal for social work', *British Journal of Social Work*, 40(8): 2450–66.

Bellinger, A. (2010b) 'Studying the landscape: practice learning for social work reconsidered', *Social Work Education*, 29(6): 599–615.

Bellinger, A., Bullen, D. and Ford, D. (2014) 'Practice research in practice learning: students as co-researchers and co-constructors of knowledge', *Nordic Social Work Research*, 4(1): 58–69.

Boyce, P., Harrison, G., Jelley, M., Jolley, M., Maxwell, C., Soper, S., Wattam, E. and White, G. (2008) 'Review of the anti-racist standards within anti-oppressive practice – executive summary', report published by Plymouth University Centre for Excellence in Professional Practice Learning (CEPPL).

Brennan, J. and Little, B. (1996) *A review of work based learning in higher education*, London: Department for Education and Employment.

Brookfield, S. (2009) 'The concept of critical reflection: promises and contradictions', *European Journal of Social Work*, 12(3): 293–304.

CCETSW (1991) *DipSW: rules and requirements for the diploma in social work* (2nd edn), Paper 30, London: CCETSW.

CCETSW (1992) *The requirements for post qualifying education and training in the personal social services: a framework for continuing professional development*, Paper 31, London: CCETSW.

Croisdale-Appleby, D. (2014) *Re-visioning social work education: an independent review*, London: Department of Health. Available at: https://www.gov.uk/government/uploads/system/uploads/attachment_data/file/285788/DCA_Accessible.pdf

Doel, M. and Shardlow, S. (eds) (2009) *Educating professionals: practice learning in health and social care*, Farnham: Ashgate Publishing.

Eraut, M. (1994) *Developing professional knowledge and competence*, London: Falmer.

Evans, D. (1999) *Practice learning in the caring professions*, Aldershot: Ashgate.

Field, D.E. (2004) 'Moving from novice to expert – the value of learning in clinical practice: a literature review', *Nurse Education Today*, 24(7): 560–5.

Fook, J. and Askeland, G. (2007) 'Challenges of critical reflection: "nothing ventured, nothing gained"', *Social Work Education*, 26(5): 520–33.

Fook, J., Ryan, M. and Hawkins, L. (1997) *Professional expertise: practice, theory and education for working in uncertainty*, London: Whiting & Birch.

Ford, K. and Jones, A. (1987) *Student supervision*, London: Macmillan Education.

Ford, P., Johnston, B., Mitchell, R. and Myles, F. (2004) 'Social work education and criticality: some thoughts from research', *Social Work Education*, 23(2): 185–98.

Friere, P. (1970) *Pedagogy of the oppressed*, New York, NY: The Seabury Press.

GSCC (General Social Care Council) (2008) *Raising standards: social work education in England 2007–2008*, London: GSCC.

GSCC (2010) *Codes of practice for social care workers*, London: GSCC.

Itzhaky, H., Gerber, P. and Dekel, R. (2004) 'Empowerment, skills and values: a comparative study of nurses and social workers', *International Journal of Nursing Studies*, 41(4): 447–55.

Jones, P. (2003) 'Educating for change: transformative learning and progressive social work education', *Advances in Social Work and Welfare Education*, 5: 69–82.

Jones, P. (2009) 'Teaching for change in social work: a discipline-based argument for the use of transformative approaches to teaching and learning', *Journal of Transformative Education*, 7(1): 8–25.

Laming, Lord (2009) *The protection of children in England: a progress report*, March, London: HMSO.

Lefevre, M. (2005) 'Facilitating practice learning assessment: the influence of relationship', *Social Work Education*, 24(5): 565–83.

Mezirow, J. (2003) 'Transformative learning as discourse', *Journal of Transformative Education*, 1: 58–63.

Munro, E. (2011) *Munro review of child protection: final report: a child-centred system*, London: The Stationery Office.

Parker, J. (2007) 'Developing effective practice learning for tomorrow's social workers', *Social Work Education*, 26(8): 263–79.

Plenty, J. and Gower, D. (2013) 'The reform of social work practice education and training and supporting practice educators', *The Journal of Practice Teaching and Learning*, 12(2): 48–66.

SEEC (Southern England Consortium) (2010) 'Credit level descriptors for higher education', Southern England Consortium for Credit Accumulation and Transfer. Available at: http://www.seec.org.uk/seec-credit-level-descriptors-2010/

Slater, P. (1996) 'Practice teaching and self-assessment: promoting a culture of accountability in social work', *British Journal of Social Work*, 26(2): 195–208.

Slater, P. (2007) 'The passing of the practice teaching award: history, legacy, prospects', *Social Work Education*, 26(8): 749–62.

TCSW (The College of Social Work) (2012a) 'Practice learning guidance: use of the PCF and assessment criteria for practice learning'. Available at: http://www.tcsw.org.uk/uploadedFiles/TheCollege/Social_Work_Education/Practice-Learning-Guidance(edref8).pdf

TCSW (2013) 'Practice educator professional standards (PEPS) and guidance'. Available at: http://www.tcsw.org.uk/Educators/

Walker, J., Crawford K. and Parker, J. (2008) *Practice education in social work: a handbook for practice teachers, assessors and educators*, Exeter: Learning Matters.

Wenger, E. (1998) *Communities of practice: learning, meaning and identity*, Cambridge: Cambridge University Press.

Wilson, G., Walsh, T. and Kirby, M. (2008) 'Developing practice learning: student perspectives', *Social Work Education*, 27(1): 35–50.

TWELVE

The concept of integrity in relation to failing and marginal students

Cherie Appleton and Carole Adamson

Introduction

This chapter considers the issue of how social work programmes can best support students deemed marginal or identified as at risk of failing. Using the lens of 'integrity' as a conceptual focus, it addresses the context in which fitness to practise is determined and the processes by which schools of social work may identify, support and manage issues of competence and practice standards. Questions that practice educators may use to determine the extent of concerns and possible options for resolution are applied to a case study and some typical vignettes are offered for reader exploration.

The practice of social work education spans academic and professional perspectives on student achievement, competency, standards and appropriate behaviour. Social work educators – in particular, those involved in practice learning – have first-line responsibility for determining who becomes a social worker (Elpers and FitzGerald, 2012; Robertson, 2013). Ultimately accountable to the individuals, families and communities with whom social work practises, social work programmes become the often-contentious territory where the determination of fitness to practise is most commonly exercised. While academic benchmarks for passing and failing are embedded within all tertiary programmes, an integral component of social work education is the applied professional definitions of competence, capability and standards of practice. Determination of fitness to practise based on judgements concerning a student's conduct, values and ethics, communication skills, or physical or mental health is a far more complex and (some would contend) less objective process. It is a judgement call that presents immense challenges for those tasked with identifying and addressing the issues within social work programmes and practice learning settings (Staniforth and Fouché, 2006), and it is this contested territory that is explored within the chapter.

A note about the concepts and terminology used here is necessary: we make the assumption that the coordination of practice learning and teaching occurs within tertiary education and that preparation for practice occurs within the academy, with exposure to practice sited within the agencies and organisations with whom the schools of social work partner. Practice teachers, in a New Zealand context, are sited within education and we engage with fieldwork supervisors or fieldwork educators who mentor, support and contribute to the assessment of students within the practice agency but who are employed primarily as social workers within and by the field. Funding systems (or lack of) dictate that supervisors in the field offer their services free, so the onus 'down under' in Aotearoa New Zealand is on the academy to provide the preparation and final assessment of a student's practice. Supervisors in the field have the responsibility of naming issues and alerting students and the social work school of any concerns that may lead to student failure. While decision-making in partnership is the preferred practice, the ultimate responsibility for excluding, removing from practice and failing a student rests finally with the academic institution. For those readers more accustomed to the active employment of practice teachers by social work provider agencies, our points about partnership and collaboration between educators and practice will hopefully maintain their strength despite the different balance in the relationship.

This collaborative implementation of social work professional standards requires a complex stakeholder partnership that may vary from country to country, while demonstrating the involvement of several key players. Determination of fitness to practise is made in the relationship between the academy, the sites of practice in both practice learning and employment environments, the professional bodies acting as voices of the profession (which may, in some jurisdictions, have the role of accrediting programmes), and the state. The state usually funds tertiary education and (in the jurisdictions in which social work is a registered profession) recognises and accredits social work programmes. Within our own practice field in Aotearoa New Zealand, the academic and practice elements are encapsulated by the phrase 'fit and proper', as defined by the Social Workers Registration Board (SWRB), a state body that both registers social workers and recognises social work programmes (SWRB, 2013). The challenge for educators is to determine a graduate's fit and proper status in a manner that addresses statutory, professional and student expectations.

Using the conceptual framework of 'integrity' as a lens, this chapter addresses the issues of at-risk students and their potential failure within the context of these multiple, and often competing, demands and expectations of academia, government, society and professional standards. It concludes by applying an understanding of integrity to examples of possible scenarios with which the reader may be familiar.

Applying the lens of integrity in relation to social work competence and the marginal student

Social work programmes are required to graduate students with both sufficient academic understanding of the knowledge bases deemed appropriate for the profession and with an assessed quality of fitness to practise exemplified not only by academic achievement, but also by the demonstration of values and skills deemed compatible with the profession. Ife (2010: 223) comments that each of these three components (knowledge, values and skills) 'is important in its own right and each also interacts with others' as social work is not a technical process without values. In compatible terminology, Furness and Gilligan (2004: 469) describe competence as an equation of 'ability + knowledge + understanding'; in this chapter, we are using the concept of integrity to describe the integral value-added combination of these competency factors as we believe that this addresses the holistic, subtle but fundamental requirement for good practice (see Figure 12.1).

Integrity is a term that occurs frequently within social work literature concerning standards, competency and capability. It is often applied broadly without definition, as if integrity is synonymous with good social work practice. Within the Code of Conduct issued by the

Figure 12.1: Integrity in relation to social work knowledge, values and skills

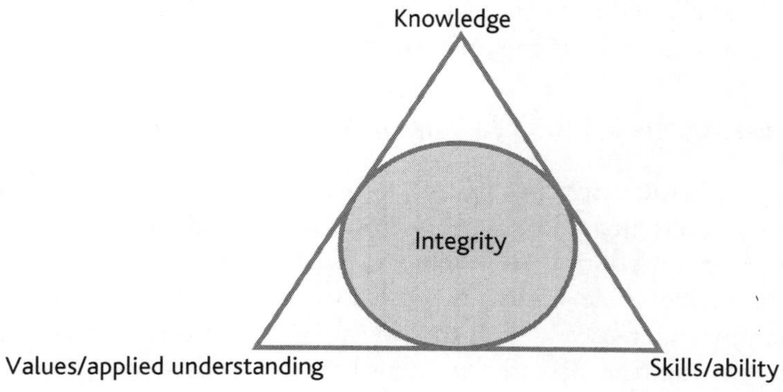

SWRB in Aotearoa New Zealand, there is a requirement that social workers 'uphold high standards of personal conduct and act with integrity' (SWRB, 2014: 4). Similarly, the Code of Ethics of the British Association of Social Workers (BASW) describes professional integrity as a value, stating that 'social workers have a responsibility to respect and uphold the values and principles of the profession and act in a reliable, honest and trustworthy manner' (BASW, 2012: 10) – comparable statements are contained within Australian and North American codes.

Further use of the concept of integrity imbues it with additional meaning, suggesting a binding together of compatible qualities within a coherent whole. Appleton (2010: 13) summarised the literature base and concluded that there is 'a re-occurring theme of integrity consisting of honesty, congruity and consistency with a person's morals, ethics, principles, values and actions'. In other words, the concept of integrity manifests in both espoused beliefs and ethical principles (alongside adherence to an external ethical code), and in actions. Embedded as it is within the contexts and processes in which social work occurs, a systems perspective applied to integrity suggests that it has a fluid and multiple identity, with strength derived from the relational connections between its elements and a vulnerability to erosion should some of these elements be either not sufficiently developed or robust and come under threat. Given the constant demands of complex social work activity and the changing contexts in which we practise, a constructivist lens further enhances our appreciation that to have and maintain integrity requires us to view it as a social virtue that is defined primarily by our relationship with others (Calhoun, 1995), and that is neither fixed nor immovable (Cox et al, 2003). From an indigenous Maori perspective in Aotearoa New Zealand, one of the participants in Appleton's research defined integrity as 'three simple words in Maori which [are] tika, pono, aroha[1]; and they mean to be right, to take the right action and to always do it with genuineness and heart' (Appleton, 2010: 82).

Addressing the issue of failing or marginal students

Tasked with the responsibility of graduating 'fit and proper' social workers, qualifying social work programmes are frequently under the spotlight of political and ideological debate over the role of our profession. Debate extends not only to graduates, but also to the programmes themselves, with the Social Work Taskforce in Britain in 2009 stating that 'Specific concerns have been raised about the … robustness and quality of assessment, with some students passing the social work degree who are not competent or suitable to practise on the frontline' (SWTF, 2009: 24).

Publication of the Narey (2014) report into the education of children's social workers in the UK appears to have raised the ante in the quality and standards debate, with similar concerns expressed by politicians in New Zealand, such as Minister of Social Development Paula Bennett's statement to the SWRB conference on 11 November 2013: 'It is time that we started asking questions as to what are we training, how are we doing it, what are the skills they are leaving with, where are the checks and balances?' (Bennett, 2013).

The Narey report and other critiques of the 'fit' between social work education and the demands of government agendas can be characterised as part of the wider ideological debate between neoliberal aspirations (reflected in the move towards competency-based training) and the social work profession's construction of its professional identity, as demonstrated in discussions promoting critical reflection, such as Eadie and Lymbery (2007), Morley and Dunstan (2012) and Van Heugten (2011). The issues that individual schools of social work face in regard to excluding or supporting at-risk students need at times, in our opinion, to be viewed within this wider quality and standards debate. As educators, we are tasked with making these decisions within the context of practice learning and teaching and this requires clarity as to the professional purpose of the gatekeeping. As with the wider role of social work, decision-making about fitness to practise lies at the intersection of the personal, professional and the political, and it requires a coherent understanding concerning who is deemed at risk of failure, what criteria are used and what procedures and processes are activated and invested in to support marginal students.

The sometimes disparate elements of assessing fitness to practise within a social work programme – academic success, practice skills and the demonstration of professional values and behaviour – are exercised within all components of a social work programme. Traditional curriculum delivery, as exemplified by discrete papers or courses within the stages of a degree, has tended to emphasise the academic achievement of students at the potential expense of the assessment of the more applied and professional aspects of fitness to practise. Integration of student abilities may be marked through combined assessment of theory and skills, or some other form of gatekeeping prior to practice learning occurring. However, the siloed construction of tertiary degrees can potentially result in, for example, the academically bright but ethically challenged student or the academically challenged but emotionally and socially intelligent student progressing unchecked through a substantive part of their degree without being offered appropriate support and guidance. It can potentially result in an overreliance on practicum coordinators, practice educators and supervisors to name issues that have manifested themselves throughout a student's academic journey. It can be argued, therefore, that the identification of and support for at-risk students might be better and earlier integrated within a degree constructed around practice learning and critical reflection (Adamson, 2011).

Defining failure and marginality is therefore located at a very busy intersection of academic and professional standards, within a bigger picture of political and ideological tensions, not the least being our profession's values of social justice, equal opportunity and the belief in an individual's capacity for change. It is important to recognise that the various terms 'fitness to practise', 'professional suitability', 'suitability to practice', 'good character', 'morally and ethically sound' and 'fit and proper' are all used in different ways and interpreted differently by individuals in practice (Currer and Atherton, 2008). Definitions of acceptable standards and behaviour may vary from programme to programme (Staniforth and Fouché, 2006).

A literature review (see Table 12.1) has identified issues that may cause a student to fail or to be considered marginal; the points attributed to the named authors are only some of those raised.

From the brief survey in Table 12.1, it can be seen that the issues arising for students and those assessing them lie not just in academic performance (although literacy and written communication skills are fundamental), but in the development of appropriate interactive, relational and values-based processes of engaging with service users, colleagues and the understanding and practice of professional identity. Also, of note in the literature is an increased emphasis on regulation and prescription, in parallel with a focus on the relational. While personal qualities and relational abilities are addressed throughout the literature, there is clearly a growing emphasis on the inclusion of equity issues and inclusive practice both for students and for the communities they will work with, for instance, Sin and Fong (2009) in relation to disability. There is, therefore, an imperative for professional programmes to be able to articulate, demonstrate, model and create learning opportunities for students to understand the expectations of growing their professional fitness to practise throughout the degree. These experiences need to enable students to build from an academic knowledge base to experiment, acquire and practise the behaviours, actions and attitudes necessary to become a professional beginning social worker practising across a variety of fields and in different

Table 12.1: Issues related to marginality and failure in social work students

Authors	Characteristics of students
Wilson, cited in Miller and Koerin (2002)	Student behaviour is outrageous or damaging to self or others (aggression, psychotic behaviour, immorality, dishonesty) Emerging patterns such as resistance or hostility towards learning, emotional immaturity, poor interpersonal skills or judgemental approaches to clients, emotional problems that interfere with ability to work with clients
Bogo and Vayda, cited in Miller and Koerin (2002)	Problems in applying theory to practice Inability to develop collaborative relationships Being judgemental and over-personalising issues Poor conflict resolution skills Lack of self-awareness, using practicum for own therapy and inability to handle feedback
Raphael and Rosenblum (1987)	High anxiety Poor collegial relationships Boundary problems Passive learning styles Difficulty in task completion
Koerin and Miller (1995) and Miller and Koerin (1998, 2002)	Ethics Mental health/substance abuse Performance on placement Illegal activities Disruptive classroom behaviours Warning signs of lack of maturity, sense of entitlement, rigid or poor boundaries, naivety and lack of awareness
Furness and Gilligan (2004)	Boundary issues such as collusion Power issues such as disrespecting or controlling service users Practice issues such as not challenging bad practice, not using supervision, placing service users in danger Being judgemental Carrying serious personal issues without addressing them
Lafrance and Gray (2004)	Personal qualities (values and attitudes; maturity; honesty and integrity; comfort with emotions; self-awareness; resolution of personal issues) Relationship qualities (how they come across to others; empathy; emotional and intrapersonal intelligence) Congruence between personal and social work values
Staniforth and Fouché (2006)	Congruence between personal and social work values Psychological and emotional challenges Reluctance to take on helping role Inability to respect diversity
Apaitia-Vague et al (2011)	Criminal convictions and placement acceptability/suitability for registration Mental disorder without adequate self-care plans
Finch (2014)	Dishonest behaviour, persistent lateness, poor communication skills, poor organisational skills and oppressive and discriminatory attitudes

contexts. It is the *integration* of the qualities of knowledge, the applied understanding of social work values and of social work skills, that we are terming 'integrity', the development of which is to be identified, assessed, supported, nurtured and monitored throughout a student's social work programme. From the working definition of integrity as espoused beliefs, personal qualities and traits, social work ethics, knowledge, and skills in action, the first challenge to practice educators becomes how students can be assisted to recognise and own integrity. The second challenge is to discover how integrity can be assessed fairly: in what ways can all parties contribute to cultivating, and systemically supporting the exploration and maintenance of integrity within the student's educational and personal/professional journey? What follows is an exploration of how integrity as an applied framework can be used to assist growing student practitioners' understanding, development and demonstration of ethical and emotionally intelligent social work practice.

'Integrity moves' within the student journey

At what point of their education do we notice that a student may have a restricted capacity to develop as a social worker? Checks and balances that can be termed 'integrity moves' (or actions that can enhance the integrity of the student practitioner) within social work programmes offer various windows of opportunity for the identification of marginal students and the activation of support systems that can assess, monitor and provide continuation or exit options for those deemed at risk of failure (see Figure 12.2). Here, we consider the systemic embedding of integrity moves within a social work programme, and subsequently address the characteristics of integrity through consideration of a case scenario.

We begin by stressing that systemic approaches to student support begin before a student enters the programme. In their literature review on student fitness to practise, Boak et al (2012: 21) draw attention to proactive measures that need to be in place before students are selected for social work courses. These include clear policies, standards and expectations of behavioural practice within professional social work academic settings. Academic staff must understand, agree to support and then consistently apply them. Elpers and Fitzgerald (2012) note that programmes should ask what would be considered professional demeanour in behaviour, appearance and communication in a traditional classroom prior to sending students out into the field. Specific 'fitness to practise' policies and procedures need to be

Figure 12.2: Windows of opportunity for identifying at-risk students

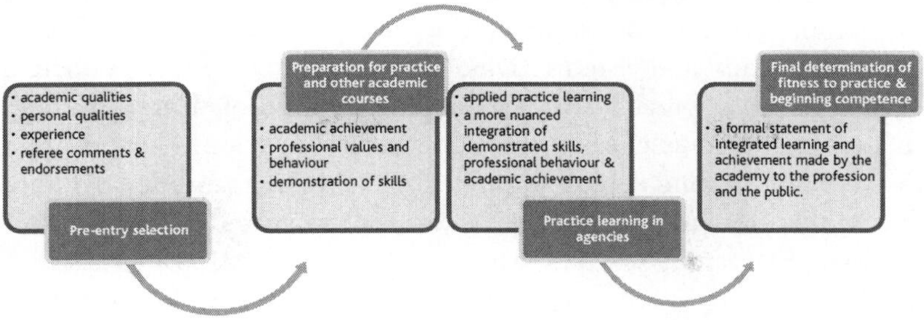

explicit and beyond the general 'academic misconduct' requirements with which all degrees operate, accepting that there will, however, be some areas (such as academic plagiarism) that are common across degrees and especially relevant to professions with codes of ethics. It is important to stress that appropriate professional behaviour is an academic requirement in a professional programme (Lafrance and Gray, 2004). This approach is transparent, upfront and invites academic staff to ensure that the expectation of meeting professional fitness to practise standards is named, discussed and agreed before students are invited to join the degree. These materials can be used at recruitment and publicity/promotional events, as well as incorporated into graduate student profiles and course materials. During selection and admission, professional standards and expectations can be further emphasised and explored with students, and the importance of learning and demonstrating how to evidence fitness to practise as they engage in their studies can be explained. Referees and references required by students when applying to programmes can directly question and invite examples of conduct and behaviours displayed that align with professional codes of conduct and ethical practice, as well as asking for an honest appraisal of students' potential skills and attributes that would align with professional values. All the aforementioned preparation is part of ensuring that the earlier definition of 'tika' (to be right) is embedded and modelled for students in the programme.

Closing the gap between selection at admission and identification of potential problems in practice learning can be approached by being alert to early warning signs and addressing issues of concern as they arise during the first year of academic courses. Some common problems may include: a student's lack of communication; issues of timeliness and timekeeping; plagiarism and honesty problems; inability to meet deadlines; non-completion of work; lack of participation in group work; non-reporting of absences; inappropriate use of mobile phones and social media; consistently submitting work with incorrect references despite correction; inability to follow instructions or change behaviour; attitude and approach taken when appealing grades or challenging ideas and systems; lack of reflection or consistently concrete thinking; and approaches to learning. Once a problem is identified, students can receive pastoral care and academic advice. This can assist them to identify and explore their circumstances, capabilities, capacity and willingness to engage their own resources and the variety of support and learning services available from the educational institution. These early conversations in the first year of study enable students to exercise a viable option to reconsider pursuing a professional course, or to put it on hold while attending to more urgent personal and/or family concerns – reinforcing 'pono' (to take the right action). This approach by academic advisors and practicum teams supports integrity and is a holistic and developmental practice that models and mirrors client-centred work.

Formal and informal encouragement and discussion by staff of student development towards fitness to practise is therefore essential throughout the degree as professionalism needs to be continuously supported and assessed. This can be nested within a wide range of teaching and learning activities that are planned, coordinated and continually examined, explored, reinforced and reflected upon to ensure integrity. Boak et al (2012: 24) note:

> There appears to be broad agreement that important elements of teaching and learning include: clear communication of principles and procedures; role modelling and explanation of desirable behaviours by staff; opportunities to practise, and to reflect on and receive feedback on practice; monitoring performance, reinforcing good practice and providing extra support where necessary; and helping students develop the skills of self-reflection.

Course descriptors and expectations of students in programmes need to clearly articulate the criteria and standards by which communication, timeliness, reflection and honesty (eg in relation to their own and others' attendance at classes, and to honesty issues such as plagiarism) can be demonstrated. It is important that professionalism be formatively assessed. This means that assessment should begin early, be conducted frequently, be implemented long-term and provide learners with opportunities in partnership with those supporting their learning to explore, understand and make the change(s) involved. As and when necessary, staff must be confident to challenge and take action regarding student attitudes and behaviours that do not demonstrate ethical approaches to learning and citizenship.

Finally, field placements during the degree are the experiential learning opportunities for which students need to be thoroughly primed as they are where 'fitness to practise' is tested in the real world. It is during their practice in the field that the development of personal and professional selves, together with the student's integration of theory and practice, can be assessed and further refined. It is where many opportunities to observe and demonstrate the third component of our integrity definition – 'aroha' (do it with genuineness and heart) – occur. However, the literature cautions against utilising the practice education components of social work education as the sole gatekeepers of integrity and fitness to practise: the issues that are named during practice education can become apparent at all stages of a student's education journey.

Discussion now turns to the positive student traits, abilities and characteristics of competence by which practice educators can identify student integrity in preparation for, and engagement in, field placements. This is underpinned by our belief that integrity is both a process and a framework that enables us as social workers to continually connect our personal cultural values and beliefs and professional worlds of knowledge, values, skills and abilities, and understandings in order to produce an authentic cohesive self. We discover our integrity on a continuous journey of building, questioning, testing and monitoring the impact of our thoughts, values, actions and their outcomes to achieve coherency and consistency. Therefore, practising with integrity involves accountability, reflexivity, self-evaluation and critical reflection and is inextricably linked to emotional intelligence.

There are many identified domains, dimensions, elements and characteristics through which students can evidence their professional suitability and demonstrate integrity. Our definition of integrity can be conceived, first and foremost, as a personal concept that is shaped and influenced by our cultural understandings and constructions. Individual integrity has been identified and described by experienced practitioners as a combination of many personal qualities and traits (Appleton, 2010). Some of these include a willingness to be open, reliable and trustworthy, to be upfront and honest about limitations, to rethink and be consultative, to search for answers, to be reflective and open to challenge, to be aware of power and how it is used, and to be able to ask for support – all components that contribute to the framework of 'tika, pono and aroha'. Boak et al (2012) see honesty in academic matters as a key indicator of behaving ethically in professional matters.

Kovach et al (2009) note that while engaged in learning their roles and responsibilities, the individual characteristics of self-motivation, independent learning, interpersonal relationships and displaying dependability are relevant. Lown et al (2009) identify compassion, empathy, positive outlook, interest in people and trustworthiness, and Dyrbye et al (2010) and Parker et al (2008) add responsibility, honesty and reliability to the integrity list. Tam and Coleman (2009) offer a social work-specific 'professional suitability' scale encompassing five dimensions and 33 elements, which include maintaining stable emotions and having good interpersonal skills. In the field of medical practice, Hilton and Slotnick (2005) offer six domains that are equally applicable to social work and where evidence of demonstrating integrity of practice could be seen. These domains encompass ethical practice, reflection/self-awareness, responsibility for actions, respect for patients, teamwork and social responsibility.

From this brief summary, we can see exemplified an active definition of integrity as encompassing personal qualities, relational skills and the development of professional identity and behaviour. In addition, integrity is the way we as educators approach, apply and administer our relational skills in the moment, the genuineness and heart with which we approach the tasks of protecting and upholding the standards and values of the social work profession. The focus of our work is therefore on those areas of helping students to identify what they are able to demonstrate already (their strengths) and what are their gaps – to be discussed and addressed in order to work towards integrity of self and thus of practice. It is through modelling many of the traits, abilities and skills identified earlier, and displaying honesty, transparency, empathy and critical reflection in a relational approach with students, that our own and students' integrity can be explored, supported and grown.

The concept of integrity in practice

This chapter continues by considering the territory of integrity in relation to failing and marginal students through the presentation of a case study to which we apply a framework based on the integrity concepts developed in this chapter. We follow this case example with five short vignettes to which the reader is invited to respond.

Case study – Alisha

Alisha is a single woman in her early twenties whose family migrated here when she was a teenager. English is her second language, which she can speak and write to an academically acceptable level, her grades throughout her degree being B to B+ on average. She is known to be a quiet student who does not spontaneously mix with her cohort, although she contributes to assigned group work and planned class activities. She has often requested extensions for assignments and she has received one academic caution for plagiarism. Alisha has been placed in a multidisciplinary statutory practice setting and her first assignment has not been handed in on time. There has been no explanation for this or contact from Alisha. Upon speaking to her fieldwork supervisor, some concerns about timekeeping, hygiene and ability to follow through on tasks allocated, and a lack of being able to work as a team member, were noted. When one of these issues was raised in supervision on practicum, Alisha was visibly upset and called in sick the next day.

Using the lens of integrity, our first area of inquiry relates to *identifying the domains, dimensions, elements and characteristics* that may have been present here. We were concerned to find out more about Alisha's levels of self-awareness, ability to be upfront and honest, interpersonal skills, responsibility for actions, management of emotions, ability to seek support, openness to challenge, attitude to teamwork, and any self-care strategies and plans.

Our second area of inquiry relates to gathering previous knowledge/experiences of Alisha prior to the practicum paper. What are her demonstrated areas of strength, and gaps, what (if any) interventions may have occurred, with whom and with what result? A consistent academic achievement was able to be evidenced and the incident of plagiarism was a genuine misunderstanding and had not reoccurred, indicating taking responsibility for actions and an ability to learn. Strong cultural values of putting others first, being responsible for family matters and maintaining strict boundaries about sharing personal information appeared to be major contributing factors impacting on Alisha's ability to get assignments in on time and on her ability to 'mix' with other students. Alisha's determination to keep her grades up and contribute fairly and fully to class group work indicated strength, and her lack of peer support within the academic environment and outside of it was seen as vulnerability. This exploration ascertains that, within the integrity framework, the right (pono) information, discussion, interpretation and understandings have been addressed.

Our third area of inquiry was to invite further information sharing, exploration, discussion of perceptions and reflection from all partners on the situation. *How were we transparent, honest, compassionate, supportive, constructive and applying a critical analysis?* We were able to identify Alisha's family matters as having an enormous impact on her mental health with the full-time work hours required at practicum increasing the stress and pressure that she had been experiencing during her studies. This had, in turn, decreased her ability to cope and challenged her integrity on several fronts, which she was able to recognise. Alisha named several unintended consequences in her professional learning experiences because of feeling isolated and trapped by her home situation. Emotionally, relationally and in all aspects of personal and professional well-being, Alisha and consequently her colleagues, supervisor and lecturers were all experiencing the challenge to integrity.

Our fourth area of inquiry centred on *exploring the constraints and opportunities we had named and discussed, identifying the desired outcome, looking for processes and practice solutions (including agreeing a plan that would help restore and rebuild integrity), and designing an evaluative framework to measure and agree progress.* This process included checking Alisha's motivation (her internal drive to address and make changes), her conviction (her confidence in being able to tackle the many issues identified) and her capacity (her ability to gather and work with the resources necessary to carry out the plan). These investigations and conversations encompass the information and understandings necessary to implement the integrity aspects of 'pono' (to take the right action).

Alisha withdrew from the practicum at this point and engaged in counselling and also received some mental health support and intervention. The academy was able to connect Alisha with an appropriate minority ethnic mentor in the community who worked with her to expand her understanding and practise of boundaries, self-care, reflective practice, use of self, ethics and teamwork. She took a six-month break from studies while she volunteered in the agency run by her mentor, and used reflective journaling and other strategies to monitor and report back on her learnings. We received regular reflections from Alisha, we met at the agreed review date to evaluate progress, she decided to take some extra time to continue to work on her personal and family issues and fully regain her health and well-being. The relationships we had established and sustained were based on integrity and premised on the concept of 'aroha' (do it with genuineness and heart). This encouraged and celebrated each step forward that Alisha took and actively demonstrated our belief in her ability to contribute positively to social work. When Alisha returned to study, she had addressed the gaps identified and further built on her strengths and personal and professional practice integrity. Alisha completed a successful practicum, passing with an A–.

We have applied the lens and framework of integrity to this case study. While recognising that each student and their situation will be different, we have paid attention to recognising, measuring and trusting our own integrity and knowing of practice. We focus on how we are identifying what is right (tika), judging what is the right action (pono) in response and applying the capacity of doing it with genuineness and heart (aroha). The reader is invited to consider their own response to the five scenarios through the application of the following questions:

- Can you recognise issues of marginality and potential failure in the following scenario?
- What factors need to be taken into consideration in order to uphold the integrity of the placement and of the people involved?
- Who are the key players? What are their responsibilities to address the issues, and how might they do this?
- What are the range of resources and relationships that are required in order for this duty of care to be exercised?
- What might a successful outcome look like?

- *Scenario 1* – a male student in his early twenties, whose placement reports that his erratic timekeeping is explained through myriad excuses and explanations such as the requirement to care for dependent family members. While a personable and enthusiastic young man, this behaviour matches academic experience of late submission of work, erratic attendance in class and unreliable participation in group exercises. The 'class joker', he has a reputation of being a party animal who burns the candle at both ends through his work on the student radio station.
- *Scenario 2* – a single mother with three children who has entered social work studies in middle age. In placement preparation, she displays extreme anxiety, with low confidence in offering her own opinion or advocating for her own needs over those of others. She has disclosed a history of domestic abuse. She alternates between being able to identify and work with her own feelings and a state of blaming others for the high stress that she experiences. From previous volunteer work, she describes uncomfortable relationships between herself and those in authority.
- *Scenario 3* – an 'A' student on her first placement in a statutory environment. The agency has become aware that she has accessed information in regard to a member of her extended family.
- *Scenario 4* – a young student between first and second placements reports to academic staff that she is currently attending class while resident at a drug and alcohol rehabilitation centre. In further discussion, she discloses a history of self-harm and depression and

feels that this experience will assist her with her stated goals of completing her final placement in a community mental health centre and of becoming an addictions counsellor.

- *Scenario 5* – a student from a refugee and migrant background whose communication skills during placement preparation evidence a perception of social work as a process of directing a client along prescribed courses of action, which reflect gender and cultural roles potentially at odds with your programme's philosophy.

Conclusion: maintaining integrity in the social work programme

Using the concept of integrity as a basis, this chapter suggests that supporting student success and working with marginal or failing students is a co-constructed endeavour systemically located within the relational space between the academy and the agency. It draws upon and calls for a particular practice approach that pays attention to and senses the necessary combination of skills and knowledge. It is an approach that highlights the integration of personal cultural beliefs, values and professional knowledge, and the skills and values of academics and fieldwork educators. It is transparently relationally based and it is supported by assessment processes that demonstrate integrity through the evaluation and development of a student's knowledge, skills and values. It is essential that the responsibility for passing or failing marginal students is shared and is seen as a partnership between all stakeholders: academic educators, host agencies, the professional staff they appoint as supervisors and, most of all, students themselves (Appleton et al, 2014).

We have an ethical responsibility to act as gatekeepers for the social work profession on behalf of society (Staniforth and Fouché, 2006; Robertson, 2013; Finch, 2014). A question that Lafrance and Gray (2004: 326) pose is: 'in a profession that espouses the basic value that all people are capable of growth and change, can we justify excluding people who may be unready rather than unsuitable?' From an empowerment stance, we argue that gatekeeping can be both an enabler (to get students from marginal communities into social work) and a means to exclude particular students (Elpers and FitzGerald, 2012). As Apaitia-Vague et al (2011: 62) comment: 'being placed in the position of assessing risk may in itself pose an ethical issue for social work educators'. After all, it can be argued that we have a responsibility to fail some students as much as we have an obligation to support the majority to pass. The desire for a social work career does not provide entitlement to complete at all costs: we are implicitly querying what is right (tika). It is a balance for educational staff between using skills to empathise and work with issues and making judgement calls and standing firm in both naming and addressing issues: this involves determining and taking the right action (pono). This dual responsibility between protection of the public and the human rights of students can cause role strain and confusion, and therefore needs to be carefully examined, understood and strongly supported by systems, processes and procedures of integrity within the school and the wider university. We are then empowered to continue to deliver social work education with genuineness and heart (aroha).

How can the academic educator best assist supervisors in this challenge? Robust frameworks to assist supervisors to identify, evaluate and address the quality of student practice need to be co-constructed and implemented within the practicum context. What does a student who is practising with integrity look, sound and behave like in their social services context? One possible process is to offer targeted workshops or coaching in this area, to reinforce and clearly name the behaviours that are required and necessary to be demonstrated in professional practice, and to understand and explore some of the possible reasons why students may not yet be able to meet them. Student learning goals and their contextual objectives to achieve them during practicum (along with specific expectations of both student and supervisors in a learning contract) further support the ability of both parties to measure progress or blocks to it transparently during an agency placement. At the point of negotiating and signing off a learning contract, time spent in carefully identifying and crafting the learning opportunities, and capturing expectations and methods of assessment, is effort well invested. A clearly constructed unambiguous contract provides all parties with a document to return to in order to measure development and improvement. The transparency and integrity of fitness to practise requirements are further supported by publishing these elements in a fieldwork handbook. The handbook brings together the information and expectations of all the parties and is inclusive of assignments, assessments and professional tasks that evidence and integrate both critical use of self in a professional setting and time management and organisational skills required by regulatory bodies.

As concluding comments to the processes and issues highlighted earlier, we suggest that the challenge of maintaining the integrity of the personal and the professional within the environment of social work education is a complex but essential task and one that ultimately determines the integrity of the institutions upon which a social work programme depends. Miller and Koerin (2002) provide a very useful ecological framework upon which to structure practice learning responses to failing and marginal students. The framework underscores the importance of practice learning teams and social work educational programmes having integrity of their own in terms of being embedded in, and making use of, the systems and structures available to support them in their role. This underpins the arguments made in this chapter that the integrity of the student social worker is best supported and enhanced by the integrity of the academic programme and the ownership of the quality of the graduate outcome within all components of the process. The existence of external reference points – for example, a statutory professional body such as the SWRB or a professional association such as the BASW – that can be contacted to consult on cases that pose ethical dilemmas or present as 'grey areas' is another important contribution to ensure the integrity of decision-making. Liability issues arise when students challenge exclusion from professional programmes (Shardlow, 2000; Staniforth and Fouché, 2006; Apaitia-Vague et al, 2011), and the responsibility is on programmes to have tight and clear boundaries and criteria, which have been followed consistently. There is also a need for good relationships with faculty and university legal services so that we can ensure that it is not just the academic criteria for failure, but also the professional requirements (such as critical reflection, clear communication, timekeeping, values-based decision-making), that are articulated in assessment processes and are enforceable. By applying the suggested integrity framework of 'tika, pono and aroha', we can work together transparently, adaptively and creatively, and draw on our intuitive, critical and analytical thinking capacities. This enables us to engage our whole being in growing our capacities to attain integrity in the work that we do.

It is with strong and ethical foundations such as these that the integrity of applied programmes that span both academic and professional identities can best be maintained, and where integrity moves, the integration of the knowledge, skills and values that we expect in our students, are best supported. We are therefore invited to apply the framework of 'tika, pono and aroha' to examine our own relationship with integrity, and to interrogate the context and systems within which our integrity is enacted, so that we are able to critically appraise the contributions we make to our social work profession. We suggest that when we as educators approach and imbue our work with genuineness and heart (aroha), we are intrinsically connecting to and building upon our sense of purpose, achievement, resilience and well-being.

Note

[1] The following translations from Maori into English are offered by the Maoridictionary.co.nz (see: http://www.maoridictionary.co.nz/dictionary-project): Tika – be correct, true, upright, right, just, fair, accurate, appropriate, lawful, proper. Pono – be true, valid, honest. Aroha – to love, feel pity, feel concern for, feel compassion, empathise.

References

Adamson, C. (2011) 'Getting the balance right: critical reflection, knowledge and the social work curriculum', *Advances in Social Work and Welfare Education*, 13(1): 29–48.

Apaitia-Vague, T., Pitt, L. and Younger, D. (2011) '"Fit and proper" and fieldwork: a dilemma for social work educators?', *Aotearoa New Zealand Social Work Review*, 23(4): 55–64.

Appleton, C. (2010) 'Integrity matters: an inquiry into social workers' understandings' (Master's of Social Work), Massey University, Palmerston North, New Zealand.

Appleton, C., Rankine, M. and Hare, J. (2014) 'An appreciative inquiry into cultivating "fit and proper" social work students', PPEP Conference Proceedings, SWRB, Wellington. July 2014.

BASW (British Association of Social Workers) (2012) 'The code of ethics for social work: statement of principles'. Available at: http://cdn.basw.co.uk/upload/basw_112315-7.pdf

Bennett, P. (2013) Opening address to 'Protecting the Public-Enhancing the Profession' Social Work Registration Board, Wellington, New Zealand.

Boak, G., Mitchel, L. and More, D. (2012) 'Student fitness to practise and student registration: a literature review', a project for the Health Professions Council by Prime Research and Development Limited, February.

Calhoun, C. (1995) 'Standing for something', *The Journal of Philosophy*, 92(5): 235–60.

Cox, D., La Caze, M. and Levine, M. (2003) *Integrity and the fragile self*, Aldershot: Ashgate.

Currer, C. and Atherton, K. (2008) 'Suitable to remain a student social worker? Decision making in relation to termination of training', *Social Work Education*, 27(3): 279–92.

Dyrbye, L.N., Massie, F.S., Eacker, A., Harper, W., Power, D., Durning, S.J., Thomas, M.R., Moutier, C., Satele, D., Sloan, J. and Shanafelt, T.D. (2010) 'Relationship between burnout and professional conduct and attitudes among US medical students', *JAMA: The Journal of the American Medical Association*, 304(11): 1173–80.

Eadie, T. and Lymbery, M. (2007) 'Promoting creative practice through social work education', *Social Work Education*, 26(7): 670–83.

Elpers, K. and FitzGerald, E.A. (2012) 'Issues and challenges in gatekeeping: a framework for implementation', *Social Work Education*, 32(3): 286–300.

Finch, J. (2014) '"Running with the fox and hunting with the hounds": social work tutors' experiences of managing failing social work students in practice learning settings', *British Journal of Social Work*, 26 August, pp 1–18.

Furness, S. and Gilligan, P. (2004) 'Fit for purpose: issues from practice placements, practice teaching and the assessment of students' practice', *Social Work Education*, 23(4), 465–79.

Hilton, S.R. and Slotnick, H.B. (2005) 'Proto-professionalism: how professionalisation occurs across the continuum of medical education', *Medical Education*, 39(1): 58–65.

Ife, J. (2010) *Human rights from down below: achieving rights through community development*, Port Melbourne, Australia: Cambridge University Press.

Koerin, B. and Miller, J. (1995) 'Gatekeeping policies: terminating students for nonacademic reasons', *Journal of Social Work Education*, 31(2): 247–60.

Kovach, R., Resch, D.S. and Verhulst, S.J. (2009) 'Peer assessment of professionalism: a five year experience in medical clerkship', *Journal of General Internal Medicine*, 24(6): 742–6.

Lafrance, J. and Gray, E. (2004) 'Gate-keeping for professional social work practice', *Social Work Education*, 23(3): 325–40.

Lown, N., Davies, I., Cordingley, L., Bundy, C. and Braidman, I. (2009) 'Development of a method to investigate medical students' perceptions of their personal and professional development', *Advances in Health Sciences Education: Theory and Practice*, 14(4): 475–86.

Miller, J. and Koerin, B. (1998) 'Can we assess suitability at admission? A review of MSW application procedures', *Journal of Social Work Education*, 34(3): 437–53.

Miller, J. and Koerin, B. (2002) 'Gatekeeping in the practicum', *The Clinical Supervisor*, 20(2): 1–18.

Morley, C. and Dunstan, J. (2012) 'Critical reflection: a response to neoliberal challenges to field education?', *Social Work Education*, 32(2): 141–56.

Narey, M. (2014) *Making the education of social workers consistently effective: report of Sir Martin Narey's independent review of the education of children's social workers*, London: Department for Education. Available at: www.gov.uk/government/publications

Parker, M., Luke, H., Zhang, J., Wilkinson, D., Peterson, R. and Ozolins, I. (2008) 'The "pyramid of professionalism": seven years of experience with an integrated program of teaching, developing, and assessing professionalism among medical students', *Academic Medicine: Journal of the Association of American Medical Colleges*, 83(8): 733–41.

Raphael, F.B. and Rosenblum, A.F. (1987) 'An operational guide to the faculty field liaison role', *Social Casework*, 68(3): 156–63.

Robertson, J.S. (2013) 'Addressing professional suitability in social work education', *The Journal of Practice Teaching and Learning*, 11(3): 98–117.

Shardlow, S. (2000) 'Legal responsibility and liability in field work', in L. Cooper and L. Briggs (eds) *Fieldwork in the human services*, Sydney: Allen & Unwin, pp 117–31.

Sin, C.H. and Fong, J. (2009) 'The impact of regulatory fitness requirements on disabled social work students', *British Journal of Social Work*, 39(8): 1518–39.

Staniforth, B. and Fouché, C. (2006) 'An Aotearoa primer on fit and proper – school version', *Social Work Review*, 18(4): 11–19.

SWRB (Social Workers Registration Board) (2013) 'Fit and proper person: policy statement'. Available at: http://www.swrb.govt.nz/policy

SWRB (2014) *Code of conduct for social workers* (vol 3, January), Wellington, NZ: SWRB.

SWTF (Social Work Task Force) (2009) *Facing up to the task – the interim report of the social work taskforce*, London: Department of Health and Department for Children, Schools and Families.

Tam, D.M.Y. and Coleman, H. (2009) 'Construction and validation of a professional suitability scale for social work practice', *Social Work*, 45(1): 47–64.

Van Heugten, K. (2011) 'Registration and social work education: a golden opportunity or a Trojan horse?', *Journal of Social Work*, 11(2): 174–90.

THIRTEEN

Cultivating discretion: social work education in practice and the academy

Avril Bellinger, Deirdre Ford and Beth Moran

Introduction

Traditionally, in the realm of social work education, practice learning or fieldwork education was consigned to the status of the poor relation (Davis and Walker, 1987; Domakin, 2014). In many UK university departments, the post designated for the organisation of, and support for, practice learning was temporary, part-time and generally assigned to a female staff member (Langan and Day, 1992). Social workers who made the transition to academic posts were socialised into developing research profiles, privileging certain forms of knowledge, following conventional processes and adopting traditional priorities in the academy. Although pedagogic research, particularly relating to practice education, would be a logical route for their career progression, it is perceived to have an inferior status within research valuation (Canning and Gallagher-Brett, 2010).

The ambivalence of higher education towards practice learning, and, indeed, towards it as a form of community engagement, is epitomised by the actions of older universities, who have relinquished virtually any vocational subject involving practice placements. In the UK, teacher training, adult education, nursing, health professions and social work have been consigned in the main to what are termed 'post-1992' universities, previously polytechnics. 'Russell Group' universities have systematically disinvested in vocational courses – the London School of Economics, Reading, Oxford, Exeter – culminating in the closure of the master's programme at Southampton in 2012. This ambivalence is not a new phenomenon; there were struggles to maintain the survival of the 'Certificate in Social Training' and of adult education in Oxford during the 1920s. Barnett House, for example, was established in 1914 and became a department of Oxford University. Initially, it trained

Oxford social policy graduates to work alongside 'the poor' through the settlement movement (Halsey, 1976). Barnett House has only survived today, however, by relinquishing qualifying social work training in 2004 and focusing exclusively on social policy research (Smith et al, 2014).

In a capitalist society, where divisions and categorisations are the norm, practice education and classroom learning are inevitably distinguished by status. This is despite the testimonies of countless generations of students who have valued placements as the most important aspect of their education (Lam et al, 2007; Domakin, 2014). The quality of the unpredictable, situated and highly complex environments in which students practise are, by their nature, hard to evaluate within the dominant paradigm of higher education, where specificity and depth of knowledge are measured. This may, in part, account for the lower value that has been attributed to practice learning in the academic setting. We propose that practice educators, supervisors and, particularly, social work academics should guard against the institutional norms, practices and micro-politics that continue to exclude practice learning as a fully equal partner in social work education. At this point, however, it is important to clarify that the intention behind this chapter is not to set practice learning in opposition to academic, or classroom-based, learning, nor to fuel the divide. We resist the notion of oppositional and binary thinking for both political and pedagogical reasons (Fook, 2002). Moreover, while acknowledging that practice education has largely held an inferior status to academic learning, neither would we argue for this to be reversed in order to privilege practice learning over that which takes place within the academy. We seek to safeguard academic rigour for students who are learning in practice as crucial to their confidence in developing knowledge and criticality as part of their nascent professional identity (Ford et al, 2005). The *context* for either element, however, is far from conducive to deep learning.

The impact of neoliberalism on social work practice

This section considers the wider context of neoliberal forces and their impact on welfare, most notably, managerialism and reductionist approaches to complex social problems. In essence, neoliberalism is the 'global economic approach which encourages a scaling back of state intervention and public spending while encouraging privatisation' (Blakemore and Warwick-Booth, 2013: 20). Neoliberalism concerns itself with markets and profits rather than social justice and human rights, and with individualism rather than the promotion of community and citizenship. A utilitarian neoliberal discourse threatens the welfare state and endorses sanctions to encourage conformity to capitalist norms. Globalisation promotes the commodification of all aspects of life, including disability and the family, with little or no scope for resistance. In so doing, collectivity, which may have acted as a protective barrier, is being systematically eroded.

'The globalisation and commodification of communications give power to those who want to demonise' (Standing, 2011: 146). One group who are targeted in this way are those perceived as requiring social care services. People in receipt of social care are all too often subjected to a deviant, deficient categorisation by the capitalist project, which, in turn, leads to overenthusiastic auditing and public distrust of how money is spent. This paradigm of New Public Management, characterised by such mechanisms as key performance indicators and other targeting measures, leads to public sanctions and benefits that are not subject to public scrutiny (Hood, 1991; O'Neill, 2002; Munro, 2004; Cooke and Muir, 2012). Social workers often find themselves operating within a libertarian, paternalist agenda where conditionality in the form of eligibility criteria, for example, constrains social policy (Standing, 2011). It is proposed that, in general, a worker's behaviour is compatible and compliant with performance measures (Lipsky, 2010), though this is not necessarily in the best interests of service users, and takes little account of competing perspectives or partnership working. The use of eligibility criteria requires social workers to ascribe the status of service users, to label them and to determine whether they are worthy of support.

An overreliance on monitoring can affect the ability of social workers to develop coping mechanisms other than those sanctioned by managers, who themselves have an increasingly powerful role, while having to manage their own 'ever-extending web of surveillance' (Gilbert and Powell, 2010: 16). Increasing regulation directly challenges the assertion of Lipsky (2010: 13) that 'the policy-making roles of street-level bureaucrats are built upon two interrelated facets of their position: relatively high degrees of discretion and relative autonomy from organizational authority'. Discretion is understood to be the active agency ascribed to front-line practitioners that facilitates the development and implementation of policy through everyday interactions with service users and carers. Lipsky (2010) suggests that in order to make sense of public policy, which is at the core of the welfare state, social workers use discretion. This enables the profession to work with uncertainty and limited resources and to respond to individuals and communities in a holistic way not necessarily sanctioned by neoliberal policy. Discretion involves using creativity and professional skills to find spaces between principles and rules (Brandon, 2005). Lipsky (2010) is clear that discretion is essential, along with traits of compassion and flexibility, in view of the complexity of the professional role in public services. He posits that a reason for maintaining discretion is the regard that it promotes both in the skills of the professional and the legitimisation of the welfare state. As a political scientist, Lipsky's analysis accords with priorities in social work education.

Social workers enjoy less autonomy and discretion, however, particularly in relation to how public funds are spent in this era of austerity. As goals become more clearly defined through performance measures and managers exert more control, so street-level workers have less opportunity for discretion, though this is still achievable, even more necessary and should be actively sought (Evans and Harris, 2004; Baines, 2011). The exercise of professional discretion, a 'series of gradations of freedom' (Evans and Harris, 2004: 871), can help to address the tensions between consumerism and citizenship, as well as promoting better working conditions for social workers. While it appears that discretion is no longer a routine aspect of practice in social care, nevertheless, 'to the extent that tasks remain complex and human intervention is considered necessary for effective service, discretion will remain characteristic of many public service jobs' (Lipsky, 2010: 15).

The impact of neoliberalism on higher education

That the university is a site of learning tends to be regarded as a given and not open to question. However, in a book focusing on practice learning and its place in social work education, it would be a mistake to disregard the challenges to higher education and its role in the development of professional practitioners. Considered one of the last bastions of reasoning and democratic action, higher education is perhaps one of the most prized trophies of the hegemonic neoliberal ideology of our time. Students have become consumers of ever-dwindling academic resources for which many incur unaffordable loans with little promise of suitable employment on completion. Neoliberalism has commodified education and the academy is now a business venture where administrators are privileged over academics. For aspiring professionals, there is potentially little room for enlightenment, less time for critical inquiry and minimal interest in anything deemed as experimental (Giroux, 2014). Critical examination of politics, power and social responsibility is no longer valued. Giroux writes that academics and students 'are scrubbed clean of any illusions about connecting what they learn to a world "strewn with ruin, waste and human suffering'" (Said, 2004: 50, in Giroux, 2014: 100). As an example, the study of economics has moved almost exclusively to elite universities, where students from disadvantaged backgrounds are a rarity, while engagement with the outcomes of economic decision-making that have caused worldwide recession and austerity is actively discouraged (Johnston et al, 2014):

> Social work practice spans a range of activities including various forms of therapy and counselling, group work, and community work; policy formulation and analysis; and advocacy and political interventions. From an emancipatory perspective ... social work strategies are aimed at increasing people's hope, self-esteem and creative potential to confront and challenge oppressive power dynamics and structural sources of injustices, thus incorporating into a coherent whole the micro–macro, personal–political dimension of intervention. The holistic focus of social work is universal, but the priorities of social work practice will vary from one country to the next, and from time to time depending on historical, cultural, political and socio-economic conditions. (IFSW, 2014)

While it is acknowledged that the manifestation of social work practice will vary depending on particular conditions, the holistic nature of social work is clearly articulated in this revised global definition. Thus, students should be encouraged to embrace the core tenets of social justice, human rights and a person-in-environment perspective (Oliver, 2013). Student social workers will need to learn the importance of 'contextual competence', develop the ability to appreciate the different contexts and practise strategically within the cultural climate which is that of managerialism (Fook, 2002: 146). This enables social workers to reframe dichotomous thinking to a position where discretion can be used to develop and maintain relationships with service users through a creative, narrative approach, while acknowledging the bureaucratic rationalist imperative. Discretion acknowledges the vital ontological importance of interpersonal relationships and how these are a 'precondition of effective social work practice' (O'Leary et al, 2013: 137). This, in turn, encourages progress towards a 'relational state' where 'the workforce would generate value and mobilise others, not just deliver preset outcomes ... citizens themselves would have power and responsibility, through their relationships with others, not just on their own' (Cooke and Muir, 2012: 15).

The impact of neoliberalism on learning to be a professional

Traditional notions of universities as institutions that are primarily concerned with the pursuit of knowledge, have been shattered by the business model that has compromised their moral integrity. Pressures on higher education from managerialist forces mirror those on practice and it is imperative that we recognise and resist the drift towards bureaucratic compliance in the service of the neoliberal agenda. If students are to graduate as practitioners able to operate to protect social justice within existing flawed structures, then programmes must be able to develop their capacity for discretion (Lipsky, 2010). As practitioners, they will have a moral responsibility to recognise when policy is unjust and to act accordingly. As a profession, social work is founded on the examples of individuals using their position to protect people's human rights even within the most oppressive regimes in which they worked, both in practice, like Irena Sendler (Mayer, 2010) and Jane Addams (Addams, 1989) and in education, like Alice Saloman (Wieler, 1988), Helena Radlinska (Brainerd, 2001) and Sattareh Farmaian (Farmaian, 1993).

The conditions of neoliberalism, capitalism-promoting growth at the expense of people and planet, should not be allowed to reduce practice to a reactive bureaucratic process. To counter this, academics should utilise a critical pedagogy of hope (Freire, 2014) to encourage a problematisation of students' assumptions about the world, and in order to promote their engagement with social justice as agents of change.

While social work programmes routinely incorporate strategies to encourage students to develop reflective skills; ironically, the teaching of knowledge tends to privilege content over meaning. The bureaucratisation of knowledge emphasises interventions and outcomes in favour of the co-construction of knowledge with service users, whose inclusion, in this sense, is tokenistic.

In the UK, for example, social work courses are given detailed guidance about the areas of knowledge that students should be taught (TCSW, 2015), as if they were discrete and uncontentious. Miller (1996), in differentiating three philosophies of education, identifies atomism as characterised by placing reliance on empirical data collected through value-neutral inquiry in the belief that this will enable control of the material world. This view of the nature of learning has justified the separation of knowledge into small units, with the primary purpose of exercising control: 'An atomistic approach reduces everything to its smallest component so that it can be analyzed' (Miller, 1996: 13). This positivist philosophy is enacted through curricula that are organised into separate units or modules. Such a traditional arrangement into subject areas is functional for teachers, who can claim their areas of expertise. It permits the measurement of student achievement in relation to their acquisition of specific knowledge. It also simplifies the administration for institutions, making transparent and equitable students' opportunity for progression. Such siloed learning, however, places the burden on the student of connecting the knowledge and using it to inform practice.

An alternative paradigm that Miller (1996) identifies as pragmatism, which arose from a critique of atomism (Childs, 1931; Dewey and Childs, 1933; Dewey, 1938). It was proposed that the world is not knowable in this way and that, instead, it is dynamic and changing. Critics asserted that knowledge is derived from scientific inquiry in which hypotheses are tested systematically. Furthermore, they believed that these methods could be applied to social problems and social experience, as well as to the natural world. Curriculum approaches based on this philosophy are recognisable in medicine and social work as problem-based learning (Boud and Feletti, 1998; Wood, 2003) and enquiry and action learning (Burgess and Jackson, 1990).

Miller (1996) also identifies a third approach, which is that of holism. He states that holistic learning derives from a belief in the fundamental unity and interconnectedness of the universe and that to behave as if knowledge could be reduced to components is to contribute to a sense of alienation. His argument is borne out by the earlier example of the economics lecturers behaving as if austerity and the failure of existing models were not relevant to their teaching (Johnston et al, 2014). Holistic teaching practices should cultivate intuition and be grounded in reality. Miller (1996: 31) argues that such learning will inevitably lead staff and pupils towards social activity that is designed to counter injustice and human suffering: 'By fragmenting the curriculum we contribute to our disconnectedness; by approaching curriculum from an integrated and interdependent perspective we begin to counter our alienation'.

Holism has not only an intellectual dimension, but also a spiritual one. It demands that teachers acknowledge the intimate connection between an internal higher self and the universe, and that we work to develop it. It places a demand on us to foster our awareness of all the connections that make us human. It is interesting to note that proponents of holistic education for children (Newmann, 1975; Noddings, 1984; Miller, 1996) advocate pupils having experience in the community and practising caring in order to promote the realisation of interconnectedness. A holistic curriculum requires practical involvement at all levels. If teaching students to care for people in the community is best done through a holistic form of education, we would argue that this has to have relevance for social work education.

In a higher education environment that defaults to an atomic structure, supporting other forms of learning can be problematic. As noted previously, courses developed with a primarily pragmatic (Burgess and Jackson, 1990) or holistic (Adamson, 2011) framework are regarded as experimental and are vulnerable to erosion by the requirements of the wider institution. Pressure to produce competent social workers for current employment conditions can lead to courses defending their quality in terms of research activity and curriculum content. This may be because it is problematic to quantify in addition graduates' integrity, humanity and sense of social justice. As Miller (1996: 31) observes:

> Because the perennial philosophy is difficult to articulate and thus to understand, holistic programmes are often difficult to sustain in schools. Holistic curriculum is also difficult to evaluate and thus is the first to be attacked in periods of retrenchment.

The same can be said in higher education.

Although theories of knowledge often incorporate analyses of hegemony and discourse, these do not usually appear to influence the way teaching is structured. Equally, pedagogical theory, especially learning theory, upholds the importance of experiential learning, yet, as the introduction illustrates, the academy does not recognise its importance. This was borne out within an integrated practice-led degree (Adamson, 2011). Even though the programme structure was explicitly designed to privilege practice, nonetheless, at the point of the formal award board, the conventional institutional procedures rendered it invisible.

A new model for social work education

One response to concerns about the difficulty of ensuring a consistent learning experience for students has been simply to propose a practice curriculum in which students are exposed to a particular set of experiences, such as witnessing safeguarding procedures in action, undertaking initial assessments and so on. Such attempts to streamline student learning in practice can act as catalysts for courses to review their understanding of the pedagogical purpose of practice learning

(Bellinger, 2010). Work-based learning as a strategy to improve student employability across subjects has also had an impact on the understanding of placements for social work. The Higher Education Institution (HEI) sector in the UK has had the sole responsibility for assessing students and for arranging their practice learning without control over the sector in which students are placed. This can perpetuate academic supremacy through institutional processes and the authors acknowledge the College of Social Work's (TCSW's) current concerns that the HEI is not a safe place for practice to be assessed. However, TCSW's solution appears to be to privilege statutory employment, students learning through apprenticeship (Frontline, 2014) and achievement through compliance.

Practice learning and ownership: recognition and equality in the academy

We argue that neither practice nor classroom learning in the current climate is necessarily conducive to the kind of learning we advocate. The pressures on each to serve the neoliberal agenda must be understood and critiqued by educators and practitioners wherever situated. Moreover, it could be argued that educators do not confront the complex dilemmas faced by public service workers and that the concept of discretion, therefore, does not apply to their work. Such a view assumes an atomistic approach to the curriculum, however, in which knowledge is prescribed rather than co-constructed. In contrast, if we acknowledge the necessity for a holistic approach to social work education, the educator is constantly confronted with the necessity to interpret theory in relation to unique and changing circumstances. Social work has always had to mobilise the systems in which it finds itself, whether these are in practice or in the classroom (Jones and May, 1992). The function of education is to educate and inspire professionals who can exercise discretion within existing systems in order to preserve social justice. We believe that the margins where practice education and the academy come together are places where extraordinary things can be achieved. We need to be suspicious and critical, therefore, of both practice and of the academy in the context of neoliberalism, and support students to learn how to exercise discretion instead of playing out the dichotomy of either university or practice education being the real place of learning.

This chapter has summarised the historically inferior position of practice learning in social work education and the inadequacy of investing in structural solutions intended to equalise or privilege it.

Such dichotomous thinking obscures the more fundamental critique of established philosophies of learning and the need for a holistic profession like social work to be approached holistically. Both practice and academia are compromised by neoliberal agendas. The challenge, then, for educators is to act with discretion within and between those flawed structures in order to maintain an unwavering focus on humanity and social justice.

References

Adamson, C. (2011) 'Getting the balance right: critical reflection, knowledge and the social work curriculum', *Advances in Social Work and Welfare Education*, 13(1): 29–48.

Addams, J. (1989) *Twenty years at Hull House with biographical notes*, Illinois, IL: University of Illinois Press.

Baines, D. (ed) (2011) *Doing anti-oppressive practice: social justice social work* (2nd edn), Halifax, Nova Scotia: Fernwood.

Bellinger, A. (2010) 'Talking about (re-)generation: practice learning as a site of renewal for social work', *British Journal of Social Work*, 40(8): 2450–66.

Blakemore, K. and Warwick-Booth, L. (2013) *Social policy: an introduction*, Maidenhead: Open University Press.

Boud, D. and Feletti, G. (eds) (1998) *The challenge of problem-based learning*, Hove: Psychology Press.

Brainerd, M.D. (2001) 'Helena Radlinska: expanding conceptualizations of social work practice from Poland's past', *International Social Work*, 44(1): 19–30.

Brandon, T. (2005) 'Classic review: street-level bureaucracy: dilemmas of the individual in public services', *Disability and Society*, 20(7): 779–83.

Burgess, H. and Jackson, S. (1990) 'Enquiry and action learning: a new approach to social work education', *Social Work Education*, 9(3): 3–19.

Canning, J. and Gallagher-Brett, A. (2010) 'Building a bridge to pedagogic research: teaching social science research methods to humanities practitioners', *Journal of Applied Research in Higher Education*, 2(2): 4–9.

Childs, J. (1931) *Education and the process of experimentalism*, New York, NY: Century.

Cooke, G. and Muir, R. (eds) (2012) *The relational state: how recognising the importance of human relationships could revolutionise the role of the state*, London: Institute for Public Policy Research.

Davis, J. and Walker, M. (1987) 'The practice learning centre: the need for new concepts in practice learning and teaching', *Social Work Education*, 6(2): 10–13.

Dewey, J. (1938) *Experience and education*, New York, NY: Macmillan Collier.

Dewey, J. and Childs, J. (1933) 'The underlying philosophy of education', in W.H. Kilpatrick (ed) *The educational frontier*, New York, NY: D. Appleton-Century, pp 287–320.

Domakin, A. (2014) 'Are we making the most of learning from the practice placement?', *Social Work Education*, 36(6): 718–30.

Evans, T. and Harris, J. (2004) 'Street-level bureaucracy, social work and the (exaggerated) death of discretion', *British Journal of Social Work*, 34: 871–95.

Farmaian, S.F. (1993) *Daughter of Persia: a woman's journey from her father's harem through the Islamic revolution*, New York, NY: Anchor Books/Doubleday.

Fook, J. (2002) *Social work: critical theory and practice*, London: SAGE.

Ford, P., Johnston, B., Brumfit, C., Mitchell, R. and Myles, F. (2005) 'Practice learning and the development of students as critical practitioners – some findings from research', *Social Work Education*, 24(4): 391–407.

Freire, P. (2014) *Pedagogy of hope: reliving pedagogy of the oppressed*, London: Bloomsbury.

Frontline (2014) 'Frontline: changing lives'. Available at: http://www.thefrontline.org.uk/our-programme

Gilbert, T. and Powell, J. (2010) 'Power and social work in the United Kingdom: a Foucauldian excursion', *Journal of Social Work*, 10(1): 3–22.

Giroux, H. (2014) *Neoliberalism's war on higher education*, Chicago, IL: Haymarket Books.

Halsey, A.H. (1976) *Traditions of social policy: essays in honour of Violet Butler*, Oxford: OUP.

Hood, C. (1991) 'A public management for all seasons?', *Public Administration*, 69: 3–19.

IFSW (International Federation of Social Workers) (2014) 'International Federation of Social Workers global definition of social work'. Available at: http://ifsw.org/news/update-on-the-review-of-the-global-definition-of-social-work/

Johnston, J., Reeves, A. and Talbot, S. (2014) 'Has economics become an elite subject for universities?', *Oxford Review of Education*, 40(5): 590–609.

Jones, A. and May, J. (1992) *Working in human service organisations: a critical introduction*, London: Longman.

Lam, C.M., Wong, H. and Leung, T.T.F. (2007) 'An unfinished reflexive journey: social work students' reflection on their placement experiences', *British Journal of Social Work*, 37: 91–105.

Langan, M. and Day, L. (eds) (1992) *Women, oppression and social work: issues in anti-discriminatory practice*, London: Routledge.

Lipsky, M. (2010) *Street-level bureaucracy: dilemmas of the individual in public services* (2nd edn), New York, NY: Russell Sage Foundation.

Mayer, J. (2010) *Life in a jar: the Irena Sendler project*, Middlebury, VT: Long Trail Press.

Miller, J. (1996) *Holistic learning* (2nd edn), Toronto: OISE.

Munro, E. (2004) 'The impact of audit on social work practice', *British Journal of Social Work*, 34(8): 1075–95.

Newmann, F. (1975) *Education for citizen action: challenge for secondary curriculum*, Berkeley, CA: McCutchan.

Noddings, N. (1984) *Caring: a feminine approach to ethics and moral education*, Berkeley, CA: University of California Press.

O'Leary, P., Tsui, M. and Ruch, G. (2013) 'The boundaries of the social work relationship revisited: towards a connected, inclusive and dynamic conceptualisation', *British Journal of Social Work*, 43: 135–53.

Oliver, C. (2013) 'Social workers as boundary spanners: reframing our professional identity for interprofessional practice', *Social Work Education: The International Journal*, 32(6): 773–84.

O'Neill, O. (2002) *A question of trust*, Cambridge: Cambridge University Press.

Said, E.W. (2004) *Humanism and democratic criticism*, New York, NY: Columbia University Press.

Smith, G., Peretz, E. and Smith, T. (2014) *Social enquiry, social reform and social action*, Oxford: University of Oxford Press.

Standing, G. (2011) *The precariat: the new dangerous class*, London: Bloomsbury Academic.

TCSW (The College of Social Work) (2015) 'Social work curriculum guides'. Available at: http://www.tcsw.org.uk/professional-development/educators/#curr

Wieler, J. (1988) 'Alice Salomon', *Journal of Teaching in Social Work*, 2(2): 165–71.

Wood, D.F. (2003) 'Problem based learning', *British Medical Journal*, 326(7384): 328–30.

Index

A

B

C

D

E

F